Building Democracy and International Governance

Efforts by governments to promote sustained domestic economic development have been mixed. Success depends on many factors including location, geography, climate, external competition, human resources, natural resources, timing, political and governmental institutions, government capacity, implementation, leadership, values—and maybe luck. This complexity means that while development experts can often identify ingredients for success, few can prescribe the specific mix needed by a particular state to achieve sustained development over the long term.

In *Building Democracy and International Governance*, author George M. Guess uses both case studies and careful data analysis to argue that federalist democracy may just be the most responsive, authoritative, and flexible system for nation building, and that there is value in confronting the challenges that lie in exporting federalist democracy abroad. Guess demonstrates the ways in which federation structures provide positive redundancy against failures, flexibility to change course and implement programs and policies, and state legitimacy and strength. Examining twelve wealthy and developing countries from five regions, representing democratic and authoritarian government structures, confederations, and federations, this book will be of interest to those teaching graduate and undergraduate courses in Political Development, Democratization, Federalism, and Comparative Political Economy.

George M. Guess is Adjunct Professor in the Schar School of Policy and Government at George Mason University, USA.

D0209459

Building Democracy and International Governance

George M. Guess

Routledge
Taylor & Francis Group

NEW YORK AND LONDON

First published 2019
by Routledge
711 Third Avenue, New York, NY 10017

and by Routledge
2 Park Square, Milton Park, Abingdon, Oxon, OX14 4RN

Routledge is an imprint of the Taylor & Francis Group, an informa business

Library of Congress Cataloging-in-Publication Data
Names: Guess, George M., author.
Title: Building democracy and international governance / George M. Guess.
Description: New York, NY : Routledge, 2018. |
Includes bibliographical references and index.
Identifiers: LCCN 2018009954 | ISBN 9781138574724 (hbk : alk. paper) |
ISBN 9781138574731 (pbk : alk. paper) | ISBN 9781351273282 (ebk)
Subjects: LCSH: Democratization. | Democratization–International
cooperation. | Government accountability. | Organizational effectiveness. |
Democracy–Economic aspects. | Economic development–Political aspects.
Classification: LCC JC423 .G921355 2018 | DDC 320.6–dc23
LC record available at https://lccn.loc.gov/2018009954

ISBN: 978-1-138-57472-4 (hbk)
ISBN: 978-1-138-57473-1 (pbk)
ISBN: 978-1-351-27328-2 (ebk)

Typeset in Sabon
by Out of House Publishing

Contents

Preface

Around the world, governments are beset by nationalist and populist movements that threaten their ability to function at best and often demand regime changes or destruction at worst. The more sensible demands are for better income and employment opportunities in poorer countries or poor regions of wealthy countries. The demands are also for better security and stability, for reduced immigration that threatens political cultures, for more power of particular ethnic groups, tribes or religious sects, and for more responsive and accountable governments that can deliver results. Weak regimes and poorly structured governments have been unable to respond effectively. This has produced more poverty, misery, and violent internal conflicts that threaten states or governments further. Specifically, regimes and governments are threatened by four major pressures. Failed states and corrupt, persistently bad governance has been the product of one or more of these forces. First, ethnic-nationalist or ethno-nationalist parties and movements are most destabilizing in poor countries where illegitimate governments retain power by force, or rigged elections and regimes change frequently because of civil wars and conflicts. These threats produce the most instability and perpetuate misery and poverty. Second, macroeconomic instabilities, driven by external trade and economic shocks and poorly designed national policies, also threaten poor-country governments most since they are typically unable to respond with proper policies to overwhelming external and internal fiscal and economic forces. Ironically, such countries often have highly educated and trained professionals in public finance and macroeconomics. But their analyses and suggestions are routinely ignored by their regimes and if persistent with advice the experts are typically sacked. Nor have such countries provided adequate services, programs and projects to meet local needs. From this inability of poor countries to provide effective governance and stability, waves of emigration from them have flowed northwards, for instance, from the Middle East and North Africa to Europe. Third, wealthy countries have had to respond to a kind of reverse ethnonationalist pressure from local nativist and populist nationalist groups that challenge arriving immigrant cultural inconsistencies and claim that they cause losses of income and employment to locals which perpetuates rural backwardness and underdevelopment. Populist can be from the left or right historically. The current trend in wealthier countries is from the right. This brand of populist nationalists have been using ethnic nationalist dog-whistling as a means to their end of gaining power and governing for populist, often racist causes against other minority ethnic groups. In the face of these complex and destabilizing challenges, both rich and poor countries have been unable to provide core sectoral services, programs and capital projects as well as investment incentives that would create local and regional economic development. Resultant regional inequalities create large groups of left-behind people in provincial areas that continue to reinforce ethno-nationalist and populist nationalist threats to governments.

As the fourth challenge to governments (see Figure 0.1), overseas aid has been largely unable to focus beyond central government state modernization and democracy and governance assistance to the operational-level sectoral and regional problems that threaten governments. Though often poorly designed and implemented, there have been smaller-scale successes. Aid has been effective in promoting skills and policies to respond to macroeconomic instability, and countries rich and poor have responded effectively to this previously serious challenge to stability. Aid has also been effective in encouraging quasi-federation sub-systems through fiscal decentralization and local government strengthening programs world-wide. Aid has also successfully supported civil society organizations to strengthen institutional checks and balances, limit corruption, and prepare the foundations for effective states.

Where aid projects have been successful, they have run up against opposing political regimes that often limit their continued work. The more successful ones compensate at the design stage or through implementation flexibility for the absence of good contextual settings for state modernization and improved governance: the lack of incentives, authority, and long-term horizon by the regime needed for reform to take hold. Aid donors in some cases anticipate these problems and try to build in remedies in their project management. Micro-level government initiatives implemented incrementally, and multi-stakeholder involvement in particular sectors, have worked well as means to address the binding constraints on improved governance (Levy, 2014: 133). Overall, large-bore aid efforts have had little effect on actual host country governments. Overreliance on NGOs where effective state partners are absent is also a constraint to state building. It is also a paradox since it could mean no overseas aid for such countries at all. Donors compromise by relying on NGOs which operate as parallel governments in many countries with few spread effects to national-level government institutions. Aid needs to be linked to regime interests if possible and recalibrated to focus on the operational-level problems that most countries face. With competing

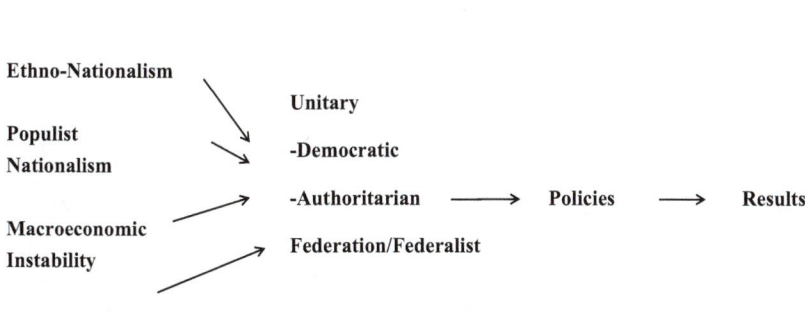

Figure 0.1 Building Effective Governments

donors offering discounted conditions to regimes in exchange for their approvals, it is often hard to gain the serious attention of regimes. Regimes imagine they have alterative choices to play off donors against each other for their personal benefit. But this mistaken impression often works at the expense of real needs and state effectiveness.

That there are four main threats to effective governance is not meant to imply that they are independent forces. As is known, countries such as Yemen have faced all four of these threats simultaneously for many decades. Many poorer country governments suffer from constant and simultaneous existential crises. Also, the threats are to country democracy, governance, and development. As recent as 2015, a World Economic Forum (WEF) survey concluded that state collapse or crisis was a major global risk. In 2013, the same survey concluded that chronic public sector fiscal imbalances were a major risk. By 2018 neither problem was considered a major global risk (BBW, 2018: 43). Macroeconomic policies have improved around the globe to ensure stability. State collapse has been limited to mainly MENA and the SSA regions and is considered unlikely to spread or contaminate state performances in other regions. Fear of a spreading scourge of terrorism that would damage state integrity and the global economy was important as recently as 2017. In 2018, it was no longer considered a major risk. Our focus is on country governance and how to improve it. The four variable framework presented here is meant to be analytic for purposes of devising better remedial policy options for both country leaders and aid donors.

Ultimately, to improve governance and create effective democratic governments, countries should move toward federation structures from either unitary, confederation, or authoritarian centralized systems. Though not the perfect solution, fiscal democratic federalism is the normative institutional objective for large, complex countries, given the alternatives. Confederations have been, and are, unable to withstand fiscal crises, external threats, and internal conflicts arising from reverse ethno-nationalism or cultural xenophobia. They suffer all the institutional weaknesses of voluntary associations built on mutual trust. Unitary governments are often overwhelmed by local-level conflicts becoming national issues; central governments waste time and are distracted by these because of structural centralization. Federations have met all these challenges more effectively. They facilitate growth and democracy and are the natural institutional architecture for complex countries and modern states. Unitary governments that fail to respond to the multi-crises of governance with at least quasi-federation mechanisms suffer from lack of redundancy and the flexibility to persist. Some federations are incomplete and consist of formal legalism rather than institutional substance. Such imitation federations can indeed lead to failed states. It is important then that formal structures be fleshed out in substance. Evidence for these assertions here is derived from a twelve-country sample of representative: unitary states (five democratic and three authoritarian), one confederation, three federations, and the European Union (EU) as a common European case of confederation. The sample represents: Europe (4), Asia (3), Sub-Saharan Africa or SSA (3), the Middle East and North Africa or MENA (1), and Latin America and the Caribbean (1). Additional country case examples are also discussed from all these regions.

Acknowledgments

The author would like to thank Laura Stearns and Misha Kydd at Taylor and Francis for their editorial support of this book project and continuing advice on how to proceed. In particular, the author would like to thank his International Management graduate students at George Mason University's Schar School of Policy and Government in Fairfax and Arlington, Virginia. Their incisive questions and critical comments led directly to the development of *Building Democracy and International Governance*. Since the subject involves threats to political regimes, governmental effectiveness and, in part, what overseas aid can do about them, he wishes to thank his many former colleagues for their criticism and suggestions over the years, from Development Alternatives, Incorporated (DAI) in Bethesda, Maryland and IMF and World Bank in Washington, DC. Of course, he would like to thank his wife Regula and their two sons Andy and Marty for their encouragement, patience, and understanding. As always, their continued support have made all things happen...

The book is dedicated to his friend and mentor, the late Paul Posner. From his years of U.S. federal government experience at GAO, international public finance and governance research, and aid field work, he belonged to the new breed of "pracademic" of which there should be more in both universities and aid agencies. He was my friend and I will miss his droll sense of the absurd and wry humor that often got me through the day.

1 Introduction
The Need for Effective Government

The growing threats are to states and the challenge is to strengthen them to withstand these mainly political forces and still be effective deliverers of services and programs. For, states are institutions requiring enough power to defend their people and territory, and to make and enforce necessary laws (Fukuyama, 2014: 37). They can be divided vertically into: ruling regimes or elites, political parties, state bureaucracies and electorates, or ruled subjects.[1] States must rule effectively enough that sales of goods and services from private, state-controlled, or state-owned enterprises provide enough revenue to finance its activities in behalf of electorates. Public budgets must be financed. Max Weber once observed that governments can be ruler-owned and patrimonial or modern and impersonal (Fukuyama, 2014: 10). The latter are legitimated by some combination of functional effectiveness, rule-based authority and electoral or performance-based accountability. States become ineffective and weak because: ruling parties, regimes, and ministries are dominated by narrow cliques, tribes, or ethnicities that govern in their own favor. Such governments rule in a legitimacy vacuum often filled by ethnic-nationalist groups through typically violent means (e.g. Liberia, Ethiopia, and Nigeria). Ineffective government bureaucracies are often patronage-ridden and insulated from citizens and their electorates at best—at worst they are silo-organized to prevent effective policy and budgetary action (e.g. U.K. and U.S.). Weak and ineffective governments are often unaccountable either for economic performance (e.g. China) or through electoral mandates from open and representative elections (e.g. Austria). Weak states can occur in wealthy or poor countries and the practical policy question is, how can this global and perennial problem be reduced?

Consistent with the objective of effective government, the frequent call is for governments that can plan and deliver policies, programs, and projects efficiently and effectively, that is, delivery performance which is least cost and to maximum effectiveness in serving client needs.[2] Because governments consist of horizontal and vertical structures of organizations and institutional processes, the tendency is to divide up this problem functionally. Thus, horizontally, the executive is often considered the purview of public administration specialists. Analysts set out to rationalize spans of control, clarify staff-line roles, and inject budget calendars with stages that employ critical analysis using formal methods to evaluate spending and taxation objectives. Such specialists also attempt to integrate budgets and program objectives to improve measurable results. Finally, specialists often try to regroup streamlined functions into differently structured organizations. The fact is, such complex processes and methods of administrative reform, state modernization, and reorganization are quite diffuse, hard to replicate, riddled with debatable unanticipated consequences, and have achieved mostly incomplete results in different contexts.[3]

Moving further to enhance state effectiveness, strengthening parliaments and elections become the responsibility of election and legislative specialists; the judiciary and judicial administration might be handled by lawyers and public administration specialists; regulatory processes are often covered by policy analysts in health, energy, transport, education, and so on. This functional specialization of reform efforts often worsens the perennial "silo" problem that besets effective governments everywhere.[4] Each specialist reforms his or her special area without government-wide integration of systems and processes. This can prevent the flow of information and orders, discourage learning, and guarantee bad policy results. This could be avoided by integrating budgets and staff to work toward specific and measurable objectives, for example, unnecessary outpatient referrals and reduced emergency referrals from care homes in the British NHS (*The Economist*, 2017p: 56). States or governmental institutions also require vertical command structures to control, sanction, and motivate staff toward objectives. Governments must be organized from the center with monopolies of force to cover territorial jurisdictions that coincide with their country boundaries. Boundaries themselves have been a historical and current source of intense conflict. Central governments are controlled by regimes that oversee the structures that extend from capitals to small villages in distant territories. Division of authority both vertically and horizontally, is a function of laws, constitutions, charters, and official accords. Governmental structures within which to exercise authority vary. Federations or federal systems, for example, feature autonomous or independent sub-national tiers of government; unitary systems do not, and all authority is deconcentrated from the central government. Authoritarian regimes that operate within any structure interpret laws to give them maximum control over all decisions affecting firms, individuals, and governmental units.[5] Limits on regime authority derive from constitutions and laws governing basic transactions and ownership and sales of property, commercial relations, civil and criminal procedures, and individual due process rights.[6] Limits also derive from institutional checks from competing civil society organizations, such as churches, media, and unions. For historical reasons, regimes span the spectrum of controls and limits on their power. In short, strengthening states is a complex task with substantial unintended outcomes anywhere.

The actual quality of government and institutions (*de facto* not just *de jure*) is revealed partly by allocation of resources, usually through planning, approval, and execution of public budgets for current services and capital works. Budgetary processes may be open and relatively transparent in contexts where citizen input, feedback and responsiveness are important for accountability. In most other contexts, allocation of resources is an opaque process governed from the top down.[7] In authoritarian regimes of both rich and poor countries, resources are allocated by what Douglass North *et al.* (2009) call "limited access orders", that is, not by legal rules but as privileges from above. In these contexts, informal networks and personal connections take precedence over formal rules and institutions. Printed budgets and other official data become almost meaningless in such patrimonial states as opposed to high-trust, modern states that allocate resources with "open-access orders". For example, in the neo-patrimonial and personalized Russian system, Vladimir Putin, as chief patron, sits at the top of a vast patronage pyramid. His patron status is legitimized by a personalized system which depends almost entirely on his popularity. His power is maintained by dispensation of public jobs, contracts, and subsidies from the treasury, with support of the formal governing apparatus that includes state security and military organizations. Intermediary or autonomous civil society institutions are either banned or tightly controlled. Effectively, opposition is banned to avoid any "centers of protest" from widening and threatening regime rule.[8] The fear by such authoritarian leaders is that rule of law could break out from independent institutions not under regime control. Rule of law as opposed to rule by law of a neo-tsar depends on independent prosecutors and judges. Their independence strengthens state institutions and preserves checks and balances; their diminution by loss of funds or institutional independence (as in Poland) threatens substantive rule of law. Neo-tsars in countries such as Russia with Putin must maintain a delicate balance, appearing to defend the people against predatory elites while defending the elites against possible popular uprising (*The Economist*, 2017o: 25). Leaders at the top of other modern illiberal regimes, such as that of Viktor Orban in Hungary, and personalized authoritarian counterparts in poor countries, such as Robert Mugabe, until recently president of Zimbabwe for 37 years, from the fall of white British-ruled Rhodesia, maintain power through deft use of similar institutional, allocative, and repressive toolkits.

Of course, budget instability and short-termism arise in both democratic and authoritarian countries; or in both rich and poor countries. Nationalism can play a dramatic role but often the causes are the much more mundane issues of political deadlock and lack of positive institutional redundancy leading to inability to plan or execute budgets for more than a few months (Caiden and Wildavsky, 1974). That weakens effectiveness by interrupting services, programs, and projects on which people depend. Bad governance derived from unstable public finances are linked to ineffectiveness. States can perhaps be badly led and well-administered for good results for a time. That time is longer in federations that have multiple levels of government that all have to fail for complete collapse. But in all cases, bad leadership and regime policies will eventually destroy any semblance of effectiveness.

The fact is that most international "bad" governance problems are messy and not actionable without serious unintended consequences. This is, in part, due to the breadth of the notions of "bad" and "governance" which are hard to attribute to anything specific in policy design or implementation. Bad governance is a way of labelling the core problem which is governmental ineffectiveness. Sorting out the precise causes and remedies is difficult even with the most formal methods. Responding to them to try and improve government policymaking and implementation requires the most precise efforts from groups of respected professionals and stakeholders to define the specific problem(s) and estimate the magnitude and range of unintended consequences. To do this, a "good" governance agenda is needed that limits itself to the planning and implementation of realistically manageable sectors, such as health and infrastructure. For, "good governance" itself is too broad a problem target or policy objective to be actionable and, for effectiveness, must be limited to issues within the major health care, transport, education, and agriculture sectors on which quality of life and development depend.

Varieties of ineffectiveness can be distinguished, some of which include inefficiency. Governments might be: inefficient and ineffective (e.g. Nigeria); inefficient and effective (some Middle Eastern countries with benevolent autocrats such as Qatar); or efficient and effective (e.g. Switzerland, New Zealand, and many U.S. state-local governments). Overall, weak or failed states lack independent systems of legal rules, legitimacy from their citizens, and functioning accountability mechanisms. A broad focus on "good" governance often means focusing on diffuse and long-standing structural and institutional problems, such as lack of checks and balances and separation of powers. Such gaps allow "doom-loops" to fester between such regime institutions and processes as: the military and foreign policy; the military and domestic policy; the regime and internal and external auditing; and regime control of budget planning and allocations. These kinds of conflicts of interest weaken governance and diminish legitimacy. A conclusion is that such structural problems can only be changed incrementally and at the margins by modifying the perverse incentives of cultural values and practices that underpin them. Reducing perverse incentives in most societies can be done at the level of sectors and programs which will improve, but clearly not lead to, perfect outcomes.

Why the sectoral focus? The short answer is scale. The longer one is that sector programs and policies affect the majority of people in most countries, those who reside in metropolitan areas and their suburbs. While over 50 percent of the world's population live in cities today, by 2050 this proportion is expected to grow to 66 percent (Ramirez-Djumena, 2014: 42). Sectors also represent the bulk of budgeted funds for programs and services in most countries and their financing depends on both fiscal policy and the performance of the financial sector. For example, macroeconomic and fiscal policies are important because budgets finance policies and their macroeconomic impact on growth needs to be estimated carefully and controlled. The urban transport sector and a deficient supply of infrastructure assets or failure to maintain those supplied are growing problems in many countries. In response, innovative models of alternative urban transport service delivery and financing are being tried with many transferable lessons. Such operational- and sector-level lessons can be scaled up, benefiting the administration and control of finances at the national government level (Guess and Husted, 2017: 4). Conversely, central government policy successes can be scaled down to the sub-national level for cities.

Additionally, health care sector financing and service delivery are also important problems with many transferable lessons available from around the world at both strategic and operational levels. Education policies are in the midst of an international revolution in cities and countries, particularly in Europe and North America. Social assistance and poverty policies offer a wide range of policy implementation and reform lessons learned, particularly from Latin America, that have already been transferred successfully to countries, both poor and wealthy. Global demand for clean energy is growing and the persistence of coal and petroleum sources continues to require smart environmental regulation and control of air, water, and solid waste pollution. Countries such as India are making important strides in solid waste management that rely on intergovernmental cooperation within the federation from both private firms and the public sector. In other poorer countries, such as Liberia and Bolivia, agriculture and natural resource policies affect more people than the above sectors of wealthier urban countries. In short, sectors serve mostly urban people and reflect general urbanization trends across all regions. Each sector offers examples of controversial policy design (including bold experimentation in some cases) and implementation. They all can be subdivided into programs and projects that may be analyzed for lessons which can be transferred to or from the national and sub-national levels. Threats to political culture values and practices by smaller sectoral reform efforts are also much smaller. They can represent the thin edge of the wedge to whole-systems strengthening and reform.

What should government structures look like if results are to be improved? Structural changes require longer-term efforts, sustained support by top-level elites and regimes, and a higher place on the policy agendas than exists in most countries. Given this reality, efforts should be at the operational level on an incremental, piecemeal (i.e. stages) basis. For, aid-driven state modernization, institution-building and civil service reform efforts have had few notable successes. Where they have made a difference, such efforts often fall victim to the withdrawal of needed top-level regime support.[9]

In the shorter-term, the best chance of sustaining good governance via domestic efforts supplemented by overseas aid is to encourage host country federations or quasi-federalist structures and processes. Federalist structures offer positive redundancy to deepen decentralized democracy, policy flexibility, single-markets for whole countries, and enhanced possibilities for systemic policy and management learning as well as more concerted policy action. Madisonian-style institutional ambition countering ambition democracy would spread power among competing branches of government and among different interests (Fukuyama, 2014: 456). A more comprehensive democracy also needs to spread power vertically as well as horizontally via checks and balances/separation of powers between the national level and independent sub-national tiers of government. Only then does a framework exist for effective government through the creation of positive redundancies and limits on power. By contrast, with exceptions for scale and culture, unitary and confederation systems have not been able to create or sustain effective and legitimate governments.[10] Confederations fall victim to the usual collective action problem of any institution requiring unanimous consent for substantive action. Creation of sustained, effective states via structural changes including federations will require long-term foresight and trial–error incremental efforts. Such efforts can enhance central governments and regimes (just as mayoral innovations often flow upwards to improve federal governance) through the creation of quasi-federation institutions that can evolve into full federations. Development of federalist decision frameworks will require sustained support of efforts by many countries around the world to strengthen their central governments enough to sensibly redefine intergovernmental fiscal and political roles and responsibilities so that sufficient authority and responsibilities are devolved to sub-national governments to meet citizen needs. For example, citizens need accountable sub-national governments that can make and enforce building codes and fire inspections. In unitary and authoritarian centralized countries, this is an unimportant central government function that is poorly performed. Though few countries have devolved core functions, many have redefined intergovernmental fiscal relations and corresponding fiscal transfer formulae, types of aid, recipient eligibility requirements, and incentives for all parties. The effect is to create quasi-federation mechanisms within otherwise unitary and even authoritarian states (e.g. China and the U.K.).

Where regimes provide the supportive will for state-building, external aid can contribute local capacity. The U.S. Reconstruction effort after the 1861–1865 Civil War was considered a successful democracy-promotion effort, supporting civil society groups and southern political organizations willing to accept black political rights. The programmatic goal was to guarantee the basic rights of former slaves and encourage the rise of biracial governments to power throughout the defeated Confederacy (Foner, 2015). States that accepted the condition of democracy received preferential financial and trade assistance. The impact of the Acts and later civil rights laws was significant in mobilizing black voters and producing black officials at every level of government. In the 1870s, they led to the establishment of the South's first state-funded public school systems; strengthened the bargaining power of plantation laborers; made taxation more equitable; outlawed racial discrimination in transportation and public accommodations; and offered aid to industries that could lead to Southern economic development which could benefit both blacks and whites. But systemic design flaws and a failure of political support from the top allowed white opponents of these programs to defeat their successful implementation through violence and intimidation (i.e. the KKK), failure to provide land (land reform that would prevent former slaves from going back to work on plantations); retreat by the U.S. government from supporting the ideal of equality (the GOP turned more conservative, new president Rutherford Hayes disavowed further national efforts to enforce the rights of blacks); and official reinstatement of segregation and inequality through Jim Crow laws. In short, Reconstruction failed because of the failure of political will by the federal government. Southern blacks were then left to the mercies of counter-reformist "Jim Crow" groups that openly defied U.S. laws and the Constitution (Mead, 2015: 56).

Such large-scale, transformational and social engineering efforts as "democracy-building" should be avoided in overseas aid programs. Aid programs are unable to sustain and target major changes in political structures and political cultures necessary for such societal transformations. They are, by definition, long term and likely to produce diffuse benefits, but also many opponents, of even incremental and smaller-scale reforms of specific systems, e.g. education. Given the need for a sector focus and the demonstrated successes of quasi-federal delivery systems, how can overseas aid enhance governmental effectiveness and spread liberal Western models of open societies and economies? The short answer to this is that to improve governmental effectiveness, the aid itself must be effective. Instead, overseas aid is often criticized for ineffectiveness, inefficiency, and corruption. The longer answer is that, first, aid must fit the institutional context and political culture. It should be targeted to problems of corruption and lack of strong institutional systems and processes that impede project implementation and diminish results. That is, the complexity of the problem is increased by the fact that both the aid and the governments need to be sufficiently effective in order to obtain in-country results. Institutions are the formal and informal rules and processes and aid should recognize them as both constraints and opportunities, for formalization, systemization, and monetization in order to enhance decision transparency. They are the "stable, valued and recurring patterns of behavior that facilitate human collective action" (Huntington, 1965). To again distinguish institutions from structures, the latter are the organizations which facilitate the rule-making and its enforcement.

Thus, the decisions and policy results of organizational structures and institutions are powerfully affected by political cultures. Political cultures are those values and practices that determine what rules are made and how strictly they are enforced. Some ignore political culture as a fluffy notion hard to attribute to results. While Fukuyama (2014: 433) mentions culture as a constraint to Middle East democracy, he fails to mention it as a factor in explaining performance differences between regions, such as Asia, Sub-Saharan Africa, the Middle East, and Latin America (2014: 386). That is hard to square with the well-known determinative features of Asian consensus and indebtedness shame culture, Islamic constraints on political and economic freedom in the Middle East, *jeitinho* in Latin America, or finding short-cuts and ways around rigid and irrational rules (*The Economist*, 2017b: 32) and the "mirroring behavior" or empathy for relaxed financial rule enforcement, also in Latin America, that weakens oversight (Vaughan, 2016). The notion that, for example, financial oversight rules are bent for groups because "we are all in it together" is an example of social reciprocity or the "mirroring" that weakens public financial management (PFM) in Latin America and other contexts as well—in both rich and poor states. These are learned values and practices, and motivational driver variables that can be changed in a relatively short time for particular transactions with the right incentives. For example, household debt in Asian countries has grown dramatically (2007–2017) fueling more consumption by the middle classes (*The Economist*, 2017q: 70). Mortgage debt has increased dramatically, driven but also controlled by tight rules on collateral and creditworthiness standards. In a short period of time, these institutional changes have marginally changed even the historic Confucian strictures against indebtedness. Political culture is a variable not a constant and can be changed. Writers such as Inglehart (1997) and Harrison (1985) recognize this and the fact that it is an important indirect force determining policy results. None of them view political culture as a single and constant determinative force.

In addition, as a second requirement, aid needs to recognize at the design stage that, as systems of values and formal practices, law is also a part of political culture. Law can be viewed two ways. First, legal systems are a constraint on governmental power, a limiting force to bring it into balance with other non-state institutions, and a requirement to make and enforce clear and impersonal rules impartially (Fukuyama, 2014: 37). Political cultures are those values affecting which rules are made and how impartially they are enforced. Second, law also affects the administration and management of public policy. Thus, rules *of* law viewed as transcendental and separate from rulers characterize modern states (2014: 10). Rulers in modern states are limited by laws and legal systems. By contrast, in patrimonial states, rulers govern *by* law which is an expression of personal power. Any limits on such sovereigns are voluntary. Confucian Chinese rulers argued, for example, that law was an unwritten rational instrument by which the state exercised authority (2014: 357). Law as an institution was affected by the cultural value that rules were made by sovereigns for the benefit of citizens. Sovereigns ruled through their legal systems. The concept of law in China was not and is not transcendental or church-derived as in the West, which is a separate and limiting force on state power.

For improving governmental effectiveness, the relation between law and public management is all important. Law should facilitate management discretion in making necessary financial and personnel choices to deliver services, programs and projects as planned. But in many country contexts, program designers and local aid officials labor under legal constraints that any minor procedural or practical modification such as a new fiscal management system requires legal or even constitutional change. Here, Roman Civil Law which applies in most of the world is different from Anglo-American Common Law. With its civil law system and culture of detailed statutory public law tradition, in Continental Europe public administration and policy is a sub-field of law. The role of the administrators is to rationally apply statutes; the statutes are promulgated by decision makers seeking the most rational approach to problem-solving. A troubling question has always been often what "rational" means? This contrasts with the role of law in public management in Commonwealth countries and the U.S. where public administration and policy studies reflect the common law tradition of precedent and broader interpretation of laws by managers. Managers act unless expressly forbidden (Wright, 2002: 9–51) and the unwritten but utilitarian norm is to act on what works or is likely to work. They are or should not be dissuaded by fear of illegal action. In Common Law countries, sanctions for error or possible illegality arise after decisions are made for demonstrable cause.

Conversely, in the state-centered public law approach to public policy and administration, managers are forbidden to act without statutory authorization. That constraint means that management tools such as financial information systems and budget reforms including shifts to program formats, require authorizing laws first. Devolution of fiscal and management authority to local governments in fiscal decentralization programs would be a legal and structural change under Civil Law systems, including the Former Soviet Union, that emphasizes statutory authority for all decisions. So, IT and budget systems are not simply economic or management tools. They become legal issues. In the U.S. and Germany, politics in principle is separated from policy formulation and implementation. In practice this rarely happens in the U.S. common law system because of the need for managerial flexibility and the necessity of ensuring political accountability of institutions to voters and publics. In Germany and to a large extent in Civil Law tradition countries, policy is strictly a matter of law.[11] The cultural and political belief is that nothing works except through law. For instance, the suggestion that the European Central Bank (ECB) should create new money to buy sovereign bonds (called "quantitative easing" or QE) in fiscal crises was viewed at first as illegal. It was illegal according to the German Constitutional Court as not just a violation of the public finance norm that central banks should stick to monetary policy and not perform quasi-fiscal policy acts such as financing. Rather, applying QE would be illegal by this reasoning because such actions exceeded its narrow mandate to manage the money supply. This would break the rules and destroy trust in government (*The Economist*, 2014: 61). For these reasons, in the U.S. tradition, policymaking and implementation are highly politicized processes which are to some extent compensated for by institutional checks and balances and separation of governmental functions.

How can overseas aid then make a difference under these legal and regulatory conditions and improve governmental effectiveness? It is important for overseas aid design to recognize that country settings where comparative lessons are to be applied will fall into one or other of these legal traditions, with some mixed examples in unitary Commonwealth countries such as the U.K. where managerial accountability is combined with a deep legal-regulatory tradition of policymaking and administration. This legal tradition distinction is important in identifying constraints to both policy formulation and implementation. The tradition can also serve as a constraint on policy analysis or appraisal before enactment and implementation. In short, aid needs to understand context and the full range of political culture influences on systems and institutions such as law. This is essential to avoid the colonialist mistake of "good enough governance" (Fukuyama, 2014: 317) which served British purposes of indirect rule in places such as Nigeria but not for implanting effective governmental institutions.

In short, policy responses for facilitating state effectiveness must be targeted and focused. An agenda to create legitimate and effective governments that deliver needed services, programs, and projects need not be all-encompassing or "transformational". The issue is how to create effective governments in countries, rich and poor? Aid design and delivery faces severe constraints that have hampered its own effectiveness. These problems are well-known: regime indifference to aid agendas; inter-donor competition for wins that become more important than results (goal displacement); aid missions of variable quality that often intrude on projects; variable quality project team and staff quality; poor project designs that often fail to anticipate obvious constraints; and interference by aid firms that manage projects. For these reasons, it is hard to compare what works and what does not to derive lessons for better aid performance. It is argued that efforts can proceed, driven by aid, through a strategy of incremental and sequential steps. As is known, small changes and improvements often lead to large gains. Aid deliverance has often been distorted by inter-donor competition, distracted by large-bore social engineering goals and micro-managed to block critical feedback and hinder development of needed incentives for management and policy improvements.

World Bank and other multilateral donor projects mostly focus on sectoral and technical policy objectives rather than whole government reforms. They have few broader social engineering projects geared to stimulating participatory democratic governance. They are not into social engineering and transformational change. Learning and diffusion of analytic methods and expanding participation of clients in policymaking (e.g. participatory municipal capital budgeting) is focused on sectors or levels of government. While many of the methods, systems, and participatory processes used for improvements in sectors such as health care and educational services are requisites of democratic and good government anywhere, they are nevertheless often not integrated into national systems. Nor do national systems emulate them country-wide.

Why then have these sectoral efforts not led to more effective government from a scaling up effect? The answer is that regimes have often been indifferent to these projects at best and, to the extent that systems and methods could or should be transferred upwards to central governments, the regimes resist this from fear of systemic implications resulting from greater analytic knowledge, transparency, and participatory clamor. In other words, the projects often work too well and become threats. Regimes are also content to let donors compete for development agenda space in their host countries in exchange for office space and in-kind counterpart funds at minimal expense to them. But where aid fiscal management projects, for instance, produce demands for greater internal audit and control institutions and stronger anti-corruption agencies, many regimes fear the obvious threats to their power bases and continued longevity.[12]

Nevertheless, to minimize waste and frustration, the majority of all-donor aid disbursements should focus on responding to sectoral problems, such as lack of health care quality or coverage, because the major causes of state failure involve conflicts reflecting the complex values and practices in political culture that often perpetuate, directly or indirectly, corruption and institutional weakness. Since operationally, political cultures determine what rules are made and how strictly they are enforced[13] it is important to devise incentives that align them with effective program and policy results. It is far easier to align incentives to operate technical systems that, for example, contribute to improved health care and education, with relatively impermeable cultures. Users need only modify their values and practices slightly to learn and operate new accounting and budgeting systems, rather than adjust to deeper changes required for social engineering objectives in democracy, governance, and human rights programs. For example, reduced restrictions on managerial authority in exchange for meeting performance targets worked in the Ecuadorian Ministry of Finance to incentivize expenditure controls and encourage better service performances (Guess, 1992: 380). Such micro-incentive systems have worked in most sectors to improve performance at the program level. If they can overcome the infamous Latin American culture of centralization to produce results and provide greater flexibility to manage budgets and programs, they can work elsewhere as well. Supported by properly designed and implemented aid projects, these micro-systems improvements can work and become additive: each project contributes to building state systems that improve overall public sector management performance and service results. For reasons of scale and minimal threats to local political cultures, micro-level and sectoral projects are more successful at professionalizing staff and developing values and practices that can be modified further at the margin to strengthen whole states. The former can be demonstrated with successful projects; scaling up to the latter from marginal changes to the culture is the harder part. Such efforts are successful in working with cultures; they have been less successful in stabilizing whole states threatened by ethnic and nationalist populist movements that destabilize service budgets and plans.

Notes

1 Karl Marx argued that state institutions merely reflected the preferences of ruling capitalist elites. State institutions were agents of their class preferences, meaning bureaucracies and judicial institutions, for example, were simply agents of the ruling elites and classes. If the adjectives "rent-seeking" and "kleptocratic" are inserted for the over-broad term "capitalist" (since even in former socialist countries some markets functioned, e.g. Hungarian property mortgages), the notion of states as passive tools and reflections of regime preferences, however contradictory they might be, is not that outlandish in poorer countries ruled by authoritarian leaders.
2 The call then is really for better governing or governments that can deliver results. To "govern: or do 'governing' are transitive verbs while the commonly used term 'governance' is intransitive and needs no object to complete its meaning. For that reason, it is almost a throw-away term and has been called an 'empty signifier' by Claus Offe (2009) 'Governance' and 'Empty Signifier?' ", *Constellations*, Vol. 16, No. 9, pp. 550–562. If nothing else, "governance" is widely used in the development industry and sells books.

3 State modernization efforts refer to broader attempts to redesign govern-mental structures and rationalize functions to improve planning and delivery of programs and projects. Functional review methods to modernize states can target whole governments or particular ministries. Civil service reform efforts are narrower and focus on meritocratic recruitment and promotion to incen-tivize action and eliminate patronage. Donors such as World Bank and U.K. Aid or British DFID have implemented projects in both areas in many countries.

4 An important early debate for development theorists was the extent to which formal structures performed basic political input functions of interest articu-lation/aggregation and political communication, and the governmental output functions of rule-making/application and adjudication, so functions such as interest-articulation could be performed by structures other than trade unions (Almond, 1960: 17), leading to the intriguing conclusion that multiple kinds of structures perform multiple kinds of functions. In Bucharest as recently as 2004, I used to buy homemade wine from the corner laundry and in Budapest, one could often buy clothes in the electronics shops. The profundity of this, its practical utility, and its potential for tautology in defining problems for improving state effectiveness is revealed in the old saw that legs were created to wear pants. The critical function not emphasized in this debate was allo-cation. To explain how that was performed one had to turn to regime and elite interests in controlling formal-legal budget processes and dividing up actual state budget shares. Regimes controlled states backed by armies and security apparatus in the many authoritarian countries. In democratic systems such as Costa Rica, Botswana, Commonwealth countries, the U.S., and many Latin American countries the traditional political functions are more or less performed by traditional structures. It is in the many poor countries with various shades of authoritarian regimes that one must decipher how status groups, tribes, sects, kinship groups, and lineage groups (Almond, 1960: 13) suffer from allocational inefficiencies that generate the ethno-nationalist leaders and groups threatening states, and otherwise combine to allocate state resources. For that reason, the focus on sectors and functions refers to the UN COFOG functions, such as health and education, for which aid can be an important influence. That is, it is known that budget functions are independent of the government organizational structures (Schiavo-Campo and Tommasi, 1999: 70). Fourteen major functions are recognized as the U.N. Functional Classification of the Functions of Government (COFOG). There are also 61 groups and 127 sub-groups (1999: 70). For example, the Social Service function includes the sub-group of Education and the sub-groups of Primary, Secondary, and Tertiary Education. Fiscal transparency and budgetary comprehensiveness are obtained by cross-walking expenditure objects across organizational units into combined functions.

5 Authoritarian states or regimes require observance of certain rules and allow limited liberty as long as it does not challenge political power. By contrast, totalitarian states exercise total control over citizen's lives. They combine sys-tematic terror, single-party rule, a centrally planned economy, command over the army and media, and an all-encompassing ideology. Some countries had both systems in their histories. Hungary in the 1950s for example, was an advanced satellite of the Soviet system but had slipped back into authoritar-ianism, with some markets operational and relatively high levels of freedom.

Marxist-Leninist ideology had been reinterpreted as Hungarian nationalism. Local intellectuals were largely in favor of their version of the communist system under Imre Nagy. But the Soviets could re-apply totalitarianism and did so in 1956 and after, until the late 1980s.

6 An important ingredient of effective democratic government is the shift from an "inquisitorial" system of judicial process associated often with discredited regimes. In such systems, judges play an investigative role which combines judicial and executive functions and violates separation of powers and checks and balances. More modern state judicial systems are "adversarial", in which judges act as referees between prosecution and defense. The adversarial justice system or sector offers lessons for analytic and evidence-based decisions which democratic policymakers can use. Policymakers in democracies should be neutral referees of evidence just like judges in adversarial systems. The hope is that lessons can be scaled up from the court system to national policymaking.

7 Fred Riggs urged that outsiders pay attention to the "prismatic" features of poor and developing country institutions. Government may have the trappings of modernity but hide the fact that structures are not what they seem and functions often quite different from organizational charts. For example, the normal flow of orders downward and information and compliance upwards often flows diagonally and horizontally in countries, for instance, MOF in Kazakhstan and normal government approval processes in Nepal. That makes it difficult to distinguish staff-line functions and to even begin to consider how a reformed ministry or government might look.

8 The 2014 Russian film by Yury Bykov "Durak" (The Fool) portrayed the dangers of being an honest citizen speaking out against injustice. After the pipes burst in his high-rise building of flats, small town plumber Dima finds they are not only endangered by the pipes but also the building itself, which is tilting and could fall over. He tries to convince municipal authorities to relocate the tenants to abandoned state buildings. But this threatens corrupt real estate moguls who profit from both their abandoned buildings and city contracts. Several of Dima's supporters are murdered and he narrowly escapes death several times, fighting corrupt bureaucrats. Even the smallest attempt to rectify routine problems with building inspections become almost impossible because they threaten established ways of state business and challenge existing authority.

9 Achievement of effective government requires definition of the state and distinguishing its components to properly focus efforts on modernization. In many countries, the distinction between regime, political parties, ministries, and state enterprises is thin. The regime effectively controls appointments and eliminates any possibility of separation of powers and checks and balances— which bodes ill for good governance. Despite the obvious framework for cronyism it can lead to stability and what have been called "stabilitocracies". For example, in Balkan countries (and elsewhere in poorer countries) ethnic-based parties and allocation of ministries by ethnicity and party are common practice (*The Economist*, 2017e: 45). In Iraq, cabinet posts are regularly divvied up between political blocs based on sect and ethnicity. Parties are guaranteed a share of spoils and power. It is said that with entrenched corruption like this, there is "little anyone can do to fix the Iraqi state" (*The Economist*, 2016: 41). Such corruption, or rent-seeking from string-pulling to bribery, destroys trust in state institutions.

10 Limited functional confederations can work, for example, trade as in the East African Community (EAC) of six countries for trade. EAC plans to scale-up to a common currency which is another building-block of effective governance.

11 This is now a problem constraining the political resolution of the fiscal balance and local management discretion issues in Catalonia that have prompted calls for secession from Spain. The Rajoy regime solution has been to apply more statutory law leading to simplistic judgments of violation requiring force to impose sanctions which generates more opposition and support for an otherwise radical demand by secessionists to solve small-bore issues.

12 Public institutions need internal audits or watchdogs to reveal mismanagement, fraud and waste. Such agencies often exist formally but are compromised by requirements that they report and vet findings to agency management first. Such conflicts of interest are common and weaken governmental effectiveness. For example, despite years of safety and poor management problems, Washington Metro (WMATA)'s inspector general (OIG) was required to hire its staff, such as forensic auditors, through the WMATA procurement office; use agency lawyers; and obtain clearance of findings that might embarrass the agency. Internal audit units should be independent or not exist at all. That governmental agencies regularly attempt to silence them is proof of the effectiveness of this kind of fiscal watchdog institution (*Washington Post*, December 4, 2017, A24).

13 For example, there is a sharp cultural difference in the occupational licensing rules made and enforced against ex-prisoners by U.S. states. California used 4000 low-level felons to battle wildfires but prevented them from getting firefighter's licenses on release. Michigan bans convicted felons from 150 occupations. By contrast, several states including Kentucky and Illinois prevent licensing boards from denial unless the crime is directly related to the job. Policy studies show a reoffending rate of 9 percent in states with the heaviest licensing burdens while states with the lightest burdens saw a decrease of 2.5 percent over the same period (*The Economist*, 2017n: 31).

2 Challenges to Effective Government
Ethnic-Nationalism, Populist Nationalism and Weak State Institutions

Societies have always faced rifts between regions, classes, tribes, ethnicities, and sects. Competition for land and territory and the resources that they command has always produced conflicts over influence. Lack of area-wide state institutions with authority to resolve conflicts between them allow rifts and conflicts to fester and in many cases to spread across country territories and to dominate entire regions. Power vacuums created by group claims from a mixture of survival needs and territorial aggrandizement are filled by groups and sects. The wars play out differentially, some continuing for generations others resulting in formation of more stable governing institutions that can exercise a monopoly of force and resolve conflicts. Historically, only some of such tribes and bands evolved into chiefdoms and later into coalitions and then functioning states (Diamond, 1999: 264–270). In poor countries such as Papua New Guinea where there are now 45 parties, 850 languages, people vote for *wantoks* or "one-talk" clans. Voting is driven by ethnicity (i.e. roots and race used to define group identity) and pork-barrel politics as clans trade votes. National policy issues in such areas as health care and infrastructure play no role in election campaigns and putting together coalitions is like "knitting with eels" (*The Economist*, 2017f: 34).

The dilemma for state-builders is that under common poor-country conditions, any resultant states have been weak, incomplete, and often regress to basic tribal and ethnic architecture and corresponding conflicts. Often for survival and security reasons, states take the form of centralized, authoritarian, and unitary entities rather than federations that could better manage conflicts and produce effective governance. For sectarian, tribal, and ethnic conflicts are expressions of the values and practices of their groups or political cultures. The conflicts have weakened states and, indirectly still prevent remedial actions. The continuing legacy is that centuries ago, arriving colonists found populations composed of multiple ethnicities, tribes and lineage groups whom they enslaved, and created extractive institutions. Mercantilist policies of extracting resources, such as timber and minerals from colonies, often relied on tribal and local group labor (e.g. Britain and tropical hardwood extraction from Belize).

The institution blocked development of open, competitive market economies and modern governing institutions necessary for socioeconomic development (Fukuyama, 2014: 235).

Resultant governing institutions after independence were fragile. They reacted to increasing national fragmentation and growing group demands with a range of responses from repression to mediation and compromise. African ethnic and tribal groups in particular were structurally and culturally complex but served colonial rulers as mere "signaling devices" which they played off against each other in political games to make them more tractable and useful for extracting resources (2014: 296). Subsequent post-independence governments continued these games in order to garner and maintain power and prestige as rulers. The regimes of many current countries still represent particular tribes and ethnicities as their clients rather than the many groups found in each "national" territory. Regimes and parties thus came to represent tribes and ethnicities rather than national interests. This built in fundamental conflicts over resources at the start and has deteriorated in many cases to wars and violent conflicts over power and territory. Arriving British in Nigeria, for example, found simple kingdoms and tribes, such as Yoruba-speaking people in the Niger delta area, with separate languages (2014: 589 and Table 2.1). The chiefdoms, tribes and local kingdoms rarely developed into modern states. Regimes and parties narrowed their representative scopes, preventing chiefdoms from becoming more modern governing institutions, thus paving the way for more conflicts and unstable governments. Of course, failure to organize beyond conflicting members of loose confederations before the arrival of colonialists made these simple forms of social organization tractable and easy game for being played off against each other which kept them weak and primitive. In these kinds of simple reactions to growing ethno-nationalism, governments have produced more sectarian and ethnic problems that exacerbate regional and class inequities. These create more governance problems for the future. The rifts have become more intense in the past decades and domestic political regimes as well as international aid responses have, in many countries, become less effective and remedial. They have both treated the symptoms of deeper historic problems without responding to the perverse incentives that frequently drive the most intense ethno-nationalist causes.[1]

The threat of nationalist pressures on state effectiveness is revealed by the fact that they have destabilized governments in both rich and poor countries. The threats can be divided into (1) existential and populist-driven, and (2) macro and micro-policy levels. Parties and movements aggregate interests in many countries with ethno-nationalist appeals. At the macro level, populists often claim fundamental and existential mandates from the "people" and often use social media to successfully convert narrower ethnic, often regional demands into nation-wide or nationalist demands. Some of these demands stem legitimately from long-standing deprivations of income and wage inequality and immigration which threaten existing and dominant group cultural values and practices. As institutions fail to respond comprehensively, such demands grow in intensity to existential proportions. Successful efforts to stabilize the macroeconomy and ensure fiscal discipline by governing institutions do not resonate and become irrelevant to the ethno-nationalist narrative. At the micro-policy level, governments face sectoral issues of: urban infrastructure and transport, health care, education, agriculture, mining and natural resources, energy supply and environmental protection. Failed responses to demands at the micro level have intensified regional and sectarian rifts. These are both causes and consequences of ineffective governing institutions.

As indicated, poor country ruling political regimes and professional governments, such as in Liberia, Ethiopia, and Nigeria (Table 2.1), face ethno-nationalist pressures from sects and tribes that further weaken their ability to govern. These countries unsurprisingly have had trouble maintaining macroeconomic stability. In regions such as MENA and Asia, the grievances of ethnicities and sects merge with the needs of gaining or retaining power, adding a religious nationalist dimension. Religious autocracies in MENA are often the product of failed dictatorships where Islamic hierarchies and practices are merged with the state, forming theocracies or the worst of both worlds. In other regions dominated by different religions such as Asia, the Buddhist regime in Myanmar (effectively a theocracy) reflects the population and violently mobilizes against minorities, including Christians and Muslims. In India, the grassroots base of the ruling Bharativa Janat Party (BJP) is led by violent right-wing Hindu nationalists against Muslims (Rohingya) and in support of its "Hinduisation" agenda, features tightened restrictions on cow-slaughter and organized vigilante attacks on Muslims. Wealthier countries, such as England and Hungary, are able to maintain stability for longer despite intense populist pressures mobilizing opinions against the resident ethnicities and sects from abroad via reverse ethno-nationalism. Such populist movements play on domestic regional employment and income grievances and successfully blame the usually long-standing economic problems on ethnicities and sects. The tragic irony is worsened by the fact that they have often escaped from the very poor countries that suffer weakened governments from ethno-nationalism at home. To cement their claims and popularity, wealthier country populists argue successfully to their voters that the values and practices of immigrants from poor, governmentally fragmented countries are permanently inconsistent with the political cultures of the wealthier countries.

Thus, the paths from radical nationalism (ethnic and populist) to governmental ineffectiveness are relatively clear. In poorer countries, tribes and sects engage in ongoing conflicts over power unrestrained by legitimate national states and their security forces. Components of

Table 2.1 Institutional Contextual Challenges, Responses, and Results

Problem	Examples	Political Structures	Response	Results
Ethno-Nationalism	Ethiopia (Oromo vs. Somali but also Ambara and Tigrayan groups); Liberia (Krahn vs. Gio and Mano groups); Nigerian sectarian tensions between Muslim North and Christian South.	Institutional Chaos and Civil War in Ethiopia 1976–1991; and Liberia: 1989–1976; 1999–2003. Nigerian sectarian wars between Hausa-Pulasi Muslims in North and Yoruba and Igbo Christians in SW and SE Nigeria 1967–1970. Liberia is a unitary state with no sub-national governments (IMF, 2012) Nigeria is a federation of 36 states and one federal capital territory (Lagos) and 774 local governments in which the states are reliant on central transfers for revenue but can also borrow and mostly avoid publishing audited budgets. With exception of Lagos state, S/L governments rely on block grants and cannot determine their own rates/bases for fees or taxes. But discretion over grant funds allows them to spend at will and run arrears that transfers cannot cover now that oil prices have dropped (OECD, 2016)	Initiated Ethiopian Ethnic Federalism 1991; Liberian Democracy at end of second civil war 2003; Nigerian electoral rules 2015	Ethiopian Official Cards still based on Ethnic I.D.; Federal Government now Tigrayan Ethnicity Dominated; Local Government Autonomy; Liberian Presidential succession.
Populist Nationalism	Spain: Catalonia region demand for independence, succession.	Unitary/Democracy	Illegal referendum to succeed which Madrid sought to stop; invoked Article 155 to take control of regional finances and law enforcement	Standoff with Constitutional Court.

(continued)

Table 2.1 (Cont.)

Problem	Examples	Political Structures	Response	Results
	Scotland (U.K.)	Part of Incomplete U.K. Federation	U.K. unitary government is ultra-centralized: 95% of tax revenues generated by London; less than 20% local own source revenues. Scotland has had substantial autonomy since 1999; in 2016, Scotland gained almost full fiscal autonomy: greater take of income taxes (higher take of Whitehall Treasury collections or reduced local taxes), can change bases/rates of other taxes, more borrowing authority, adjustable block grant based on Scottish GDP growth formula. Scotland is one of world's most powerful subnational states along with Canadian provinces and Swiss cantons (*The Economist*, 2016a: 56)	
	Hungary	Unitary/Democracy	Unitary system and illiberal democratic regime.	
	E.U.	Confederation of 28 member states with 24 languages	"Incompletely theorized agreement" (Petersen, 2015: 37 citing Cass Sunstein); standoff between euro-federalists wanting deeper integration (i.e. political, banking, and debt) and German fiscal restraint positions	
	Former Yugoslav Federation	Imposed federation (to 1991)	Break-up and war	Independence for most republics; continuing tensions Serbia-Kosovo.

Canadian Aboriginals or First Peoples	Iroquois Confederacy (Canada and America 1500s)	Confederation united warring tribes. Chief Hiawatha (Mohawk) united League of Five Nations 1570s prevented war among tribes and made alliances with Dutch and English. Most Indians did not evolve beyond tribes. Local Indian groups up to the 1600s had fought among themselves as much as offering resistance to European outsiders. King Philip's War (1675–1676) united them for a time against the British. By contrast, Iroquois, Mexican Mayas and Aztecs, Peruvian Incas, and Colombian *Pueblas Indigenas* evolved into political organizations (Morison, 1994: 40). But their main geopolitical role remained allying themselves with Europeans. For example, Indians allied with the English Crown against Louis XIVs New France plans for Canada (whom they called *les sauvages*). In the 1640s, the British kept them loyal with superior woolens and powerful West Indies rum (Morison, 1994: 152)
U.S. (1781–1791)	13-state Confederation evolved into Federation	Failed because of opposition to power shifting from states to weak central government in 1780s; John Calhoun argued for state nullification of laws not liked; civil war (1861–1865) sparked by confederation of southern states which also failed and evolved into national federation.

(*continued*)

Table 2.1 (Cont.)

Problem	Examples	Political Structures	Response	Results
	Brazil	Federation/Democracy	Stable democratic system with robust civil society and solid institutional checks and balances	
	China	Unitary/Authoritarian	The central government provides more fiscal transfers to cover devolved expenditure assignments; there are no revenue sources exclusively assigned to sub-national governments. Local governments have no discretion to modify tax rates or bases and are agents of the central governments to execute expenditure responsibilities (Wang and Herd, 2013: 33)	
	Russia	Unitary/Authoritarian	False federation masking autocratic neo-tsarist unitary system	

states dominated by particular sects use state resources to attack other minority sects and tribes. States are weak to begin with and such almost perennial power games and battles weaken them further. The result is either a period of chaos and civil war or accession of one tribe or sect to power. The path is often an ethnic-controlled party and this leads to at least temporary stability. Stability can be enforced by a long dictatorship, such as Robert Mugabe's in Zimbabwe for 37 years. Often bad policies are corruptly implemented and a country becomes destitute. The treasury subsists on royalties from its natural resources which keep the regime in power. As Mugabe's policies ran up a 500b percent inflation rate from printing money, he once noted that "traditional economics" did not fully apply in Zimbabwe. Many dictators make similar claims until deposed by failed economic policies and destructive politics. In many cases, post-independence rulers gain popularity by tribal affiliation and anti-imperialist rhetoric, rather than any evidence of competence. Again, Mugabe's rule was perpetuated by playing both ethnic and populist nationalism cards. The ethnic and racial cards were used first against white British colonials then the racial card against white farmers; at the African Union his rantings against whites and colonial injustices were always given rousing ovations. As a populist, he also played off the rival Ndebele group, threatening his hold on power by using the North Korean trained 5th Battalion against them (*The Economist*, 2017u: 40). Presence of a large population of poor ethnicities and uneducated believers in slogans and platitudes passing as policies enabled such rulers as Mugabe to gain and retain power for lengthy periods, even as "president for life" as he was. These almost comic, cyclically predictable ruling episodes weaken states further and make them more patrimonial, less modern and less effective. In 2015, Zimbabwe received an 11.5 percent Knoema/World Bank effectiveness rating out of 100 percent. Despite this low ranking, it actually rated higher than that of Liberia and Nigeria! In short, such rulers are able to leverage the anger and resentment of mostly ill-educated populations derived from poverty and bad governance (i.e. bad policies) against rival tribes, ethnicities, and races to gain and sustain power. It has been a winning formula in both poor and rich countries.

In the wealthier countries of Asia and the Middle East, ruling elites also play the dominant racial or religious card to gain power and sustain it against rival races and religions. Asian states are generally stronger and have been able to maintain macroeconomic stability while providing adequate services and programs. As in the Middle East, the "social pact" is services and social safety nets in exchange for quiet political support. Regimes, such as that of Malaysian Prime Minister Najib Razak, control a ruling party (UMNO in that case) composed of dominant ethnic Malays and their religion Islam. Ethnic gerrymandering of electoral districts often works in these countries to control delicate multi-ethnic coalitions in order to maintain power. Such regimes typically provide enough services for followers, such as rural infrastructure, to keep them content and quiescent. But overall, the governments are still ineffective. In the wealthiest countries, such as those in Europe, parties successfully employ populist methods to mobilize followers against the importation of problems from poorer ethno-nationalist countries. Hungarian blockage of immigrant flows from other countries has been a successful example of this negative strategy. The U.K., with its approval of Brexit largely to keep immigrants out, is another. Both governments are rated effective yet unable to mobilize against imagined threats to their very successes in policymaking and enforcing democratic safeguards. Hungary has been able to maintain itself in isolation despite E.U. membership, retaining the benefits of membership while using its imagined weaknesses to mobilize populist followers. The U.K. has voted to leave the E.U. because of its highly representative electoral system that facilitated voice by left-behind voters. The governments remain effective in both countries but threats to their democracy and governance loom on the horizon.

Few countries, regardless of levels of wealth, have been able to deal with the technical policy causes of the allocational inefficiencies that in part lead to the regional and income inequities which have been driving the ultranationalists. Well-performing governments have strong institutions which are able to affect budgetary outcomes at three levels: aggregate fiscal discipline, allocation of resources consistent with strategic priorities (allocational efficiency or AE) and efficient use of resources in implementation of policies (technical efficiency or TE) (World Bank, 1997: i). Inefficient allocation is evident in poorly allocated resources for such sectoral policy areas as education, health care, infrastructure, and economic development. Failures at this ground level have increased local problems to which populists have responded successfully at the national level with electoral victories. Predictably, few of the populists have successfully responded to either macroeconomic, sectoral level, or other policy challenges once in office. Efforts, domestic and aid driven, to strengthen states in order to deal with radical nationalist agendas have not been very effective. As will be seen, more of the efforts at the operations policy level have been successful. In some cases these sectoral developments have strengthened national governments and regimes to both make more effective policies and to withstand the populist pressures for immediate and unrealistic improvements.

One sectoral policy ignored in poorer countries that is less ethnic-related is: urban development. Urban migration has historically been a channel to escape poverty from rural areas suffering from effects of the elements (e.g. drought, floods), poorly conceived agricultural policies (e.g. tariffs), land tenure insecurity (i.e. lack of title to become real property and thus debt collateral) and lack of employment opportunities. Large urban agglomerations in Africa and Asia (e.g. Lagos, Mumbai) have been poorly planned and lack basic services, housing, and connectivity. Cities are designed for two main classes of people via gated communities linked to nearby consumption centers. They are not magnets for agro-industrial and manufacturing jobs absorbing rural migrants that they were and still are in Europe and Latin America. Most urban immigrants remain poor in Africa and Asia and are viewed as a problem to be ignored, not as a human resource opportunity by urban and national policymakers (*The Economist*, 2016c). This creates additional pressures on regimes for effective national and urban governments to which few countries have responded.

Regional Ethno-Nationalism

African Cases

Colonists arrived and exploited and manipulated local ethnicities to aggrandize power and to permit them to extract natural resources quickly. This was an example of the aggressive mercantilism practiced by most colonial powers. Building permanent, effective governing institutions was rarely on their agendas. In Africa, a long list of colonial powers plundered the continental populations.

Botswana

Nevertheless, some positive legacies exist. Botswana had become the model for "good enough governance" in SSA (Fukuyama, 2014: 316), meaning the objectives that aid donors and reformers should adopt elsewhere in the region. Defying the odds (the famed "resource curse") with judicious use of diamond revenues to benefit the economy and people; building strong public financial management institutions to support sound macroeconomic and fiscal policies; and building a modern state governed by rule of law in the British tradition, Botswana is the exception. In 2015, for example, its budget was in surplus (0.20 percent GDP); HDI was 0.98 (higher than the U.K.!); government effectiveness was 72.1 percent (same as Hungary) (Table 2.2) and unemployment was 17.6 percent. These are wealthy-country effectiveness figures! In short, the British colonized Botswana, Nigeria, Ghana, and Sierra Leone. They provided property rights, independent judiciaries, and rules of law for commercial and individual transactions. These were partial cultures that, with the right incentives, policies, and regimes to support them, could become parts of the political culture—as they have in Botswana.

By contrast, the concept of "resource curse", illegitimate states and bad governance was largely inherited by Congo from its former Belgian colonial masters. The Belgians exploited Congo from the end of the nineteenth century for 70 years. It exploited and withdrew vast resources of: diamonds, copper, gold, tropical hardwoods. After Belgium departed, mining companies tied to the regime exploited cobalt which is now used for electric cars. Congo has never had a president peacefully cede power. Since 2001, Joseph Kabila has ruled a corrupt and incompetent state. Since 2016, a local chief has led a bloody insurgency in diamond rich Kasai state against the government, further destabilizing the illegitimate regime from improving the quality of life of the inhabitants of this desperately poor state. The effectiveness of its governance is revealed by its low HDI score. Congo ranks 176th out of 188 HDI countries with a rating of 0.43 or very low human development.

The "resource curse" hypothesis focuses on the long-term negative consequences for the economy from resource production and taxation. For example, the volatility of export and tax revenues from natural resources may worsen public finances. And in oil countries such as Ghana, resource revenues can corrupt or trigger and sustain violent conflict (Cust and Mihalyi, 2017: 38). Ghana devised rules for saving the financial windfall from the discovery of oil (in 2007 and 2010), then violated them and over-borrowed, requiring an IMF surveillance program in 2015 (2017: 37). For that reason, effective governments concentrate on the "presource" stage, or the period between discovery and the start of production. This can be the "curse" if they fail to anticipate the influx of investment and foreign currency on both the economy and governmental regulation and policymaking. Thus, as indicated by Botswanan prudence in managing diamond revenues, neither the resource nor the *presource* curse is preordained. Note that institutional strength or weaknesses in both countries depended on the rules made and how strictly they enforced them, i.e. the political cultures. Botswana enforced its fiscal sustainability and discipline rules after discovery of the resource; Ghana did not.

South Africa (RSA)

Both the Dutch and British colonized the Republic of South Africa (RSA) whose institutions have facilitated its growth as a member of the exclusive transitional country club (BRICS). In contrast with the neo-patrimonialism of many African states, then president of RSA, Nelson Mandela, voluntarily gave up office after one 5-year term, unlike such figures as Kenneth Kaunda of Zambia (30 years) (Fukuyama, 2014: 288). This suggests a more modern institutional context, in part the result of a British legacy that invested heavily in hospitable places (where roads could be built easily or settlements could be accessible from the coast) such as RSA, but did "colonialism on the cheap" (2014: 292) elsewhere in Sub-Saharan Africa (SSA). Another factor in RSA state formation contrasts with institutional contexts in other regional countries. In the RSA, a larger political unit already existed (the Zulu kingdom) on which an institutional core could be built as opposed to the context of many smaller tribes locked in almost hunter-gatherer conflict in loose confederations found elsewhere in SSA (2014: 295). Political authority in RSA could be extended over a more defined territory of people that identified with the national boundaries as citizens. Eventually the state could become the nation.

The rest of SSA is largely characterized by colonists who came, pacified through wars and/or deals with locals, exploited their labor, extracted resources for the home country, and did colonialism on the cheap. That pattern left no real concept or legacy of a modern impersonal state and its needed functions. Most SSA states during that period and after independence became patrimonial, or largely the property of rulers and their clients, and both governmental effectiveness and economic performance have suffered since. Rule has been by law rather than of law, which fails to limit sovereigns in their will to stay in power for decades without legitimating elections of any kind (e.g. Robert Mugabe in Zimbabwe whose rule has just ended).

Nigeria

Another former British colony, federalist Nigeria evolved from brutal civil war to a state of relative stability owing largely to changes in its electoral democracy. Elections are an important component of the modern state and of Western political democracy. The major source of continuing Nigerian electoral tension reflects the deeper North–South religious conflict (see Table 2.1). In 2015, after the president stepped aside peacefully following the election, for the first time in history, Nigeria worked out better institutional arrangements: running mates had to come from different religious traditions and regions and the winning ticket now has to secure at least 25 percent of the vote in 75 percent of the states. The rules force political parties to build coalitions that bridge divides (Kifordu, 2011: 439). The stark ethnic and religious cleavages both are effects and causes of state weakness in Nigeria. The 250 ethnicities were subdivided in 1960 into an "ethnic gerrymandering" system of specific districts, allowing them to control jobs and funds. Most funds are from central government transfers to the 37 states, few of which have any revenue sources of their own. The central government collects the oil revenues (50 percent of general government revenues are from oil) and transfers 50 percent of them to the states. Eventually, the new electoral rules can help, if followed, to strengthen state institutions. SSA is a region where power-sharing among elected elites is not typically considered a viable option (Kifordu, 2011: 440). Because empowering another group that could repress your own is not rational, fair institutional rules that enforce power diffusion and sharing for national benefits can work. It may help that in Nigeria, a federation, power is being diffused over three levels of autonomous government, enabling diverse coalitions to form and widen representation. If one level of government fails, there is at least one more that can act as a buffer to keep the programs and services going.

Ethiopia

As examples of state failures, in Ethiopia and Liberia, conflicts for power between shifting ethnic group alliances degenerated into multiple civil wars costing millions of lives between the 1970s and the early 2000s. UN efforts were important in ending the violence and restoring peace to Liberia. This produced a successful Liberian presidential term and the first transfer of power from one elected president to another since 1944 (*The Economist*, 2017b: 49). Ethiopia also suffered years of brutal civil war. It recently developed an ethnic federalist system to manage pressures on the regime from tribal and ethnic conflict, provide national unity, focus on effective governance, and represent all ethnicities. The government is now a strong, technocratic regime with powerful military support, ruling through a single party. The ethno-federalist system established administrative divisions along ethnic lines but has ended up increasing ethnic tensions between disempowered groups (i.e. the Oromia and Amhara) (King, 2017: 71). The design has followed failed partition schemes elsewhere that use ethnic I.D. cards and allow its federal government to be dominated by one ethnic group (*The Economist*, 2017a: 50). It is now an asymmetric federation that attempts to manage tensions between stronger ethnic groups such as the Amhara that want a strong unitary state (that they can likely dominate) and the coherence of the ethnic federation which diffuses power and provides a semblance of at least vertical separation of powers. Ethno-federation is a weak compromise, institutional design that likely paves the way for the next ethno-nationalist Ethiopian conflict over power which largely reflects its geography.

Italy also was a minor player in the push to colonize and plunder SSA. For example, it colonized Somalia and Ethiopia. Conflicts for power between shifting ethnic group alliances in Ethiopia and Liberia degenerated into multiple civil wars costing millions of lives between the 1970s and early 2000s. Ethiopia suffered years of brutal civil war and a brutal Mengistu dictatorship which oversaw the Derg "Red Terror" of the 1970s, whose policies resulted in famine-induced collapse of the economy. His disastrous programs were pitched as "pan-Ethiopian nationalism". Ethiopia recently instituted ethnic federalism to manage pressures on the regime from tribal and ethnic conflict, provide national unity, effective governance and represent all ethnicities. The central government is a relatively strong, technocratic regime with powerful military support, ruling through a single party. The weakness of ministries together with support for "regionalization" leaves a half-way reform point between centralization and decentralization of authority and power. The policy twist here in 1995 was "ethnic self-determination" which would serve rural needs

and build support for the dominant EPRDF party (Peterson, 2015: 18). The ethno-federalist system drew administrative divisions along ethnic lines and has ended up increasing ethnic tensions between disempowered groups (i.e. the Oromia and Amhara) (King, 2017: 71). It also facilitated public financial management reform and can boast the lowest fiscal deficit of the sample countries (-1.1 percent GDP). But it still remains, like British federalism, "an incompletely theorized agreement" (Cass Sunstein, cited in Peterson, 2015: 19). Nevertheless, the arrangement supported by the regime and military has provided needed stability. As indicated in Table 2.2, of the three African cases cited, Ethiopia has the most effective government.

Liberia

By contrast, in Liberia the brutal civil wars that devastated the country for 14 years (1989–2003) led, with international pressure and support, to developing an electoral democracy that attempted to represent the different ethnicities that are based in counties. That is, representation is crudely based on ethnic geography. The wars killed an estimated 250,000 people. The U.S. was not an active colonist in SSA but was important in the founding of Liberia as a refuge from slavery. This was more symbolic than substantive. The U.S. provided only minimal support in human capital or institutional development. Nor did it build up a modern, legitimate state with a monopoly of force to stem the growth of the patronage and warlords (such as Charles Taylor) that destroyed the country for decades.[2] The ethnic and tribal conflict between the Krahn, Gio, and Mano groups caused by an extreme version of state weakness led to complete state failure (Fukuyama, 2014: 300). Nevertheless, this institutional development, born of brutal war and state collapse, produced a successful Liberian presidential term (Ellen Sirleaf) and the first transfer of power from one elected president to another (footballer George Weah) since 1944 (*The Economist*, 2017b: 49).

Unfortunately, economic and fiscal performance is still weak (see Table 2.2) and the state is still reliant on indirect taxation which is a poor foundation for modern development. President Sirleaf was unable to improve the health and education sectors or curb corruption substantially while in office. She did not modernize the state though major gains were made in the area of public financial management and fiscal policy (USAID, 2014). Liberia remains a unitary state with no sub-national governments (IMF, 2012). Like other weak states, Liberia relies on rents, royalties and indirect taxes and fees from natural resources, as well as VAT taxes (i.e. sales) and aid support rather than direct personal income taxes (declared and withheld). Direct taxation requires consent of the people, support for the regime and state performance, and is an indicator of state capacity.

Table 2.2 Challenges to Effective Government Macroeconomic Governance Regional Equality

Country	PCI 2016 (a)	Ue 2017	Inflation 2017 (b)	Budget Deficit (2016)	HDI 2015 (1.0 highest); CPI 2015 (100 highest)	Govt Structure	Challenges	Govt Effectiveness 2014© (% rank)	% Immigrants 2015(d)	Vertical Imbalances (share of subnational in total government tax revenue)(f)	NR rents as % GDP 2015(g)	Subnational Discretion over Tax Rates/ bases(f)	Regional Inequality (2015) (h)	Top 2 Parties Share of Vote (i)	Voter Support for Top 2 Parties
Ethiopia	$707	5.7	23.4	-2.4	0.44/33	U/D	EN	17.7	0.8	0.0	12.7	0.0 (f)	0.33	91.2/95.4%	
Nigeria	2178	13.9	16.0	-1.1%	0.53/27	F/D	EN/MAC	10.5	0.7	15.3	12.5	0.0	0.33	76.6/67.2%	
Liberia	455	3.7	6.9	-5.3	0.42/37	U/D	EN	2.3	0.7	0.0	28.1	0.0	0.28	90.9/98.9%	
Egypt	3685	8.1	8.5	-9.8	0.69/36	U/A	PN	30.4	0.5	2.0	8.5	–	0.49	97.0%	
Spain/ Catalonia	26529	17.1	2.1	-3.3	0.88/58	U/D	PN	84.6	14.0	20.0	0.14	R60.0/L30.0	0.79	73.4/55.6%	
U.K./ Scotland	39899	4.3	3.0	-3.3	0.91/81	C/D	PN	92.8	13.0	3.6	0.71	0.0	0.83(5x)	65.1/82.4%	
Hungary	16100	4.1	5.6	-2.0	0.82/48	U/D	PN	72.1	4.7	15.8	0.47	16.0	0.77	62.0/65.0	
E.U.	35632	9.1	0.5	-1.3	0.85	C/D	PN	–	–	–	–	–	– –		
Brazil	8650	12.6	3.7	-8.9	0.76/38	F/D	MAC	34.9	0.9	32.0	5.0	75.0	0.56	79.5/75.1%	
Malaysia	9360	3.5	3.1	-3.1	0.79/50	F/D	PN	73.2	8.3	3.4	8.2	3.4	–	47.5%/50.8%	
Indonesia	3604	5.3	4.5	-2.5	0.69/34	U/D	PN	33.4	0.1	8.1	6.3	25.4	0.56	53.2%/ 46.9%	
China	8123	4.0	2.3	-3.0	0.73/36	U/A	PN	66.3	0.1	0.0	4.0	5.0	3.50x	1 party	1 party
Russia	8748	5.0	6.1	-2.4	0.79/28	U/A	PN	51.4	7.7	6.5	16.3	0.00	0.73	1 party	1 party

(a) Per capita nominal GDP (World Bank, 2016, https//data.worldbank.org/indicator/ny.gdp.pcap.cd).

(b) Average annual consumer prices (CPI); inflation.eu–worldwide inflation data; harmonized inflation Europe (HICP).

(c) World Bank: Worldwide Governance Indicators (WGI); (World Bank, 2015, https//knoema.com).

(d) UN: "Trends in International Migrant Stock: 2015".

(e) Xiao Wang and Richard Herd (2013) "The System of Revenue Sharing and Fiscal Transfers in China", Working Paper 1030. (Paris: OECD), p. 7.

(f) "Fiscal Federalism Network" (2017) www.oecd.org/tax/federalism; IMF (2012) Serdar Yimaz and Varsha Venugopal (Atlanta: GSU Andrew Young School of Policy Studies, Working Paper 08-38, 12/08); with exception of Lagos state, states and localities have no discretion over local tax/fee rates/bases; they have discretion over and receive most of their funds from formula block grants from the central government; Nigeria is called a "centralizing federation" by Rotimi Suberu in *Routledge Handbook on Regionalism and Federalism*, edited by John Loughlin, John Kincaid and Wilfried Swenden (New York, 2013).

(g) "Total Natural Resource Rents % GDP" (World Bank, 2015). https://data.worldbank/ny.gdp.totl.rt.zs; IndexMundi 2015: sum total of rents from forestry, oil, minerals, oil and coal; the world average level of revenue from natural resource rents dropped from 4.7% in 2011 to 1.73% in 2015 reflecting the sharp drop in world prices for major commodities such as coal and oil; but economic dependence based on consumption and demand remained about the same, e.g. based on the "other" source of Nigerian government revenues (which includes overseas aid grants from governments and international organizations and is derived from subtracting direct taxes and social contributions), it still receives 69.0% of its revenues from commodities—general government just receives less money (*Government Financial Statistics Yearbook 2015*, IMF, 2015); "Local Government Discretion and Accountability in Ethiopia"; Russian subnational governments have virtually no discretion over the rates and bases of their assigned revenue sources (Jorge Martinez-Vazquez and Jamie Boex, "Russia's Transition to a New Federalism" (Vazquez and Boez, 2001); China is a unitary autocratic capitalist state with quasi-federation features. Most Chinese subnational revenue sources are assigned without discretion or shared with the central government. But China can set land use tax rates up to a centrally determined ceiling and can set the rates for business receipts and income taxes as well as O&M "taxes" (surcharges are fees) (Robert R. Taliercio, World Bank).

(h) The UNDP Inequality-Adjusted Human Development Index (IHDI) adjusts the HDI for each dimension across the population. It is the actual level of HD accounting for this inequality, while the HDI is an index of the potential human development that could be achieved if there were no inequality. The IHDI is the HDI discounted for inequality. Higher scores indicate higher regional inequality. The scores for China and U.K. are supplemented by estimates of the per capita GDP differences between richest–poorest regions. Regional differences are a product of deteriorating: productivity, skills, income, and educational trends met with weak policy responses.

(i) Ethiopia 2010 and 2015 EPRDF party; Nigeria 2011 and 2015 APC opposition coalition and PDP; Liberia 1st round 2011 and 2017; Spain 2011 and 2016 PSOE and PP; U.K. 2010 and 2017 Conservative and Labor; Hungary 2010 and 2014 Fidesz, Jobbik and Unity MSZP; Brazil 2010 and 2014 PT and PTSB 1st round; Egypt 2014: 2 candidates for president, el-Sisi and Sabahi with el-Sisi winning 97% of vote in election boycotted by other parties including the Muslim Brotherhood's Freedom and Justice Party; Malaysia 2013: ruling Barisan National (BN) cluster of 13 parties with leader Najid Razak won 47.3% of the popular vote but 133 of 222 or 59% of the seats; opposition cluster of 3 parties won 50.8% of the vote but only 40% of the seats 89 of 222 which was an increase in parliamentary control; the opposition won more popular vote but under the electoral system it lost; there was an 85% turnout which is the highest in their electoral history; the system is single-member district/plurality vote election or SMD/PVE; Indonesia 2014: 12 parties divided into two coalitions: minority (PDI-P) headed by Joko Widodo and the majority Gerninda coalition headed by Prabowo Subianto; the minority coalition won with 53.2% of the popular vote gaining 63% of parliamentary seats; the majority received 43.7% of the popular vote and 40% of the seats; turnout was 70% and e-voting coverage is spreading across the 33 provinces; elections are overseen by the General Elections Commission (KPU).

Other Colonized African Countries

Other SSA countries were colonized on the cheap by a variety of powers. The Spanish, for instance, colonized Equatorial Guinea, the one Spanish-speaking country in SSA. Partially from its centralized autocratic model of governance and from global demand for commodities such as oil, diamonds and copper, the country was ruled by the "grotesque dictator" (2014: 286) Teodoro Obiang for 35 years. To this day, it remains an authoritarian, patrimonial state, held together by this weak state from even further chaos and war driven by international weapons and mercenaries and local tribal allies who would take power and rule for their own interests.[3] Germany colonized The Gambia and Cameroon after marginal support for tribes in a series of nearby wars.[4] Portugal colonized Angola, Mozambique, and Guinea Bissau. Suffering from decades of violent inter-tribal contests for power after independence, countries like Angola are still ruled by long-serving dictators (Eduardo dos Santos over 35 years) and still rely on commodity exports to supply funds for the treasury. Simple, patrimonial and kleptocratic regimes allied with international interests that fueled these and subsequent wars over local commodities. In short, the ethnicity itself is not the driving force of war and conflict but rather the weak patrimonial state. Such states have used ethnicity as a tool to mobilize followers to maintain or take power (Collier, 2007).

Given the weak states that at best use ethnicities to maintain power and at worst to simply rob treasuries and repress citizens, the question is what can be done to create modern states in SSA? Despite the persistent weaknesses of central governments, the major advances have been made at the sector policy levels. For example, Rwanda suffered from the genocides of the 1990s that decimated the country and destroyed health levels. Since the late 1990s, it has decentralized the financing and management of its health care system. With strong commitment from the central government and support from WHO to make and enforce technical norms and transparency and accountability standards on NGO providers, the system has by 2013 reduced TB, HIV and malaria rates by 80 percent and increased life expectancy by 60 percent. Local health care financing is provided by performance-based central transfers that provide enforceable norms and performance metrics as incentives for results. The government has implemented a national health insurance system (*Mutuelles de Sante*) that now covers 80 percent of the population. The result is a replicable model for SSA that could be used to scale-up reforms to other sectors and to the central government, which has improved its capacity to govern by implementing this program (Aud, 2017).

In such SSA states, patrimonial states, brutal dictators, large security apparatuses, and endemic corruption between such elite actors has prevented effective government. The standard practical notion of strengthening state capacity and effectiveness relies on greater numbers of professionally competent officials, stronger financial controls to reduce corruption, greater accountability to voters through election reforms and devolution of authority to local officials that can be held responsible. But it should also be noted that effective delivery of programs, services and projects depends on the availability of electricity at least, safe drinking water at best. Even the most democratic and professionally trained officials would have trouble under such conditions. Thus, more effectively governed countries such as Ghana and Botswana (discussed previously) have greater than 75 percent electricity coverage for their populations. In less effectively governed places such as Liberia, Ethiopia, and Nigeria, about 55 percent to 85 percent of their populations are without electricity coverage (*The Economist*, 2017r: 4). Lack of electricity damages health care. For example, 36,000 Nigerian women die in childbirth annually during pregnancy because of darkness in clinics. Clinics are also unable to store vaccines in fridges, which limits their ability to prevent basic diseases. Small firms in Ghana lose roughly 50 percent of their revenues during frequent blackouts and the cost to the country is about 2 percent GDP/year (*The Economist*, 2017r: 3). For these reasons, current initiatives to increase generation and the falling costs of renewables should enhance governmental effectiveness across the SSA region.

According to some, SSA regional governance has improved more recently from 1990–2014 (Radelet, 2016). The suggestion is that colonial legacies and practices do not necessarily determine contemporary outcomes. Radelet finds evidence for this in the increased number of skilled leaders and policymakers, and better socio-economic policies in particular countries. For example, poverty and mortality rates are down significantly and incomes have increased in this period (2016: 8). In an era of declining commodity prices, these conclusions are important. But the bulk of them have been obtained by regime support for local and sectoral reform initiatives such as that in Rwanda. To the extent that these kinds of programs can be planned, implemented, and partially financed by aid, the future of the SSA is looking up.

Middle East and North African Cases

States in the MENA differ from Africa and Asia (to be discussed below) in that sectarian, religious-driven populist conflict has been the threat to regime stability. The main destabilizing religion has been Islam and sects within Islam. While organized and aggravated harassment has been largely divided along religious as well as ethnic lines, the reaction of most regimes remains the same: to play them off (or buy them off) in order to maintain power and control over subject populations. In general, states are already closed, authoritarian, patrimonial, and supported by resources from narrowly structured oil and gas economies. Economies have diversified little from dependence on oil and gas exports. As in many authoritarian contexts, the regime pact is for political and social obeisance in exchange for free goods: health, jobs, education, and incomes. But few governments deliver effective results. For example, MENA governments such as Egypt, Morocco, and Jordan score very weak, with Egypt and Morocco at 22.1 and 50.5 respectively, and with Jordan slightly better at 59.1[5] (see Table 2.2). Average MENA governmental effectiveness declined from 39 percent in 2010 to 35 percent in 2016. Specifically, policy agendas are unlinked to growth, development or improvements in the quality of life. While some countries, such as Egypt, raised targeted cash transfers to the poor tenfold in two years to 1.7m households, 67 percent of the MENA population lack bank accounts and therefore access to finance; firms are unable to obtain equity and debt financing because of undeveloped capital markets (Azour, 2017: 8). Whatever governmental effectiveness means, it has to include modern financial policies. Most governments in MENA lack sensible financial policies, an oddity given the spate of financial expertise and professionals that live and work in most of these countries. With the most tolerant strand of Islam and the most stable, liberal regime, Jordan is the best governed large, complex country and also the wealthiest country in MENA with the highest quality of life (74 HDI). In a reversal of the colonial mercantilist model, most MENA workers supplied for construction, manufacturing and services are imported and indentured labor to support regime projects and private firms. Civil services are reserved for local, mainly male citizens.

In addition to the normal kleptocratic tendencies of poor, dictatorial states such as those found in SSA, citizens in MENA have intense beliefs and values and must abide by the religious practices of political cultures that have constrained the development of modern states. The most Westernized countries in MENA, those with the most relaxed and tolerant versions of Islamic practices such as Jordan, are clearly the most stable and effective. MENA ethno-nationalism is religious, driven by states fused with mosques into theocratic regimes that lack the most basic checks and separation of powers. In this region, countries must contend with "militant and anti-democratic Islamist groups" (Fukuyama, 2014: 433), which is qualitatively different from the transitions and developments in other regions such as Latin America or Eastern Europe. Groups such as the Muslim Brotherhood have never accepted the principle of separation of church and state. They have long traditions of violent religious militancy and usually seek power to enforce their agenda of creating "illiberal theocratic states" (2014: 433). The Shia-Persian political philosophy is different, separating the temporal state from the spiritual Mosque for over five centuries. There, the tensions between Western modernizers and Islamic clergy for power and forging appropriate responses to European imperialism were intense but dominated by temporal leaders.[6] The current Iranian theocratic context was created largely by a clergy rebellion in 1979 to challenge the soul of Shia orthodoxy (Amanat, 2017). The clergy and its security apparatus, the Islamic Revolutionary Guard, remain powerful enough to set both policy and security agendas and enforce them. For the Islamic populists of both Shia and Sunni sects today, however, their agendas are facilitated by almost exclusive reliance for followers among the uneducated, rural poor, and marginalized communities within urban areas. Predictably, the religious recruiters are mostly middle class and well-educated. Democratic development historically in other regions such as Latin America has depended on organization by the middle classes into parties to contest elections (2014: 432).

It is a cause-effect relation almost as simple as: no elections, no middle classes, almost exclusive education in Islam, and no Western liberal democracies. In addition, to the extent that nationalism is an "identity dislocation" problem for individuals torn from kinship and locality ties by the forces of modernization—technology, urban jobs, new cosmopolitan values—the rise of political Islam is a response to the half-modernized states in MENA. As in other regions as well as wealthy countries, the left-behind respond by ballot box if available, by mobilization and violence facilitated in MENA by radical religious values and practices, to fight against changes from the cosmopolitan urban West.[7] In practice, some of this translates into violent competition for power and territory across national boundaries between Sunni and Shia sects and the shades of religious schools of thought within each of them, in addition to the more secular and stateless Kurds who also vie for territory and power in parts of MENA countries.[8] The territorial and religious conflict in Lebanon is split between geographic thirds: Shia, Christian, and Sunni, with values and practices mixed in urban Beirut. In Iraq, the three main sects and even more radical off-shoots (Shia Hezbollah, vs. Sunni Al-Qaeda and ISIS vs. Kurds) have fought against each other for decades. For example, Iraq currently comprises separate countries: a Kurdish North, Sunni West and Shia South. This sectarian conflict, though, is not a battle between urban–rural resulting from identity dislocation. All sects are, to some extent, dislocated in MENA, an entire region left behind. The results for effective governance and quality of life (HDI) have been devastating.

Thus, for practitioners and aid designers, some important questions are: why have generations of Arab elites failed to create strong, accountable, and effective models of governance and education? What does political Islam mean in practice? What lessons does the ISIS model of governance hold for policy and administrative reform in this region? The deeper cultural, religious, and colonial boundary reasons for ineffectiveness have been noted. To the extent that they prevent change, what can be done? The specific problems are immense. While Arab bureaucracies are the largest in the world in public sector wages as shares of GDP: Iraq (18 percent), Saudi Arabia (11.2 percent), Egypt (8.2 percent), they are treated as employment agencies for families and friends of the royal families and elites—they are not accountable to publics or parliaments for services and programs. Public bureaucracies are often petrified, feather-bedding or make-work operations with high absenteeism levels on which few monitor or report. Efforts to change laws for state modernization and civil service reform are blocked by public sector unions and conservative religious groups concerned about women working across MENA. Better chances for improvement lie in sectors and at the local level. For example, school and teacher performance is monitored, and evaluations are based on those performances in West Bank and Gaza local schools (*The Economist*, 2015b). Note that these problems or solutions are not particularly religious or related to anything as abstract as "political Islam" or as tempting as grand plans for new political boundaries. They can and have been fixed by marginal changes to incentives in each sector to deliver particular levels of government and services.[9]

Because of the internal problems noted above, largely illegitimate Arab states have broken down further, reverting to ethnic and religious identities. It is often argued that new boundaries from those drawn by the Sykes-Picot Agreement in 1916 would help create legitimate states. But new boundaries would likely produce new efforts to grab land and expel rivals (*The Economist*, 2016d: 7). Such diagnoses distract from the real efforts needed to build modern, functioning states. Tyrant-toppling theatrics, electioneering, and campaigns for good governance mixed up with concepts of democracy[10] distract from the needed real work of building legitimate states (*The Economist*, 2016e: 38). Despite the grotesque brutality of ISIS, its perverted efforts offer lessons for what is needed to build such states: intolerance for corruption, decentralization of authority, discretion, and funds to local administrators, taxation regulation of enterprise rather than ownership, and secular and legally enforced respect for human rights and diversity (2016e: 39). Factionalized politics in MENA has worked to ensure anarchy. The indirect cause and intervening variable between states and effectiveness is the influence of radical and armed Islamist groups. Both their religion and politics favor autocratic governance. The deeper cause is sectarian conflicts, often between Islamic families of different sects going back over generations, that translate into revenge and blood feuds that inhibit the inter-group compromise and cooperation necessary for forging effective policies. Despite all this, policies and regime compositions do matter. The key to successful policies is to target local units, functional sectors and build on the positive lessons of these efforts to build modern states. If they can evolve from unitary to federation structures, so much the better for effective country governance. The current cultural and religious obstacles to creating decentralized democratic federations across the region require incremental, bottom-up steps to build such states piece by piece.

Asian Cases

Attempts at state comparison, diagnosis of threats to regime stability, definition of effectiveness constraints and the devising precise remedies in this region are all made difficult by the wide diversity of religions, languages, regime types, and colonial histories. But behind this diversity of institutions and histories is a relatively consistent set of common values and practices or political cultures, some of which include religious practices. They are distinct enough to serve as independent variables that correspond to specific policies. Many have noted that a weakness of the "political culture" concept is precisely this inability to link cause and effect, to actually explain why particular policies exist. Political culture is the behavioral expression of language, religions, social values, and trust. These values influence what rules are made and how strictly they are enforced. The task of linking behavior to policy results anywhere is difficult and beset with attribution problems. But in this region, the methodological task is much less difficult. What cultural features can be linked to state ineffectiveness and poor policies?

The Asian region is characterized by strong, ancient states and associated institutions such as armies and security services. Ethnicities of different religions vie for power and control of land, jobs and cultural status. The most efficient way to gain control of these resources has been through ethnic or religion-dominated political parties that then control political regimes. Given the greater institutionalization of countries in this region, conflicts become intense and long-lasting. For example, Sinhalese (Buddhists) and Tamils (Hindu) in Sri Lanka fought a 26-year civil war (1983–2009) that killed 100,000 people. The conflict between the two religious ethnicities dated back centuries before the British (ruling it as Ceylon) and the Portuguese controlled the island and prevented self-rule. The peculiar feature of conflicts over language, cultural status (ethnic feelings of marginalization) and state support for the dominant Buddhist religion is that Sri Lanka is quite an upscale country. With a per capita annual income of $3870 (slightly higher than in Indonesia or Egypt), the Sri Lankan HDI is 0.77, meaning high human development. Governmental effectiveness in 2016 was 53.4 percent, ranking it between Indonesia and Malaysia (Table 2.2). The civil war between the LTTE (Tamil Tigers) and Sinhalese was brutal but, for non-combatant civilians, relatively civilized. While the pogroms carried out by Sinhalese against Tamils in the century before the most recent conflict were brutal and close to ethnic cleansing, the more recent civil war was more formalized. Tamil Tigers, for example, often gave advance and precise warnings of their planned bombings both around Colombo and from the sea by Sea Tigers attack boats. The 26-year conflict ended when LTTE withdrew demands for a separate state and agreed to forge a federal solution to the country's problems. The Sinhalese seem to have backed off on the requirement that they speak the national language.[11]

As other countries in this region, Sri Lanka is religiously diverse: Buddhist (70 percent); Hindu (12.6 percent); Muslim (7.4 percent); Christian (7.4 percent); and Catholic (6.1 percent). In theory, religion-fueled ethnicities should practice tolerance and live peaceably. They are, after all, "believers" in peace, harmony, and eternal verities. In practice, evidence of economic and cultural differences in the division of spoils by governments, and the resentments stirred up by party leaders using social media, produces intense conflict. Many of the conflicts such as those over land tenure, cultural status, and jobs seem simple to outsiders and easily remedied by the many known and successful program and policy options. The outsider learns and asks: why fight over these small-bore issues for so long when larger issues remain unresolved? But their intensity is driven by long-standing feuds and hatreds and facilitated by weak conflict-resolution institutions that are not viewed as legitimate by the "country" as opposed to particular groups.

An important conclusion for this region is that, at least in the wealthier Asian countries, intense ethno-nationalistic threats to the regime over long periods of time do not necessarily weaken governmental effectiveness or diminish overall quality of life. That speaks to the deeper institutionalization of countries in this region that has served as a stabilizing force. Long-established bureaucracies have clear roles, recruitment and promotion criteria, formalized processes and routines, tight management controls, and top-down vertical command structures. In contrast with MENA and SSA states, governments actually do control and service national territory. Where did these states come from? Prior to contact with the West, Asian states reflected strong national identities, shared cultural values, and were some of the most ethnically homogeneous societies in the world (Fukuyama, 2014: 336). Political development began, not with rule of law as in Europe, but with the state (2014: 337). In short, the tools and systems for effective government existed; the task for democracy-building was to limit the power of states through law and representative government.

Japan

In East Asian Japan, the predominant cultural values and practices are: deference to authority, group harmony, personal shame for failure, and predictability of values. High trust in institutions such as banks and governmental ministries and families are more important than formal links. These values and practices have led to such policy results as: decades of economic deflation and recession; preference for harmonious contracting (sole-source) over competitive bidding leading to the crony-capitalism of the construction industry; and unquestioning deference to official explanations, such as that of Tokyo Electric Power Company (TEPCO) and the Japanese Nuclear Safety Commission (JNSC) during and after the Fukushima nuclear accident. Institutions are centralized, opaque, or closed-door, and unresponsive to citizen needs. Individually, risk-aversion works into a common preference for life-time jobs. Common problems in this region, not usually found elsewhere, are excessive activity to appear productive, and *karoshi* or death by overwork! One could say then that "but for" these specific values, the policies and practices would not have occurred or be occurring.

Across the region, such values and practices translate into: strong, authoritarian governments and regimes ruling highly deferential populations that work hard. Incomes, employment and growth figures are generally high (Table 2.2). In Japan, as in China, the difficulty in creating a modern state was to limit its actions by law. Law in both places was an administrative arm of the government.[12] In 1889, Japan reviewed the English Common Law system of decentralized, judge-made law and the codified Napoleonic European Civil Code, and adopted the latter as more consistent with its cultural practices. The Mejii Constitution in place until 1947 rejected the English model in favor of the more conservative and semi-authoritarian Bismarck constitution of the German Empire (Fukuyama, 2014: 342–343). Japan and most other countries of this region have rule *by* law (sovereign rules by law) rather than rule *of* law (rules binding on the sovereign for accountability). This legal structure reflected underlying authoritarian values that persist to the present in other regional countries as well (e.g. China, Thailand, Japan, and Malaysia).

As is known, the Chinese state bureaucracy is the oldest in the world (roughly 1800 years before Europe (2014: 354), with modern impersonal and meritocratic recruitment and promotion systems. It registered citizens, levied taxes and regulated society long before such institutions in other parts of the world. In Japan, where institutions ultimately came from China (2014: 354), officials are screened and advance by competitive exam; political patronage appointments were almost impossible—but it also meant few opportunities for lateral or mid-career entry (2014: 340), devices modern bureaucracies employ to bring in new talent and innovative methods. The Chinese civil service is highly respected and trusted, much more so than local governments, which are viewed as generally corrupt (2014: 381). Township and Village Enterprises (TVEs), for instance, even turned themselves into often semi-corrupt profit-making enterprises (2014: 377). Later, the Chinese state was colonized not by patronage systems as in most countries, but by a disciplined Leninist party that sought to subordinate it for its ideological purposes through a parallel hierarchy (2014: 372). Governance in China is still conducted through this fused or unified Party as political regime and professional bureaucratic state institution.

Malaysia

Other regional regimes have used racialism and religious sectarianism as resources in populist nationalist style to gain and control power. The most authoritarian regimes, such as that in Myanmar, have resorted to religious-driven ethnic cleansing to legitimate themselves. In Buddhist-majority Myanmar, the dominant army has been "cleansing" and evicting the Muslim minority Rohingyas through violent pogroms to legitimate its role in the governing regime. It is effectively an ethnic militia with wide support from a majority of the Buddhist population. As indicated, the Asian region is characterized by multiple religions and minority groups often used by a wide variety of dominant groups controlling regimes. Minorities are played off much as SSA tribes by colonial powers to maintain power. Where the game fails to produce the desired result, more violence, civil war, and chaos is the typical result.

For example, in Southeast Asia, Malaysia is an example of a strong regime presiding over a federal structure with regular democratic multi-party elections. Elections for parliamentary seats have been fair and power is actually contested (the minority coalition actually won 50.8 percent of the 2014 vote but only 40 percent of the seats); turnout is high (70 percent); and macroeconomic policies are sound, as indicated by the range of positive indicators in Table 2.2. Governmental effectiveness is also considered very high. Nevertheless, the Prime Ministers' (Najib Razak) minority but winning coalition (dominated by the UMNO party) has used the ethnic and religious card to solidify its power. Malaysia is a Muslim majority country and the largest minority groups are ethnic Chinese and Hindu Indians. A preferred mechanism, reflecting what has been done in many electoral systems worldwide, including the U.S., is gerrymandering. Here, Chinese are crammed into large urban constituencies, meaning their votes count for less than the Malays in sparsely populated rural districts which tend to favor UMNO (*The Economist*, 2017s: 33). Najib has also adopted traditional populist policies to garner votes: cutting taxes, civil service bonuses, rural infrastructure. Prime Minister Najib is currently deciding on the timing of a parliamentary election in 2018 for optimal use of his ethnic-religious and populist policy resources: between civil service bonus instalments but not during seasonal flooding that could depress turnout in rural areas (2017s: 34).

Taiwan

Taiwan is another strong Asian state in East Asia like China, but with a strong democratic tradition. Its political history suggests that regime composition matters for the facilitation of strong institutions that permit changes in regime power and ensure independent limitations on the goverment. With these ingredients, destructive factionalism that has been common in SSA and MENA, for example, has been held in check. Sensible macroeconomic policies ensure growth and revenues that finance sound socio-economic policies such as education, health, and social safety nets that enhance regime legitimacy. A distinguishing feature of Taiwan is that it is a quasi-federation rather than a full federation system. An important component of the governmental effectiveness problem and aid design issue is evidence that federation is the most successful structure to respond to multi-level, sectoral issues. Some view federalism or federation as a process structured by a set of institutions in which states or subnational units are represented in central government policymaking (Rodden, 2006: 30, 31, 36). But the necessary legal institutions and political structures need to be in place to ensure subnational autonomy and representation, i.e. actual subnational fiscal and political autonomy and election systems that reflect their preferences/needs. That means federation is more than just a process; otherwise, these would be merely formal federations and substantive confederations. Though not all democracies are federal systems or federations, they can be associated in the long-term with democracy and growth. The essence is substantive subnational representation, often measured by public spending through transfers, programs, subsidies, and direct expenditures.

Several exceptions reveal that quasi-federation institutions or traits can operate within unitary systems: Taiwan and Costa Rica are good examples. In Taiwan, democracy began at the local level in the 1920s and spread to the central government in the 1947 Constitution that created a republican form of government with strong checks and balances. Taiwan is considered to have "traits" of federalism. The federalism issue in Taiwan is often confused by some with that of its being a potentially devolved province of the PRC (which is a unitary government). And it hardly considers itself a devolved PRC province (any more than Belize would consider itself a province of Guatemala, as is still shown today on official Guatemalan maps!). Costa Rica is a small country that has been a strong representative democracy since 1948. As will be discussed further below, its small scale allows it to combine federalist traits in its unitary form of government, for instance: local fiscal and political autonomy and elected mayors to provide an overall inclusive government.

Indonesia

Indonesia is another unique unitary government in Southeast Asia. Laws such as (22/1999) made it one of the largest decentralized countries in the world. Since, 1999, Indonesian sub-national governments have gained considerable political and fiscal power and many new responsibilities (OECD, 2016). That program was called "big bang" devolution and considered to be one of the fastest and most comprehensive decentralization initiatives ever attempted by any country (Guess, 2005a). The devolution featured not only political and fiscal authority but also assignment of central government expertise to local governments to assist in implementing the law. The Indonesian state is strong, macroeconomic measures are sound, and the HDI level is considered to be medium. But compared to Malaysia in this region, the government is not considered very effective. The Malaysian division of authority to govern its 34 provinces and 508 municipalities assigns tax collection to the central government and gives more control over provincial governments.

But Indonesian local governments have gained authority, responsibility and expertise over the past two decades and the country could now be called a decentralized democracy. Municipalities rely on devolved taxes including property taxes collected locally, and formula-based transfers from the central government. Roughly 25 percent of revenues are considered "own-source" which is much higher than Malaysia or China (Table 2.2). Local governments also receive funds from the provinces and shared revenue with the central government, together with the ability to borrow on international markets for capital works. Borrowing is limited by the quite liberal rule that debt must not exceed 75 percent of previous year budget revenues (OECD, 2016). In short, this is a quasi-federation operating within a unitary structure. As indicated in Table 2.2, the election system is well-administered, vigorous, with results overseen by an elections commission (KPU) and ensures results that are considered fair enough to produce legitimate governments. To the extent that the Joko Widodo regime has used the ethnic card, it has not significantly altered results or led to any threats to regime stability.

Pakistan

Since the 1947 partition with India, the Islamic Republic of Pakistan has been a relatively homogeneous Muslim country that is nominally democratic. But the country is governed by Islamic law, and ruled by the army and its intelligence service, the Inter-Services Intelligence or ISI. The regime is fragmented between secular and Islamic forces in policymaking. Secular institutions are in practice subordinate to Islamic law as enforced by the military.[13] Professionally, the government and regime are composed partly of a quasi-feudalist landed elite that has no intention of giving up its privileges and creating a modern, centralized state (Fukuyama, 2014: 33). Of today's Muslim countries, only Pakistan has this social structure of large landowners dominating masses of peasants (2014: 430). The rest of the regime is controlled by the military. An uneasy tension has existed for decades between a secular, largely middle-class educated population and Islamic institutions, such as the religious madrassas schools, and the Taliban serving the less-educated rural peasantry.

Formally, Pakistan is a federation (Rodden, 2006: 39). The basis of this classification is that the four provinces (Sindh, Khyber, Punjab, and Baluchistan) have substantial sub-national authority. A formal federation was completed with the creation of local- or district-level governments in 2000. However, the provinces and districts still rely heavily on central transfers for financing, despite their relative political autonomy from the state. They are not however, independent of the religious authority and their pervasive applications of blasphemy laws as well as the intrusions of other non-state restrictions. Overall, these parallel institutions indirectly supported by the state, control swaths of national territory as well as budget shares and vie for control of the legal and policy agenda. For its part, the military has used the "line of control" issue with India over the de facto border between India and Pakistani controlled Kashmir. The military has mobilized Muslim extremists over this "nationalist" issue for decades in order to maintain its own legitimacy and that of the regime. Predictably, that has led to substantial Islamist violence in Pakistan. The regime does not rule over all national territory: the Tribal Areas (FATA) are a separate area which it controls but provides few services or even security controls.

The result is a nuclear-armed country with weak institutional and governance measures. The per capita income is low ($1410, which is lower than Nigeria and Egypt); the HDI is low (0.550 which is about the level of Ethiopia and Nigeria) and governmental effectiveness is scored only at 27.4 percent which is higher than Ethiopia but lower than Indonesia) (Table 2.2). Despite these numbers, there is a substantial middle class, a vibrant civil society, and media to serve as indirect checks on state action. In this context, smaller secular state reforms have been attempted. In 2001, fearing threats to its legitimacy from growing unrest in rural areas and recognizing poor service and program coverage, the military government of President Musharraf, through its National Reconstruction Board (NRB), shifted from a deconcentrated model to a quasi-federation structure by devolving authority and funding to a new level of local government-called districts. Three levels of government below the provincial level were created: 96 districts, 337 towns and 6033 union councils (Guess, 2005a: 337). As in Indonesia, this was a home-grown and designed attempt at fiscal decentralization. Rather than begin with a pilot program, the designers (NRB military and civilian members of an NGO called the Good Governance Group) decided to cover the entire country. This was due in part to fear that top-level regime support could be withdrawn and that provincial officials who were opposed could reassert their authority and block the reform. District funding is still 95 percent derived from central transfers.

But even without significant own-source authority, conditional transfers to sectoral programs such as education and health have improved performance. For instance, one of the metrics for education transfers, as part of the fiscal decentralization program, has been percentage enrollment and promotion of girls in schools. More recently, the Pakistani province of Punjab (population 110 million) has become a world leader in educational reform. Dismal public schools had allowed a grade 1–12 dropout rate of 97 percent; there were 867 terrorist attacks on educational institutions between 2007–2015 many of them girls' schools; and teacher salaries absorbed 87 percent of the provincial education budget much of which was wasted either on paid no-shows ("ghosts") (40 percent of total teachers) or on patronage teaching jobs in exchange for votes and political election work (*The Economist*, 2018: 14). With grant and technical advice support from British Aid (DFID), the chief education minister of Punjab began a major reform. The province has placed 10,000 schools in the hands of charities and non-profit educational organizations. One, known as the Citizens Foundation (TCF) has merged schools, identified and removed 6000 ghost teachers using biometric attendance registers, subsidized poor children attendance at cheap private schools, designed a modern curriculum based on best practices, increased attendance, and so far improved performance on tests (*The Economist*, 2018: 13). The allocational inefficiency problem in education was largely the misspending of funds rather than an insufficiency of them. Institutional pressures from elected officials and reactionary teacher unions as well as poor supervisory management systems impeded educational systems performance. Reform efforts based on Punjab's example have spread to Sindh and Khyber provinces and are on the way to being scaled up to the national level as a country model.

Despite these sectoral gains, Pakistani regime stability is threatened still by Islamist groups that control core institutions such as the courts and which collude partly with the ISI and the military. For example, feudal landlords were empowered by the British which produced a Latin American-style pattern of few landed barons with most of the productive agricultural land and many serfs with smaller often uneconomic plots for anything beyond subsistence. A post-independence land reform effort was declared "un-Islamic" by the Supreme Court as recent as 1990, allowing large landowners to maintain their economic power and turn it into political authority. Feudal politicians once controlled 42 percent of the seats in parliament (*The Economist*, 2018a: 24). Behind the theocracy is a dominant political class that controls unused land and prevents evolution of the state to a modern democracy. A shift from strictly feudal in-kind transactions that preserved the servant class and allowed landowners to beat them regularly (to prevent stealing!), to the current situation of reduced parliamentary control (down to 25 percent of the seats), high urbanization, and a cash economy that allows migration has threatened many of the feudal barons. But political and economic tensions from such forces still constrain investment and growth and, above all, the development of a modern state separate from Islam (in practice, the "Islamic Republic" is a theocracy), with an independent rule of law rather than through attempts to rule arbitrarily by law.

China

China is a fast-emerging modern state with an autonomous bureaucracy and quasi-federalist features of political and fiscal decentralization.

High state performance of policymaking and service delivery functions represent the qualities of Asian states leading, for example, to high Malaysian governmental effectiveness and the fiscal and politically decentralized features of Indonesia (Table 2.2). China is another variant on the strong state tradition of Asian stability and quality service outputs. The state faces no real populist nationalist or ethno-nationalist threats. The Party State has made an issue out of monitoring, controlling and harassing the main minority (Uighurs which are an ethnic group and also Muslims) group on its Western frontier with Central Asia. But it is hardly a threat to state stability or effectiveness. One historic reason for this is that, in contrast with SSA and MENA states, where bureaucracies are subordinate to regimes and militaries, the bureaucracy has always been autonomous in China. While there has never been a formal rule of law in China since the Qin Dynasty, there has always been a bureaucracy operating with written rules and stable expectations. China is considered the first modern state. The bureaucracy is autonomous despite formal subordination because regimes need bureaucracies to govern properly. In China, over centuries, all regimes have become actual prisoners of the large bureaucracy which, in fact, controls much of China. As far back as the Ming Dynasty, the Chinese bureaucracy limited and put a stop to much of the autocratic behavior of the emperor (Fukuyama, 2014: 75). But there are limits to even this autonomy. Mao's Cultural Revolution (1966–1976) was ideologically driven and with the assistance of other autonomous institutions such as the army and security forces, he was able to impose his rule by law, overwhelming the bureaucracy, undermining the operations of government and terrorizing the party itself, similar to Stalin's purges in the 1930s (2014: 362). Today, China has two pyramids of authority: the state and the Communist Party. While the Party parallels the state and outranks it, high officials are often members of both institutions.

Despite unitary structures, then, China has autonomous institutions: horizontally (the state bureaucracy) and vertically (subnational governments). Formally, China is a unitary state with power and authority derived from the communist party apparatus that controls the bureaucracy and the rest of the state, including subnational governments. There are 31 provinces, 330 prefectures and 2800 county-level administrations. In such a vast and administratively complex setting, relations between the center and periphery have always been tense and intergovernmental fiscal relations constantly in flux. The relation between them is roughly that of budgetary guardian and spender roles. The center (Party and central ministries) tries to control spending and debt by local units that seek to spend more resources in order to finance services and infrastructure (local and county governments). Local borrowing has been threatening the central government fiscal position (Guess and Ma, 2015). It was recognized recently by the central bank chief in 2017 as one of the two main threats to national financial stability, along with state-owned enterprise or SOE debt (*The Economist*, 2017t: 38). The problem is that shared resources and transfers do not cover local needs. Local governments receive about 50 percent of total tax revenues and are responsible for 67 percent of total government spending. Local governments tried off-budget "financing vehicles" or (LFVs), which were set up as SOEs to escape central controls (consistent with their spender roles). This allowed them to borrow opaquely, with debts reaching an estimated 24 percent of GDP.[14] In 2014, FVs were banned and municipalities were allowed to issue bonds and use the funds to redeem LFV debt. The plan was to convert all debt to bonds, making debt transparent. Now municipalities use complicated forms of PPPs and LFVs to reclassify loans so they no longer appear in official statistics. Implicit guarantee relations still exist between LFVs and local governments even though they were formally and officially separated.

Again, the intensity and agility of local government "spender" role behavior highlights the quasi-federalist nature of Chinese central–local relations. The vertical tensions and distrust persist between the center—which believes that local authorities need to be controlled, and the periphery—which believes that it needs more revenue and fiscal autonomy (2017t: 38). Creation of the new Central Commission for Discipline Inspection (CCDI) in 2017 was intended to intensify the anti-corruption campaign of President Xi Jinping and to clamp down on local officials who ignore the orders of the central government (*The Economist*, 2017h1: 45). Given fiscal space provided by national growth, the sub-national debt problem is not yet a crisis and can be remedied by clarification of intergovernmental fiscal roles and shifting to a full federalist system. China might be described as Stalinism without collective farms and totalitarian coercion. That brutalist regime model produced rapid accumulation, industrialization, and growth. Now, distribution of resources equitably and efficiently is required in China and the existing institutional architecture of the past cannot do that. In the present context of a large and growing middle class with greater demands on markets, and the need for sound macroeconomic and financial policy results, the constraints of a patrimonial regime driven by an outmoded ideology work against state modernization and evolution of the state into a modern, impersonal, but responsive government.

Myanmar

Other examples of poor-country Asian ethno-nationalism as a cause and consequence of weak states and dysfunctional state structures include Myanmar, formerly known as Burma. In Myanmar, ethno-nationalism takes the form of ethnic cleansing by the dominant Buddhist Bamar group against the Muslim Rohingyas. The pitfalls of the brief democratic experiment (that left the army in control of state institutions) and the manipulation by the military of ethnic and religious identities laid the foundation for even more intense sectarian conflict. The deeper roots of this are: the tangled roots of colonial rule; the army's "Burmanization" project (favoritism for dominant Buddhists and forced assimilation for the many others); and hate speech by radical monks all left unchecked by a weak state and enabling politicians. The Burmese nationalist movement—which had been traditionally a domain of the ruling elite— has now gone mainstream, which bodes ill for Myanmar's political future (Wade, 2017).

Kyrgyzstan

Kyrgyzstan is an ancient Central Asian country that was more recently colonized first by the Russians and later by the Soviets. The tribes and existing alliances between the Turkic people who brought Islam to Central Asia in the tenth to twelfth centuries were eased into the tsar's Kyrgyz area provinces by the Russian army in the 1860s. The Russians gave land to the new Russian settlers, producing revolts by locals in the 1900s. The Russians then classified the local Kyrgyz and Kazaks as separate nationalities and proceeded to place them on collective farms during the Stalin era of the 1930s (King,1996: 352). The Russians and later Soviets had transferred ethnic Russians to develop and work industries and occupy land and housing. In Central Asia, locals often had to learn Russian while other ethnicities such as Uzbeks and Kyrgyz also learned Russian. Few Russians bothered to learn the local languages for their supervisory roles. The roots of present ethnic violence were mainly land and housing associated with colonization and failure to liberalize and modernize the state.

With respect to poor-country problems, terms such as "culture of poverty", "culture of corruption", and "cultural tendencies to self-destruction and violence" are commonly used as if they were permanent features of national landscapes. But persistent ethnic and religious violence are often institutionally determined and therefore can be remedied by marginal changes in economic and behavioral incentives. For instance, Kyrgyz–Uzbek ethnic violence around Osh in Southern Kyrgyzstan has caused hundreds of rioting deaths over many decades. But the causes of this ethnic hatred and violence are institutional: lopsided distribution of justice through the police and courts; high unemployment among Uzbeks; official obstacles against use of the Uzbek language, and organized crime (*The Economist*, 2013: 46). To the extent that these two ethnic groups have successful traits (e.g. impulse control or discipline, insecurity about attainment of standards, and belief in their own exceptionality) they can overwhelm the larger more divisive institutional forces in the political culture (Chua and Rubenfeld, 2014) and co-exist.

India

During the "great" colonial games of the late 1800s to early 1900s between Britain and Russia, India was a sprawling country that once included Pakistan, Burma, Nepal, and Bangladesh. It is now a democratic federation with a robust civil society and autonomous sub-national governments. But many remain uneducated by the poor state system of schooling and the caste system that inhibits socio-economic mobility. Society is fragmented by castes and religious sects, often pitted against each other (e.g. Hindu vs. Muslim). The current regime and government of Prime Minister Narendra Modi has aggressively pandered to the conservative Hindu nationalists rather than to the merchant class. His BJP party relies on electoral gains from stirring up communal splits, such as the specter of illegal immigration from states such as Syria and Bangladesh (i.e. Muslims). He has replaced old secular elites with religious conservatives at the head of universities and other state institutions. Civil society has been weakened by this rising tide of authoritarianism or "majoritarianism" that prevents reasoned debate, discussion, and dissent (*The Economist*, 2017c: 8). As noted by Kaplan (2016: 77) modern nationalists often demand ethnic straight-jackets, mobilizing illusions of group purity and inborn national traits. As in Myanmar and elsewhere, this often has led to ethnic cleansing and genocide. The fact that ethnic cleansers have often been former Communist apparatchiks is not ironic. It is part of their desire to retain power by pulverizing individual identities and setting group against group (2016: 77). According to Kaplan, "Former Communist states from the Baltics to the Balkans have escaped these strictures and entered a world of individual rights beyond ethnicity" (2016: 77). Such progress now is under threat in both rich and poor countries as nationalists successfully mobilize against anyone perceived as "non-native".

Notes

1 Nationalism can work to build nations, as it has in Latin America. But it usually is destructive of both regimes and societies. Driven by authoritarian leaders in either democracies, or dictators in authoritarian regimes supported by state security forces, it quickly becomes destructive and unworkable. The ethnic purge of Bulgarian Turks by the Communist regime in 1989 was "the last cretinous crime of twilight totalitarianism" (Kassabova, 2017: 140). These were indigenous Turks that had lived in Bulgaria for generations and mixed with the local population. Though considered a 5th column problem by the regime, they accounted for only 8 percent of the population at the time. The fear was that "they" could reproduce and outnumber "us" (2017: 141). The regime decided to rename them (from Turkish to Slavic and Arabic ones) and forcibly Christianize the remaining Turks to get them back to their true roots in what was called the "Revival Process". This would assimilate "them" before they assimilated "us"! The ethnic hate campaign, like others in modern

countries today that employ populist reverse ethno-nationalism techniques and tools to aggrandize power, was a pointless and poisonous distraction from the real problems of failed economy, empty shops, environmental problems, lack of human rights, and especially the rising tides of Glasnost and Perestroika that would end their reign throughout the region and even Russia for several decades (2017: 142). The Bulgarian state opened the border with Turkey and sent those who disagreed with the Revival Process on the Big Vacation, meaning expulsion to a land in which they had never lived. Media support provided by the state organs showed doctored films of murderous Muslim nationalists in the nearby Yugoslavian war and included a fictionalized portrait of the Islamization of the Rhodope region in the seventeenth century. Even this was perhaps the earliest "fake news" in that most converts to Islam in the Balkans did so voluntarily as far back as the ninth century—to escape persecution from the Orthodox Church and for easier upward mobility for members of the land-holding nobility. For imposition of Christianity in the Bulgarian kingdom of the ninth century had been an "astonishingly bloody" affair (2017: 224). In short, nationalism is unworkable in countless ways (2017: 139).

2 In Russell Banks' searing novel *The Darling* (New York: Harper, 2004), set in Liberia and the U.S. from 1975–1991, Hannah, a member of the Weather Underground, flees to West Africa where she and her Liberian husband become friends with none other than Charles Taylor.

3 See Robert E. Klittgaard's classic: *Tropical Gangsters*.

4 See William Boyd's classic: *An Ice-Cream War*.

5 World Bank Governance Indicators, Annual Update 2015 (World Bank, 2015).

6 MENA governments are largely closed organizations with rigid routines, staffed by small-print mentalities. This is demeaning to ordinary citizens who need services from them. Theocratic governments such as Pakistan are often swept up in paranoid religious nationalism rather than experimenting on how best to deliver needed services. More secular governments, such as Egypt, still lack the common touch with the people whom they are supposed to represent and serve. For example, Egyptians are noted for their irreverent sense of humor yet the government is quite smug and humorless. Actions are routinely brought against citizens for such offenses as: "insulting Islam" (for portrayals of fundamentalists; for tweeting images of Minnie Mouse in a niqab); for "offending Islamic beards" (portrayal of a cleric) and "contempt of religion" (for blogging that 1/3 of Egyptian women cheat on their husbands) (*The Economist*, 2017z: 44).

7 The conflict between anywhere and somewhere values is not new. E.M. Forster captured the split in the early twentieth century in *Howard's End*. In that novel, the Schlegel family was internationalist and cosmopolitan in outlook and committed to gender equality and mobility. By contrast, representing the rural provincials of today, the conservative Wilcox family were passionate in their belief in empire and English superiority.

8 The sectarian struggle within Islam is the most obvious manifestation of a religiously inspired governance problem and is a regime-destabilizing force. Judaism suffers from some of the same problems. As noted by Cohen on the issue of American Jews, Orthodox Jews and the Israeli governments over the fate of West Bank-Gaza: "…the vast majority of American Jews are not Orthodox, and they resent the hold that the very religious have over Israeli political life. As we see with Sunni and Shia Muslims, interreligious fights are the most ugly" (Cohen, 2017).

9 A political and aid design solution must take into account the specifics of the sectarian conflict. The Good Friday Agreement of 1998 resolved decades of Northern Irish "Troubles" by carefully drafting constructive ambiguities and avoided stark binary choices that could fuel more violent conflict between Protestants and Catholics. The Agreement included paths to reunion for the opposing sects and ensured trade and commerce as the "great healer" between the parties (*The Economist*, 2017a1: 49). Aid can also add to such agreements providing benefits to locals who need sectoral services, programs, and projects to increase their incomes and employability.

10 The importance of professional election administration and the need for independent election management bodies (EMBs) to oversee elections should not be underestimated. Free and fair elections are necessary ingredients in seating legitimate governments. Greater electoral accountability can also be achieved through changes in voting districts from multi-member to single-member with plurality rather than majority vote requirements. But even advanced countries such as Italy still allow only a third of parliamentarians to be elected by the latter rules. And legitimacy can also be derived from economic and service performance as in China. Elections are a necessary component of democracy. But they are not the sine qua non and such systems may be established by benevolent rulers as well. Elections, however free, fair, and courageous in Iraq, for example, have not legitimated the government in the minds of citizens since the territory is effectively partitioned into separate countries.

11 Fights over which will be the national language that will be taught in schools and used for signing are often proxies for deeper resentments and hatreds. The Macedonian conflict over this with Albanians living in its eastern sectors is actually between Slavic and Muslim culture or Orthodox vs. Islam. Outsiders also marvel at the hatred of and by Greeks just south of there who both claim Macedonia as their name dating back to the biblical Philip of Macedon. The Slavic Macedonians (FYROM) have the 16-point Vergina (or Greek Argean) star on their flag and currency (which dates back to third century BC Greece). In the mid and late 1990s this was almost enough to spark a war (prevented by UN intervention). Since the flag and currency look the same today, the conflict may be replayed again.

12 Thus, the question is whether an independent set of laws and rules limit the actions of the state? Are they superior to the state (Anglo-American constitutions and laws or rules of the separate law), equal to it (theocracies in MENA), or subordinate to it (e.g. the Russian Orthodox Church and laws made by the state, i.e. rule by law)? Transcendent secular rule systems limit state actions in Anglo-American countries; transcendent religious rules limit the state less in theocracies (e.g. blasphemy laws in the Islamic Republic of Pakistan); and in subordinate systems, states and regimes become embodiments of the church, holy emperors or tsars anointed by the church and have few independent limits on their actions.

13 That Pakistan is actually a theocratic government was underscored recently by the sacking of the Law Minister for granting rights to an unapproved religious organization. Consistent with military support of Islamist organizations (e.g. Taliban) against Indian Kashmiri rule, it supported the Messenger of God group opposed to religious liberty and in

favor of strict enforcement of blasphemy laws on any evidence of disrespect for the prophet. The most recent conflict was triggered by law ministry "weakening" of the oath in the electoral law requiring all candidates to swear that they believed Muhammed was the "final prophet in Islam". The group claimed that changing the federal election law to allow the religious minority Ahmedis group to enter politics was an insult to the prophet Muhammed in a country that is 95 percent Muslim. The position of the powerful Messenger group is revealed by its adoration of Mumtaz Qadri, a man who recently assassinated a provincial governor for defending a woman accused of blasphemy. Conflict between the groups' protesters and the state was brokered by the army as "guarantors" (Constable, 2017). Thus, the agreement was signed in behalf of the state by the army between the army and the group.

14 To put this in perspective, in 2010 China had a private sector debt of 250 percent of GDP. But the public sector debt was only 58.2 percent of GDP of which only 23.7 percent was the local government component. Despite the frequent worries that local government debt will threaten the national financial condition, in fact China has substantial fiscal space, plenty of reserves and a strong regulatory apparatus that has been clamping down further on local government borrowing.

3 Wealthier State Populist Nationalism

North American, European, and Eastern European Cases

Poorer countries are not alone in their inability to respond effectively to the intense and often populist group demands that fragment their governing institutions. Ironically, a growing number of wealthy country governments are also unable to anticipate and manage conflicts or to respond to regional, sectarian, and ethnic demands: Scotland, England, Hungary, and the E.U. In other cases, such as Italy, states are unable to reform their own institutions and policies without serious populist demands. They are just petrified by process and bureaucracy, paralyzed by internal rules and special interest control of the agenda, and traditional political parties that are unable to forge workable programs to move forward. The driving forces for the other wealthy countries beset by populist nationalism are often fringe parties and populist movements. These are able to effectively mobilize opinion against ethnic and sectarian minority immigrants (from the poorer countries suffering ethnonationalist pressures) and domestic urban cosmopolitan values that favor more liberal immigration rules.

Strictly defined, populism is the belief that society can be divided into two antagonistic classes: "the people" and the powerful. The "people" are presumed to have a single will. The powerful are presumed to be devious and corrupt: determined to feather their own nests and adept at using intermediary institutions (courts, media companies, political parties) to frustrate the people (*The Economist*, 2017w: 50). Common populist slogans such as "power to the people" in wealthier countries translate as cultural code for: "our kind of people", not foreign immigrants or elites. Traditional populist policies have allocated funds for local public works, welfare, free tuition, and child subsidies (especially around election time), higher corporate taxation, and even new income support payments, as the Polish PIS party has done to entrench political support for its regime.

For example, the powerful Tunisian General Labor Union (UGTT) successfully pressures the Tunisian regime to hire more workers. Public sector wages already absorb 14 percent of GDP and state employees are

57 percent of the workforce. Such pressures are not unusual and, while costly, may not be destabilizing. Italian populism is based more on the frustrated economic expectations of the younger generation who view more public spending on the past (pensions) as opposed to their present (education, training, and loosening up a rigid job market) to be inherently unfair. Anti-immigration is not part of the Italian populist complaint. Their ballot box expression of this generational frustration (rather than regional or income-based) has been to support new parties such as M5S (*The Economist*, 2018b: 35). Some populist policy proposals are also badly conceived from a lack of comparative insights on how they have performed elsewhere under similar circumstances. For example, implementing privatization schemes in places such as Tunisia to eliminate public sector wage costs may be more destabilizing since they throw workers out into economies with limited private sectors unable to absorb them.

Thus, wealthier countries, particularly in many European countries and the U.S., are fighting viruses of populism, driven by forms of reverse ethno-nationalism in which often white supremacists tout their ethnicity and campaign against immigrants of sects and ethnicities from poorer countries with large non-white populations. There are at least 39 populist and radical right parties across Europe that have now held at least one parliamentary seat. Election results in 22 countries show support for these parties to be higher than at any time in the past 30 years. The exceptions are Portugal and Spain where leftist political activity is more intense than rightist organizations (Tartar, 2017: 40). Populist nationalism has been the rising pattern in wealthier countries such as the U.K., U.S., Russia, Hungary, Spain, Germany, and even Poland (whose citizens have been objects of British anti-immigration advocates themselves). Western civil society institutions and norms are viewed by populists as tools of rival cosmopolitan elites with "anywhere" values. In mass societies, voter ignorance and unfamiliarity with technical policy issues is often just below the surface waiting to be exploited by demagogues, nativists, and populists with social media to amplify their extremist messages. Rather than bold leaders, the demagogues are actually cheerleaders for the past who hit strong chords from their left-behind political bases. Support for and confidence in the major parties to respond to these pressures has been declining along with the rise of splinter parties of both hard left and right.

Most wealthy countries have macroeconomic stabilization policies in place that have functioned well over the past several decades. This will be discussed further below. But populist causes are successfully mobilizing regional, group and class opinion against perceived unfairness measured by wage and income inequality; lack of wage growth; loss of employment; lack of investment; and favoritism for newer immigrants often from entirely different cultures with their values and practices inconsistent with long-established local patterns.[1] Some of this may be driven by the familiar expectations/reality gap (Huntington, 1965) and thus incurable by more rationally designed or even successfully implemented policies. Fueled by social media to raise unreasonable expectations, this gap often produces destabilizing societal effects energizing populist demagogues.[2] That is more troubling in that, given that it seems to be a permanent gap, it may not be curable by sounder fiscal and economic policies. Most of the other *macroeconomic* components are well-known and measured, for example, unemployment and lack of wage growth, and thus represent the product of accumulated policy deficiencies over many years. Perpetual populist demands for equality and more benefits by nativists constrain the forging of better policies. For example, attempts in Australia at structural reforms to shift away from narrow export dependence on mining and mineral resources have been consistently stymied by populists and single-issue parties that have harnessed frustration with mainstream parties to claim the balance of power in parliament.[3] Australia still lacks a coherent energy policy and suffers from the highest electricity prices in the world though it has some of the largest coal and gas reserves on the planet (BBW, 2017: 33). In the medium-term, shifting political structures toward federalism, with autonomous subnational levels, guaranteed local fiscal autonomy, and a central level empowered to preserve the national interest under specific conditions, is the best means to resist populist demagoguery and sustain growth and development.

Spain and Catalonia

Catalonia is a part of the Spanish political culture of values and practices and a province of Spain. The Spanish Empire in Latin America was a Castilian venture but included Catalan viceroys and forebears of presidents. Latin Americans are perplexed by the secessionist movement in Catalonia since they have struggled to preserve their own cultures too (e.g. Mexican Indians) but also want to be full citizens of each country (e.g. the Mexican tradition of *mestizaje* or racial mixing dating from the Revolution of 1916–1917). Nevertheless, regional grievances exist in countries such as Argentina over the inequity of central government–local government fiscal flows and poor services such as infrastructure, health and education that have actually turned into referenda on secession. But Latin America has a tradition of employing nationalism as a tool to build nations rather than separate them into smaller parts. The Brazilian populist dictator of the 1930s, Getulio Vargas, for example, crushed the "arrogant imposition of regional interests" in Rio Grande do Sur, which endangered national unity (*The Economist*, 2017y: 32). In many countries of this region, the nation-building process was not peaceful or easy which may account for the lack of substantive interest in secession.[4] Still, wealthier European states face the destabilizing effects of regional populist demands and have been unable to respond in nuanced, flexible, and creative ways. They veer from letting voters decide (e.g. referenda which often leave issues unsettled) to heavy-handedness (security crackdowns which generate support for secessionists) and in some cases use both options. Rather than ethno-nationalism fracturing states, such as in SSA and MENA, such governments suffer from the forces of populist nationalism.

For example, the centralized Spanish unitary system, absolutist civil law tradition, and irresponsible hardline moves by both Madrid and the Catalonian independence movement to secede without real debate even in the Catalan parliament or *Generalitat*, have left Madrid with two stark but false choices: capitulation and loss of face, or exercise of legal control to prevent secession. The dictator Francisco Franco once enforced a fiercely homogeneous and centralized vision of the Spanish nation, denying and repressing the distinct languages, cultures, and histories of the people he ruled—until his death in 1975 (Abend, 2017: 13) After him, the democratic state of Spain was divided into 17 autonomous communities, reflecting the distinct peoples and cultures of Basques, Andalusians, Castilians, and Catalans.

But as with unitary and confederation states, the organizing principle of the nation as a shared basis of identity was and is an alliance, treaty, agreement, or a peaceful coexistence arrangement that would be enforced by mutual goodwill (i.e. *convivencia*) (Abend, 2017: 13). These problems have been common to all historical and current confederations, from the 1573 Warsaw Confederation (Lithuania and Poland into a "Catholic state" that was to be tolerant of non-Catholics) up to the E.U. Put another way, the union works until there are severe internal disagreements, and then it does not work. The prosperous Northeast Spanish region of Catalonia has a unique language, history of subjugation, and singular cultural traditions. It could be called "indigenous" as the term is used in other countries such as Canada, or given a unique legal status and protection as the Romansch regions in Switzerland, or allowed to hold their referenda as the U.K. did Scotland in 2014 and Canada did Quebec.[5] But all three of these countries are either federations or quasi-federations. In Spain, intergovernmental fiscal roles and responsibilities have not been properly assigned to serve efficiency and responsiveness needs. Catalonia suffers from the mandates without the money problem faced by many decentralized countries, both federation and unitary. But pro-nationalists have parlayed this familiar issue into the radical solution of total independence—which could end both E.U. and central government funding in order to gain more revenue autonomy to finance needs. Spain was already one of the most decentralized countries in the world, with exclusive control by its 17 autonomous regions over vital functions as: education, public works, and language (Cercas, 2017). Catalonia rejected more revenue-raising authority in 1975 and has since relied on transfers from the center. But this gave Madrid more fiscal control and entrenched centralization further.[6] Since the flow of contributions to budgets in a national fiscal union depends on formulae, Catalonia is a net contributor to poorer regions. That is largely because Catalonia accounts for 20 percent of GDP and 25 percent of total Spanish exports. Catalonia rejected a fiscal union arrangement (common in federations) and now seeks to keep more of its revenues (*Economist*, 2017d). In this delicate context, Madrid bluntly applies more law. The 1978 Constitution declares Spain indivisible and Article 155, which allows Madrid to strip regional governments of autonomy in times of crisis, has generated more intense opposition. The Article has never been invoked before. Making it hard to use law as a tool for political compromise and solution, civil law courts and officials routinely apply the letter of the law without having to cite precedent or allowing equity considerations to permit managerial discretion as would be required in Common Law judicial systems—the result, as here, often intensifies conflict and makes political compromise more difficult.

In its unitary system, Spanish regions are part of the central government rather than autonomous sub-national governments, which inhibits efforts by all parties to diffuse the conflict. One remedial option is to change its fiscal and political status to be more autonomous but less reliant on central transfers (positive or negative balances, and both current and capital). The Canadian federation, for example, devolved local economic development authority from the federal government in Ottawa to the Tsawwassen First Nation or indigenous people (which of course have their own history, language and culture). This moved them from dependence on fiscal transfers and continuance of their tax-exempt status to fiscal and political autonomy. They now pay sales, income, and property taxes in exchange for regulatory and political autonomy. By creating investor certainty to make and enforce contracts, the new status has led to an economic boom (BBW, 2017a: 32). Another realistic option is to hold a valid election for independence sanctioned by Madrid that ensures proper turnout and includes a minimum threshold for independence (e.g. 51 percent or even 67 percent since it is an existential question) (*The Economist*, 2017: 18). The final needed step, in our view, to resolve this crisis and provide sustainable governance for Spain is to adopt the opposition Socialists' view and transform Spain into a federation. Nevertheless, in a modern display of how nativist passion can overcome the forces of institutional rationality and fiscal prudence, Catalonian nationalists decided in October, 2017 to pursue full independence from Spain. Populist nationalists of the pro-independence movement still hope to sever Catalonia from both Madrid and Spain and then itself from the E.U. That would be a minor victory for political rhetoric and a major defeat for fiscal sanity and governmental effectiveness.

Scotland

The case of Scotland provides support for the thesis that devolved fiscal and political autonomy even within an incomplete federation (i.e. the U.K.) can work, with appropriate policy responses by the central government, to overcome populist nationalism. Fiscal autonomy and the experience of governing worked in Canada to diminish the power of the populist-separatist Parti Quebecois (*The Economist*, 2015: 10). As seen, it has also worked in Canada on issues of First Nation local economic development. It seems to be working in the "devolved administration" of Scotland. While Britain is the most centralized rich country in the world after New Zealand, since 1999 it has devolved authority to Scotland (and Wales and Northern Ireland). The U.K. is gradually realizing that the cult of centralized government created in the age of early mass production is not suited to modern demands for tailoring and customization. The fact is that innovations worldwide usually come from mayors and regions and not central governments. The new tax band and adjusted block grant system in 2016 now provides maximum fiscal and political authority to the treasury in Edinburgh. Its own source revenues have increased as the result of a formula that allows greater withholding of tax receipts, previously collected and retained by the central treasury in Whitehall. Grants are reduced for increased tax receipts. But Scottish fiscal risks are reduced by a sensible transfer formula that adjusts and compensates for lower GDP growth. Local borrowing authority has also been increased which should incentivize better fiscal performance and more investment in infrastructure to spur more growth. The agreements devolve more fiscal and tax authority but also responsibility for maintaining the overall financial condition. The risks of full responsibility are diminished to some extent by the adjusted block grant that cushions any loss of grant funds for better economic performance (and also diminishes the potentially perverse incentive this created). The devolution of fiscal powers also makes it more difficult for the SNP (Scottish National Party) to disavow responsibility for Scotland's problems and promise all things to all people in classic populist fashion (*The Economist*, 2016a: 57). Since the favorable Brexit vote of June 2016, heightened economic and financial fears together with greater acquisition of local autonomy from Whitehall have diminished Scottish interests in another independence referendum and any eventual secession from the U.K. The SNP now argues that the road to substantive independence lies in good governance (*The Economist*, 2017j: 49).

United Kingdom

To prevent nationalism from further regime weakening of the U.K., many believe that it needs to evolve into a full federation (*The Economist*, 2015: 10). It is now an English-dominated hybrid four-state confederation.

The British union is a delicate balancing act, created by the Act of Union in 1707, held together because the English have subsumed some of their identity and all of their institutions into those of the whole: Britain. It is a nation without a state. And it is the only rich country where the population of one constituent part is greater than all the other parts put together: California 12 percent of the U.S.; Bavaria 16 percent of Germany; Ontario 38 percent of Canada; but England is 84 percent of the U.K. (*The Economist*, 2015a: 57). This is incomplete in theory and practice, unstable, and bodes ill for the future, especially after the vote to leave the E.U.

The U.K. has three serious problems that render its government vulnerable to destabilizing nationalists and nativists. First, despite extreme fiscal and political centralization that prevents responsiveness and accountability, its system is paralyzed by a historic fetish for "delegate" democracy. Leaders successfully thrive on avoidance of the "trusteeship" of having to take hard decisions. This clogs the system further at the top. The costs of Brexit, for example, were not explained clearly to British voters by Conservative Party leaders: Treasury projections indicating the drops in income from decreased trade; the trade-offs between greater "freedom" from immigration and regulations now and future losses in income; and the overhang from the up to 20 ongoing commitments to the E.U. budget which will have to be covered in an exit bill of up to $50b to cover these costs. Of course, the independent and respected Office of Budget Responsibility (OBR) did forecast weaker economic performance as well as an increase in public debt (the public sector borrowing requirement) owing to diminished revenues from likely future trade complications and departure of firms in particular sectors such as finance, auto manufacturing, and aviation to E.U. countries. But Brexit campaigners successfully countered this information to its followers as elitist and untrustworthy, much as the Trump administration has done to respected institutions as CBO which forecast very specific and dire consequences from its disruptive trade, tax, and fiscal policies. Thus, in the U.K., this and the misleading claims of Catalonia independence, confirm Goethe's statement that "none are more hopelessly enslaved than those who falsely believe they are free". Moreover, misleading claims by Brexit supporters were not challenged effectively and aggressively by opposition party leaders (i.e. Labor) who acted as passive delegates to the voter's will. That was an abdication of leadership responsibilities to fully reveal the reasonably estimated costs of proposed policies and to provide a critique of the supposed benefits. Delegate-style leaders put such complex issues to popular referenda votes and have argued again successfully that the will of the voter amounts to an iron law.[7] The result has been the multiple referenda offerings to the voters by leaders that should have been handled either by bolder elected leaders or perhaps decisions to the contrary from what voters decided, e.g. by even The House of Lords.

Instead the decisions stand of Cameron's Brexit decision based on referenda, and Theresa May's short-sighted decision to confront the E.U. with a more united front.[8]

Second, leaders fear relinquishing central political and fiscal control from Whitehall/Westminster. The U.K. is the most centralized rich country system in the world.[9] This has been increasingly hard to justify as more English mayors are being elected and some local governments even have North American-style city managers. Evidence is clear that innovations in governance, business, and even public finances originate at the bottom local level and filter upwards to improve policymaking and operations of central governments around the world. Third, the two U.K. party platforms and leaders are increasingly irrelevant to the needs of voters in a large, complex, multi-cultural society. The populist revolt in the U.K. and elsewhere consists of so-far unbridgeable cultural conflicts between "somewheres" that are rooted to place, socially conservative, and suspicious of change and "anywheres" that are cosmopolitan, socially liberal, internationalist, and comfortable with change (Goodhart, 2017). The Conservative Party is led by, what might be termed, a stale gerontocracy supported by a narrow base of the old white working class and less educated. This party has become almost a fanatical sect formed around Brexit. Labor leadership offers worn out and demonstrably failed statist solutions and giveaways peddled in the 1960s that ended up requiring an English bailout from the IMF. These rigid partisan features make it harder to win pluralities of voters and then to form majority coalitions of like-platform parties from which to govern. Such is the institutional paralysis that the U.K. faces today. Evolution to a complete, full federation (the U.K. union should be federalized) would at least allow more institutional redundancy and responsiveness by the overall system to withstand nationalist pressures that have justifiably derailed both parties and their leadership.

Hungary

Hungary is a strong-state, unitary government, relatively higher income country with solid macroeconomic performance (Table 2.2). Still a unitary system with reliance on central transfers, local governments have been delegated functional responsibilities and can borrow for capital asset financing (Bird *et al.*, 1995: 71). It has minimal regional inequality problems and transfers from the center to local governments are sufficient to cover most needs. Foreign investment, economic growth, and employment levels are all high. Hungary has a relatively homogeneous population with few immigrants. But it has had a long history of mistreating Roma, the main minority and, of course, local Jews in WWII by the fascist Arrow Cross and its successors in the Jobbik Party. Hungarians have long had strong nationalist leanings, some derived from being treated as the junior partner in the Dual Monarchy of the Austro-Hungarian empire and then by mistreatment at the hands of the Nazis during WWII, and Soviet Communists after WWII. Noteworthy is the Hungarian tradition of support for strong, authoritarian governments, buttressed by formal-legal authority that precisely circumscribes the limits of dissent. The Hungarian "revolution of 1989" or transition from a Communist regime to a genuine multi-party system and its vital role in the unraveling of the German GDR (East German Communist regime) are significant in that they were conducted by reform Communists themselves (Judt, 2005: 610). Two decades of ambiguous tolerance, including the opening of the Hilton's first hotel behind the Iron Current in 1976, culminated in the shift toward what can now be called "illiberal democracy".

Viktor Orban's ruling and highly popular Fidesz Party is a collection of rightist groups from ethno-racists such as the Jobbik Party (including its uniformed *Magyar Garda* unit of jack-booted troops) to traditional nationalists who want standard policies such as nationalized industries and more subsidies for farmers (Guess, 2007: 3). The sudden arrival of waves of Iraqi and Syrian Muslims and North African immigrants in 2015 opened up the country along its traditional fault lines. Fidesz took the opportunity to pursue a successful populist, ethno-nationalist position of no immigrants from these regions or requirements from the E.U. that they provide asylum to them. In this ethnic and racially based intransigence, Hungary has been supported by similarly constituted political regimes in Poland and the Czech Republic (both unitary regimes with quasi-federalist mechanisms). In its popular anti-immigrant policy stance deriving from dominant cultural values and practices, Hungary is similar to the historic stances of Japan. Japan is a unitary state on a sovereign island, and not a member of a confederation with rules that require democratic tolerance like the E.U. But in both places, political cultures favoring white, European (or Japanese) racial stock overwhelm interests in inclusion or diversity. Both countries have low percentages of immigrants and very low annual asylum acceptance rates.

The Former Yugoslav Federation

After the end of WWI and the 1919 Treaty of Versailles and the end of the Ottomans, this Balkanized area became the Kingdom of Slovenes, Croats, and Serbs. Yugoslavia became the name in 1929 of this multi-ethnic, multi-religious, multi-state federation with its six republics and two provinces led by governors and at the federation level by Josef Broz Tito (1945–1980). Yugoslavia became a functioning federation with a fiscal transfer union, and a federal army (JNA). Each republic had its own central bank and the entire federation was directed by the Yugoslav Communist Party (Silber and Little, 1995: 64). This was the peculiar feature of the federation: it was a one-party state governed by the Communist Party. So long as the leader was considered legitimate and was able to balance ethnic and republican interests for the benefit of the federation, the system worked. When Tito died in 1980, the delicate balance was upset, allowing the rise of nationalist demagoguery to overwhelm the system. Nationalist demagoguery can overwhelm even the strongest institutions if the conditions are favorable.[10]

In 1988, Slobodan Milosevic began mobilizing populist, ethnonationalist support for "oppressed Serbs" in Kosovo and against Albanians (the Muslims living there) and the provincial Vojvodina leadership which he claimed subverted the "fatherland" (occupied by Slavic Orthodox Serbs). Kosovo was the historic location of the Field of Blackbirds 1389 holdout of Serbs against the Ottoman Turks. It is now portrayed as an unjust displacement of this hallowed Serb ground by Muslims. Kosovo Serbs were portrayed by Milosevic and his followers in Belgrade as downtrodden martyrs for Serbdom (Silber and Little, 1995: 61).[11] He thus led a successful populist "Anti-Bureaucratic" revolution against the federation using the secret police (SDB) to get crowds and workers behind him. Given the centralization of party control and the lack of contestability, he successfully manipulated federation institutions, claiming authority from the federation when he needed it and then used it in behalf of the Serb republic when that suited his power-grabbing aims. He capitalized on the death of Tito (a Croat) and the Soviet collapse in 1989 that broke up Yugoslavia into constituent countries and republics, all of which left minorities stranded in someone else's country. This was partly the legacy of what Wilson and his colleagues failed to resolve at Versailles 70 years earlier (Judt, 2005: 673). The catalyst was the Serb fever of the 600th Anniversary of the Kosovo Battle whipped up by Milosevic. The other significant issue was fiscal (as in Catalonia): Belgrade grabbed 50 percent of the federation budget drawing rights for its public sector workers in back pay (2005: 673). Slovenia, with 8 percent of the population, contributed 25 percent of the budget, withdrew first from the federal fiscal system. Belgrade sent the JDA army to stop it from secession but withdrew; then the Croats fought with the rebellious Serb minority backed by the Yugoslav army. The five complex internal wars could be viewed from the simpler historical lens of the repressive Croatian Ustasha (Catholic) security apparatus vs. Serbian Slavs (Orthodox) and their obvious Russian cultural link. Then, after Croats and Bosnian Muslims declared independence in 1992, the Serbs attacked the new state of Bosnia (later Bosnia-Herzegovina) and its capital Sarajevo (2005: 674). To muster more populist support, Milosevic turned back to Kosovo to expel or exterminate Albanians (Muslims) there and was finally prevented from further nationalist destruction and ethnic cleansing by NATO in 1999.

In short, centralization and demagoguery over religious-ethnicity issues overwhelmed the institutional strength of the federation that had worked so well to make Yugoslavia unique and prosperous for years. The institutional structure was simply unable to contain ethnic and populist nationalistic forces after the death of Tito. Demagoguery for years had a difficult time, in that ethnic identity in Yugoslavia could not really be ascertained by speech or appearance (Judt, 2005: 675) and many had believed they had been assimilated into the multi-ethnic community and protected by federation law and judicial institutions (i.e. formal and informal processes and rules of the game). On paper, that was true. But Slobodan Milosevic's demagoguery, stoking resentments over underlying ethnic and religious differences, slight though they might seem to the outsider, opened up centuries-old animosities over land, power, and even the results of long-forgotten (by some) wars. The Serbs successfully stoked the hysteria of a potential Muslim jihad when most Muslims were quite secular. Enver Hoxha had made sure of that in his neighboring Stalinist Albanian regime (1940–1991) by banning religion altogether! To this day, Albanians from Albania are still only nominally Muslim. The resultant Yugoslav break-up and nationalism exploited religious identities which were hardly more distinct than the several Romansch dialects from different Swiss valleys in one canton (about which Graubunden locals will tell you are substantial, obvious, and reflect cultural differences obvious to anyone!).

The EU Confederation

The E.U. is a partial federation governed from Brussels by a government created top-down to represent 28 members (soon to be 27). Created by the 1992 Maastricht Treaty (derived from the intentions of the Treaty of Rome in 1957), it is a customs and monetary union but not a debt, fiscal, political, or banking union. Thus it is incomplete in theory and practice. There is no independent sub-national level; authority flows from the Treaty which, despite the limit of "subsidiarity" (i.e. no E.U. action if it can be taken at national, regional or local levels; Judt, 2005: 715), is largely a top-down governance operation. Sub-Brussels governments have no real stakes or representation because the budget covering the E.U. area is miniscule. The budget and policy processes are top-down and secretive. The E.U. budget (around $120b) in 2017 was 1.23 percent of total E.U. GDP; or 1/50 of total E.U. public spending; 50 percent of this budget goes to agriculture (CAP); and 33 percent for regional aid through "cohesion" grants. The E.U. has been described as a system of representation without taxation! A policy problem with such a small budget is that the ECB by default must provide both monetary and fiscal stability which it (or any central bank) cannot do. Institutionally, since there is no E.U. ministry of finance or MOF, there can be no E.U.-wide fiscal stimulus or macroeconomic stabilization policy effort to deal with the periodic economic crises that can easily result in recessions or depressions.

The budget and policy processes are opaque and top-down. The Council of Ministers as the main policymaking arm and the European Parliament (EP) are responsible for proposing and adopting the E.U. budget (*The Economist*, 2017h: 15). But it is a low-stakes operation, concerning only CAP and rural development cohesion grants (plus administrative expenses for Brussels and Strasbourg) that are miniscule in proportion to European member states' GDP. The fiscal policy debate is one-dimensional, dealing only with expenditures and not revenues because the E.U. cannot raise taxes. Regardless, there are two kinds of generic budget-policy processes. The first is top-down where the regime and its close advisors and their associates develop and adopt options which the executive agencies (here the member states) must implement. Debate over costs and consequences, technical inputs such as forecasts, and public interest inputs are limited in a closed budget-policy process. The second kind is the more textbook style operation where assumptions are challenged, premises are revealed, options are developed and consequences forecasted.[12] Technical costs and benefits are weighed and passed upwards with preferred options selected by an MOF or Parliamentary committee. Spending ministries and parliaments are then responsible for implementation, monitoring, and evaluation of results. The standard examples are macroeconomic targets squared off against revenue forecasts to develop budget scenarios consistent with targets. The E.U. budget/policy processes do not encourage counterfactual "what-if" thinking. In this they inhibit any links with wider stakeholders in member states that prevent both policies and budgets from attaining either wider support or legitimacy. This process opacity and centralization appears undemocratic and may be an important cause of how populist groups have gained anti-E.U. traction with voters.

The failure to employ formal policy analytic methods in one scheduled and legitimate annual process has been the cause of the ill-defined policy problems leading to bad policy results which have weakened E.U. legitimacy further. For example, the E.C. defined the 2010–2012 Euro crisis as a problem of public sector profligacy, generalizing from the Greek case. From 2010, Greece had borrowed cheaply because the use of the Euro made its goods expensive and debt was there for the asking on good terms. Given local political pressures, this led to excessive spending, unsustainable borrowing and provided few incentives for the regime to increase its own-source revenues with more taxation. A deeper problem was undercapitalized member banking systems and weak criteria and creditworthiness review practices for loan origination. This stemmed from the lack of an E.U. banking and credit union. The proximate cause of the Euro crisis was private borrowing from banks to firms and households. In Ireland, Spain, and Portugal, the level of private debt was over 200 percent of GDP. The problem was mortgages in Ireland and Spain, and corporate debt in Portugal and Spain. Instead, the E.C. defined the problem as public sector profligacy and imposed austerity fiscal consolidation programs around the E.U. that deepened recessions and made it harder to reduce the level of private debt. The rigid imposition of the wrong policy also widened the split needlessly between E.U. members (northern savers and southern spenders) that led to the fall of several governments and widespread public resistance. The institutional rigidity problem derived from a noted feature of the political culture: a formal-legal mindset. That led to the enforcement of legal strictures rather than to efforts at political management, leading to more problems that still fester: illegal immigration from MENA, North Africa and SSA, and now the impact of Brexit.

Members lack substantive representation as part of the E.U. governing structure: states are nominally represented by the Council of Ministers and the E.P. This is important because representation of states in central government policymaking is clearly part of the essence of federalism (Rodden, 2006: 36) but not of confederations. The E.P. does not control governments like a national parliament; it lacks any connection to voters who decreasingly turn out for elections and who decide on national not E.U.-wide criteria. Nor does the European Parliament control spending or curb the executive—the European Commission (E.C.). The European Commission has one power over recalcitrant E.U. members, invoking Article 7 against member states that threaten the rule of law. In response to the Polish regime's recent weakening of its constitutional tribunal and orders that Supreme Court justices resign, the E.C. now views this as a severe weakening of judicial independence sufficient for the application of sanctions through Article 7. But other members who have made similar transgressions against rule of law would oppose an Article 7 application by the E.C. and vote to support Poland. This legal dimension is another dilemma for any confederation structure.

Instead, the E.P. behaves more as a lobby group, spending more and augmenting its own powers (*The Economist*, 2017h: 14). Worse, member states treat the E.U. as an external, international organization—one which merely grants them funding and regulates loosely their economies but cannot impose any taxes. The E.U. regulates in blanket fashion (one size fits all) with a rigid civil law approach to governing that excludes discretionary action. Few exceptions are made for national differences with repeatedly perverse consequences that upset nationals and trade relations in member states. For example, the Georgia-E.U. Deep and Comprehensive Free Trade Agreement (DCFTA) requires certificates of origins for all its agricultural exports. But it cannot certify the 10 percent of hazelnuts coming from the breakaway and Russian-backed republic of Abkhazia (*de facto* independent after wars of secession of 1992–1993) and must therefore ban them from being mixed with Georgian exports. This punishes Abkhazian farmers for the Georgian inability to prevent the taking of national territory, a geopolitical conflict out of the control of farmers in both countries. The rigid application of law to reach absurd conclusions has also been a problem, as noted, by enlarging an intergovernmental fiscal problem in Catalonia into a deeper political and constitutional crisis for Spain.

The US Articles of Confederation (1781–1789)

Previously independent states often pool troops and capture gains from cross-border trades with loose alliances or confederations. Easy to form, they require unanimous agreement for significant action and can easily be dissolved. Lacking enforcement mechanisms, they often suffer from problems of instability, free-riding, and collective action. That is the history of the Articles of Confederation (Rodden, 2006: 32–33). It was a formative attempt in 1781 to create a loose union of 13 states. Before 1963, the government of the British Empire was de facto federal but the colonies had no security for their rights through this informal arrangement (Morison, 1994: 362). The Articles formalized the power of the Continental Congress and most importantly states ceded land to the Congress after which Congress established a territorial policy (1994: 365). But the Articles did not give Congress the power to tax or to regulate commerce and rested on the goodwill of the states to preserve a perpetual union (1994: 366). James Madison noted in the *Federalist Papers* that the Articles were nothing more than a "treaty of amity" and an "alliance" between independent and sovereign states (1994: 366). There were no sanctions which, to Madison, were essential to law and that proved to be the undoing of this form of union in the U.S. as elsewhere. The federal government was tightly constrained. As in the E.U. Council of Ministers, member U.S. states under the Articles had to obtain unanimous votes before taking significant action. For borrowing money, raising an army, concluding treaties or appointing a commander in chief, only two-thirds of the states were required to assent (1994: 365). But, the unanimity requirement for most domestic policy and national issues meant the Articles could not deal with growing regional differences. Hamilton argued also in the *Federalist Papers* (#19) for a centralized, unitary system to replace the Articles. The Articles demonstrated the same institutional flaws which were unable to control the policy or finances that characterized the eighteenth-century German confederation—sovereignty gone awry (Rodden, 2006: 153). But 200 years later, Germany is a full federation with constitutional safeguards, separation of powers, checks, and balances, and Länder (states) retaining widespread autonomy over taxation and spending decisions. Institutional evolution is possible.

Notes

1 Poorer workers who often form the base of fringe and single-issue parties oppose the rootless cosmopolitanism of cultural-liberal elites in many countries, rich and poor. They resent these elites even more than financial elites.

This angry block of voters are more comfortable with community and majoritarian values and care less for the procedural niceties of the liberal order and multiculturalism. They are also impatient with due process via affirmative action for minorities and hanker for strong leaders that provide seductively simple answers to complex policy problems (Bardhan, 2017).

2 Successful populist movements are often led by demagogues. Who and what are they? Demagogues are not necessarily evil or dangerous people. They are usually gripping orators who have experienced your personal pains—being culturally put down, sacked, part of a family bust-up, in poverty, feeling loss of racial or religious solidarity or identity to newcomers. They speak your language and know instinctively what makes you tick. They offer plausible, simplistic, and collectively disruptive solutions.

3 Austria fits the pattern of voter frustration with colorless centrism and rising inequality. More parties are formed on single or narrow issues which makes coalition-building and governance harder. Spain produced a minority government after two ballots and ten months of political deadlock in 2017. Loyalty to the main parties has plummeted in most rich countries, increasing support for fringe parties that add to fragmentation in parliaments (*The Economist,* 2017g: 48). Needed to supplement this growing inclusion of voice in governments are less colorless centrist leaders and new centrist parties that defend open societies and economies, such as Emmanuel Macron and *En Marche* in France.

4 Da Cunha chronicles the "scorched earth" campaign of the Brazilian army in the 1890s to "pacify" the backlands from disturbances and uprisings and to bring them the fruits of civilization. A sanitary engineer working with the army, he documents their barbarity and frequently takes the side of the *sertanejos* or backland race constituting one-third of the nation's population but forgotten by the state for 300 years. He says:

> It was not the backland fanatics who were at bottom to blame but their countrymen of a higher stage of civilization who had left them in a centuries-old darkness, failing to prepare them for sharing the higher responsibilities of democracy ... This entire campaign would be a crime, a futile and barbarous one, if we were not to take advantage of the paths opened by our artillery, by following up our cannon with a constant, stubborn, and persistent campaign of education, with the object of drawing these rude and backward fellow countrymen of ours into the current of our times and our own national life.
>
> (da Cunha, 1944: xv)

5 Should the verdict of referenda be allowed to stand for existential questions of national integrity and finances? Referenda are important reforms used in Switzerland for national and local questions, with verdicts held in check by a final constitutional court. But often they lead to inconsistent results that muddle policy and diminish support for governments that appear not to know what they are doing, for example, votes for higher education and large tax cuts. More importantly, they unleash populist forces driven by social media and sound bites that produce policy disasters like Brexit (*The Economist,* 2017i: 58). In the U.S., referenda were useful reform tools circumventing

corrupt state legislatures. Then, as now, referenda reflect widespread alienation from politics and anger at the governing class, that is, a perfect storm for populists. U.S. state fiscal questions often have a higher threshold than a 51 percent simple majority to protect minorities. There are no national referenda. The question turns on whether one believes representatives should be passive delegates responding to the voter will or active trustees or guardians of the national interest. For the latter to work, parliaments and legislatures have to be qualified and active to judge the practical functioning of government and its policies. With distorted electoral systems that produce safe districts and which favor minority rural and parochial interests at the expense of cosmopolitan, urban growth and modernization, that competence cannot be assumed in most countries.

6 Control of budget spending is essential for fiscal discipline. Standard drivers of loss of control are (1) over-responsiveness to special interests resulting in subsidies and direct expenditures to them; (2) fiscal reporting systems that fail to provide valid and timely fiscal decisions, and (3) weak cash management systems that are unable to match spending obligations and revenue availability during budget execution (Guess, 2015: 176–177). But a more serious impediment to state effectiveness is the legalistic pre-decision compliance control systems that exist in Civil Law countries and the legislative line-item controls in Common Law countries that turn the state into a rigid executor of regime will. Modern states register financial transactions in general ledger FMISs (aka GFMISs) in real time, cutting out layers of unneeded approvals and potential corruption points. Transactions are examined postdecision by internal and external auditors. State reforms in many countries have often been driven by the bureaucratic systems changes required for full implementation of FMISs. On the other hand, unreformed states often ensure that FMISs are only partially installed to prevent embarrassing revelations.

7 The two currents in the trustee–delegate dilemma were noted by Musil (1995: 1096–1097). One states that man is good by nature and collectively knows what is good for him. The other states that they do not know or want what is good for them and must be guided and forced to do the right thing. Leaders could respond to the first current by becoming their agents or delegates in office; to the second by being trustees of the public will and acting in their behalf. For leaders, the contradiction between the two currents could be resolved by the notion that they could then love mankind after changing it by force (or more moderately, acting as their trustee without detailed consultation). More seriously, the positive political economy justification for unitary governments (which even Alexander Hamilton favored), with strong executives and officials acting as trustees, is to prevent self-seeking, private goods over the common interest and debt-servicing crises of the subnational governments that would require federal bailouts (Rodden, 2015: 54, 56).

8 The proximate cause of the Brexit vote was growing impatience with the urban governing elite in London and other advanced cities by voters in the poorer industrial hinterland (or rustbelt) known as JAMs or "just-about-managing" families and unemployed workers, also embittered by culturally different immigrants from the E.U. The legitimacy and sustainability of fiscal policies that ignored the rift between services-rich boomtowns and forgotten, post-industrial regions (the north–south divide) was called into question by

the Brexit vote. In a classic case of a poor definition of a policy problem, indifference of the central government toward regional decline attendant on the shift from manufacturing to services was successfully blamed on membership in the E.U. (even though the economic and demographic changes had been evident for 30 years). These same forces threaten the model of devolution and flexible governance. The difficulty is that the model is successful in advanced OECD Commonwealth countries for fiscal discipline and macroeconomic stability while less capable in allocating shares of income, employment and growth to non-advanced cities—small and medium-sized towns in the provinces. Allocational efficiency has not worked even for OECD Commonwealth countries between socio-economic classes and regions. Allocations between sectors such as health vs. education are made easier, perhaps, by the fact that they are less technical and more political choices (i.e. reflecting the inability to compare interpersonal utility preferences for such services). But even for sectoral planning, MTEFs in peripheral countries do not function well.

9 Regime weakness, instability and unresponsive, centralized governments are not new problems here. Some have suggested that the U.K. has turned into a petrified democracy, frozen by rules and protocol, over-centralized and out of touch. After outlasting three Prime Ministers in a row, including Anthony Eden and Harold McMillan, Queen Elizabeth in 1962 suggested she was surrounded by a "confederacy of quitters"!

10 The German National Socialist party victory in pre-WWII Germany revealed that populist nationalism energized by a skillful demagogue can overwhelm deeply civilized and strong democratic institutions by perverting and distorting, then hollowing them out of dissenters. Neutralizing especially non-state civil society institutions such as the media effectively counters opposition to newly composed populist nationalist regimes. Favorable contextual ingredients include: a bad economy with high unemployment, stagnant incomes, and extreme income inequality; plausible external enemies (e.g. unnecessarily harsh Versailles Treaty conditions, and "5th columnist" scapegoats); and an electoral system that in the name of representational equality magnifies the voting power of provincial rural areas to balance out the urban cosmopolitan population centers. But a sensitive democratic election system registers dissatisfaction and magnifies it in varying degrees. Regimes and budgetary systems should respond via fiscal transfer reformulations and quasi-federalist sub-systems to reduce allocational inequality and prevent fringe movements and zealots from capitalizing on apparent injustices and indifference to left-behind people and regions.

11 The 1389 defeat of Prince Lazar's forces and Christian Slavs by the Muslim Ottoman Turks created martyrdom for the vanquished: a kind of standing pool of purity from which to receive the Eucharist, enabling Christian Slavs to go to heaven. Fans of the "Grey Falcon" poem believed that an individual could procure salvation by refusing to save others from suffering and war. Unlike a "kind Caesar" from an effective state, martyrs, including priests and philosophers, wanted to be right rather than do right. While defeated Slavs knew that Christianity was better for man than Islam because it denounced the prime human fault—cruelty, they could not go forward (West, 1993: 915). Slavic Christianity could not even rid itself of cruel, medieval perversions

such as lamb sacrifice, of an innocent animal so that believers could remain good. "The power of the rock over their minds" prevented them from moving beyond a sense of their own righteousness and virtue. In this metaphysical self-sacrifice they betrayed generations of those who came after in Serbia and any country where common sense is needed to forge a governing coalition to improve life.

12 Policy-budget processes are similar on paper to Professor Surway's 5-Button Process of Successful Reasoning: (button 1) observe events and problems, (button 2) define the problem more precisely, (button 3) develop hypotheses on remedial options and solutions, (button 4) develop and measure consequences of remedial options, and (button 5) observe implementation for consistency with hypotheses on options and solutions (Musil, 1995: 1030). Of course, Professor Hagauer was trying to apply the process to his personal problems and not to those facing technical policy professionals in separate ministries and institutions, vying for influence over their final budgets and policy results to satisfy external and internal stakeholders with their narrow, increasingly ideological, and often unsubstantiated views.

4 Macroeconomic Instability

The third kind of destabilizing force on states that prevents effective governance is macroeconomic shock and instability (Figure 0.1). To the extent fiscal and monetary policies cannot stabilize key macroeconomic variables, in addition to contributing to weak economic growth, users of basic services and programs suffer. Public budgets cannot be planned beyond the very short term and their implementation is interrupted by constant funding shortages. Consumers must deal with price inflation and firms cannot pay for imports priced in dollars or euros in often deflated local currency. Macroeconomic instability at a minimum results in unreliable service, program, and project delivery. At the strategic level, macroeconomic instabilities are evident in phenomena such as: deflation, hyperinflation, deep recessions, high unemployment, low investment, greater poverty, and income inequality, all of which produce severe economic losses. Often, the sources of instability are the large fiscal deficits and public debts derived from ill-designed fiscal policies.

Latin American regimes in particular suffered from hyperinflation and high unemployment in the 1970s to 1980s and chronic inability to finance their suffocating public debt burdens and high annual fiscal deficits. Part of the problem was that the relatively weak states were unable to extract significant amounts of tax revenues from their own populations (Fukuyama, 2014: 260). Political instability was high and many regimes in that region were overthrown. Note the mutual causation: illegitimate and weak states unable to extract tax revenues inflated money supplies producing severe macroeconomic problems that led to public frustrations and regime overthrows. The ill-conceived policy responses, in short, were derived from prior failures to tax and spend sustainably. Argentina has been a textbook case of the evils of economic nationalism: self-generated cycles of rapid growth, inflation, devaluation, default, and economic collapse (2014: 277). As indicated in Table 2.2, Brazil is again having macroeconomic problems (12.6 percent unemployment and the highest fiscal deficit of sampled countries, -8.9 percent), largely due to its political scandals and populist economic policies.

Instead, effective governments should be able to respond to such destabilizing forces with sound fiscal and monetary policies. Fiscal policy is important in that it provides financing for the key sectoral policies, programs, and capital projects that serve not only public need but also as seeds for institutionalization of state capacity. Wealthier countries with effective governments have institutions that make and enforce the hard policy choices needed for stabilization, e.g. tax increases, public spending cuts, and monetary policies to control inflation or stimulate growth, that have strong regulatory links to the commercial banking system. Independent central banks are indicators of macroeconomic policy maturity and stability. Wealthier countries also have the advantage of automatic stabilizers that allow them to rely less on unpopular discretionary policies such as budgetary austerity. Wealthy countries such as Switzerland and some poorer countries, including Chile, have made the necessary fiscal choices for stability automatic by making and enforcing automatic budget rules to control deficits and debt levels. Relying on other automatic, counter-cyclical stabilizers, when prices increase and incomes fall, unemployment and welfare benefits kick in to provide social safety nets and prevent the recessions or depressions that can threaten regimes. Such fiscal stabilizers did not exist during the 1930s' Great Depression. Now they are part of every wealthy country policy toolbox and also explain why public budgets are a much greater share of wealthier country economies than in the 1930s. The stabilizers and social safety nets are part of the liberal economic and social-democratic governance reforms that have benefited the populations and stabilized economies of the wealthier countries for nearly a century. Poorer countries without automatic macroeconomic stabilizers attempt to build up foreign exchange reserves for use in crises. Such reasonable policy responses under conditions, where political regimes are unwilling or unable to make the hard discretionary choices necessary for stabilization, require consistent budgetary fiscal discipline to control deficits and debt. As noted in Table 2.2, these compensatory efforts have been largely successful in most countries.

But some countries still ignore decades of practical policy remedies and lose control of their macroeconomies. Populist politics driven by traditional electoral power concerns and ethno-nationalism are often the culprits. Countries such as South Africa, have been wracked by fiscal profligacy, mismanagement, and looting of the state treasury by corrupt officials. While the deficit and debt levels are not nominally large (-4.9 percent and 53 percent of GDP respectively), poorly conceived fiscal management policies have led to excessive borrowing to pay interest costs on its debt. Lack of growth (from other badly designed macroeconomic policies) meant that it has not been able to grow its way out of the debt trap. Debt service payments (15 percent of budget expenditures and 3.5 percent GDP) now crowd out the budgeted funds needed for essential services. It spends twice as much on debt service as higher education each year (*The Economist*, 2017x: 77). Should spending increase to reward ANC voters who can prevent it from losing its parliamentary majority before the 2019 elections, loans would be even harder to roll over (especially by banks to SOEs), inflation could increase, and the currency could weaken further (2017x78). That would drive up debt service payments beyond 15 percent of the budget.

Large fiscal deficits and debt often reflect weak state institutions, unable to manage the public finances. They may also reflect populist regime policies that seek to preserve jobs, votes and their own elected tenure.[1] The annual budget deficit is termed the public sector borrowing requirement in Commonwealth Countries. It correctly indicates the borrowing necessary to finance the excess of expenditures over revenues but provides no guidance on its sustainability, given the macroeconomic requirements over the medium term. For, deficits or not, sufficient public spending is needed to maintain aggregate demand in recessionary contexts where private consumption and investment are weak. There are limits beyond which the growth payoff from additional spending can be undone by the damage to consumption and investment from additional (or poorly designed) taxation to keep the budget in balance over even the medium-term. Taxes have to be designed to minimize distortions to the economic incentives of firms, investors, and consumers. Beyond this limit, norms of tax policy design and fiscal discipline are often violated, leading to unsustainable fiscal deficits and public debts (Guess and Husted, 2017: 27).

Central governments have three traditional functions: (1) macroeconomic stabilization, (2) efficiently allocating societal resources and (3) altering the distribution of resources (Musgrave, 1959). Strong, professional central governments, whose policy decisions affect the welfare of an entire nation, are absolutely necessary to perform these functions. Stable, predictable employment levels, lower inflation rates, accurate demand and growth estimates, and effective fiscal policies are needed by investors, consumers, and governments. Stabilization policy refers to the role of governments in maintaining employment, price stability, and economic growth through fiscal and monetary policy (Fisher, 2007: 25). Instability in any of these variables affects the others in largely predictable ways. For instance, weak consumer demand for goods and services, reluctance of banks to lend and investors to borrow for investments means slower economic growth. Failure of government to step in and increase purchases and investments either through greater deficit spending or increases in tax revenues will perpetuate weak growth. Included in the traditional functions is the need to anticipate and control threats to them from sub-national debt and overspending. This requires modern systems of accounting and public financial management to enforce fiscal discipline. Governments around the world regularly face these policy problems and dilemmas.

Such challenges and requirements mean that strong economic and fiscal policymaking and implementation institutions are required to achieve macroeconomic stability sufficient enough for growth. Mentioned have been the horizontal checks and balances and separation of powers necessary to prevent conflicts of interest and abuses of power. Institutionalized checks on government prevent politically short-term decisions from interfering with the need to put necessary medium and long-term policies in place, such as counter-cyclical spending and tighter interest rates to control inflation. Modern states have independent central banks, single treasury accounts policed by strong internal control and audit institutions supported by strong ministries of finance. In patrimonial states, these institutions are subordinate to regimes that are often more interested in maintaining power and political control than macroeconomic stability.

Evidence of strong institutions can be found in political cultures: the values and practices that affect which rules are made and how strictly they are enforced. In Chile, for example, the independent central bank has held down inflation since the 1970s when the country adopted a liberal economic model. It also adopted a fiscal rule, similar to one used by Switzerland, that requires governments to balance budgets over an economic cycle. The persistence of these institutions that make and enforce rules strengthens the larger state, enhances its legitimacy and facilitates its ability to implement sound policies, programs, and services, such as effective macroeconomic policies (inflation at 2.1 percent and budget deficit only -2.8 percent of GDP). Evidence for the effectiveness of its policy and governance institutions lies in its high governmental effectiveness score (82.7 percent) as well as the fall in its poverty rate from 40 percent in 1990 to less than 10 percent in 2017. In a region tagged often for a culture of corruption, Chile scores relatively high (66 percent) in the 2015 Transparency International corruption perceptions index. This suggests institutions are strong enough to limit government, facilitate its effectiveness and inhibit abuses of financial and political power.

Similarly, despite vast diamond resources, Botswana has built strong, modern state institutions focusing on financial management and control and effective macroeconomic planning. It is a unitary state with authority diffused over multiple parties that elect parliamentary representatives. Governmental branches are independent and civil service rules are strict and merit-based. Senior civil servants in many cases are personally liable for misappropriation of funds below their chain of command. The country uses its diamond receipts to benefit the population (Fukuyama, 2014: 312) and is still considered a model for "good enough" governance for the region. Fiscal and monetary policies have been conservative, evidenced by fund reserves for stabilization and debt service payments. The country has built outstanding structures of control. Civil servants receive high compensation and function within well-defined lines of authority and accountability (Good, 1994: 502). More recently, the country's institutions have weathered corruption scandals and national development bank (NDB) bankruptcy, but largely because of its institutional strength, it remains a beacon for effective governance.

Malaysian macroeconomic institutions and performance have also been solid. One of the few Asian federations, Malaysia's per capita income is relatively high ($9360), with low levels of unemployment (5.3 percent), inflation (4.5 percent), and budget deficits (-2.5 percent GDP) (Table 2.2). Its quality of life (79 HDI) and governmental effectiveness are high (73.2 percent) (South Korean effectiveness is 80.3 percent). Malaysia is a democratic federation with strong electoral institutions and party contestability for power. In 2013, the opposition minority won the popular vote but remains a minority within parliament (by seats) because of the electoral system (similar to the effect of the U.S. Electoral College favoring sparsely populated districts). The electoral system is otherwise advanced and modern: election by single-member districts for higher accountability and plurality vote election rules to encourage turnout. The 85 percent turnout in 2013 was the highest in national history.[2]

Costa Rica defied odds like Botswana and developed an effective, democratic state but without any natural resources other than its forests, which have turned into a source of tourism and international financing and goodwill for sustained tropical management and preservation. Costa Rica has also used its water, sun, and wind resources to become completely self-sufficient in energy. Its modern state and path to democratic accountability began in the 1940s when the political class supported changes at the time that would make it the institutional exception in Central and Latin America. It is a small, unitary state with consistently high macroeconomic and quality of life indicators (0.77 HDI is very high human development); inflation (1.7 percent), and governmental effectiveness (67.0). Current policies favoring consumption (wages) over investment (education and infrastructure) have meant weaker macroeconomic performance (budget deficit -6.9 percent of GDP and unemployment 8.3 percent). But Costa Rica is building on a strong base of decades of high educational and infrastructure investment, so that cuts in these areas are not destabilizing. Its electoral democracy has been the envy of the region, featuring power contestability and regular changes in party control of the government. Elections are overseen by a strong institution: the Supreme Tribunal of Elections (TSE) to prevent any efforts to tamper with election administration from balloting to counting.

The notion that micro-institutional development can strengthen the state and overall governance is evident in Romania. In 2002, the government created the National Anticorruption Directorate (DNA) because of the perception and actual experiences of high corruption—for normal service transactions as well as contracting with the state. The DNA was created as an independent unit, separate from the rest of the judiciary, to investigate and prosecute high and medium-level civil and criminal offenses. It has investigated and solved thousands of cases and its public support is consistently higher (60 percent) than either the parliament (13 percent) or the government itself (23 percent). By creating an independent institution (from both other branches as well as the judiciary), the DNA is an example of a mechanism that strengthened Romanian horizontal checks and balances. Additionally, solid support for Romanian local government over decades has also strengthened vertical checks and balances which indirectly have strengthened the state. That is, subnational hierarchical reforms contribute to a quasi-federalist system that strengthens the overall bureaucracy. Local governments deliver services effectively, supported by central transfers and a substantial delegation of tax and spending authority from several laws. They have financed infrastructure needs with repeated borrowing and repayment from banks and international markets. Many local governments have been rated highly by Fitch for the transparency and quality of its annual and medium-term budgets, and their control of revenue collections and spending. Such micro-sectoral institutional developments have multiplier effects on national governance and public support for regimes. Romanian mayors are well aware of this and ensure that debts are immediately repaid in order to borrow more, produce infrastructure that benefit citizens, and hopefully get reelected.

It should be no surprise that poorer countries with weaker institutions suffer from macroeconomic shocks to which they are mostly unable to make effective responses. An extreme example of an ineffectual response to mostly self-made problems has been that of Robert Mugabe in Zimbabwe. As noted above, bad policies corruptly implemented impoverish a country, leaving treasuries to subsist on the royalties of its natural resources in order to keep regimes in power (the real resource curse!). As Mugabe's currency-printing policies ran up a 500b percent inflation rate, he merely noted that "traditional economics" did not fully apply there. To confirm this again and to ease the dollar shortage, he issued a parallel currency called "bond notes" (2BNs = $2) on the theory that paper value equals actual currency exchange value. The plan was to issue $12m in BNs and pay off national debts. Such desperation policies try to assuage followers and keep regime in power, ignoring or changing the advice of highly trained and educated staff in MOFs, treasuries, and central banks.

To a lesser extent, other poor country regimes have to deal with normal macroeconomic shocks (falls in commodity prices, reduced demand for national exports) as well as varieties of ethno-national and populist nationalist forces working to destabilize them. Bad policies fail to stimulate aggregate demand which perpetuate stagnant incomes and unemployment levels. This intensifies the very poverty and regional inequality that in turn stimulates more ethno-nationalistic demands for quick and simplistic changes, such as parallel currencies and wasted public spending on make-work programs. While some country regimes, such as Zimbabwe (and Venezuela) add to their problems with absurd policy responses, in general poorer countries have been unable to respond to the three forces effectively. It is hard to imagine even wealthier countries dealing with all three, but this is also starting to happen as will be noted below (e.g. Brexit). For example, note the low HDIs and governmental effectiveness ratings of low per capita income in Ethiopia, Nigeria, and Liberia in Table 2.2. Note also their poor macroeconomic performances: high inflation, and unemployment. Note that moving up the income scale slightly (from $2178 in Nigeria to $3604 in Indonesia and $3685 in Egypt) is associated with a major jump in governmental effectiveness (from 10.5 to 33.4 and 30.4 respectively) as well as a major drop in inflation levels. The latter countries are able, despite their relative governmental ineffectiveness, to respond more effectively. Their HDI levels are correspondingly higher at 0.69 each.

Table 2.2 suggests income differential can explain much of the low HDIs and governmental ineffectiveness scores. But to achieve higher income has always been complex in theory and practice because it requires sustained higher growth for long periods. The path to achieve growth in order to achieve governmental effectiveness and quality of life is not straightforward. In the short term, only sound macroeconomic policies can provide the stability necessary for this to happen. But almost intuitively, this cannot happen in weak institutional settings. Immediate demands by populist leaders for change, jobs, and incomes overwhelm nuanced analyses and normally incremental and piecemeal policy-making systems. Instability breeds more instability unless the cycle can be stopped. Perhaps the most feasible model is Indonesia, where low per capita income (only $707) still has allowed governmental quasi-federal fiscal decentralization initiatives to improve regional and local quality of life (HDI 0.69), keep inflation and unemployment down, and maintain fiscal discipline (deficit only -2.5 percent GDP). The low governmental effectiveness ranking (33.4 percent) so far has not impeded these macroeconomic and quality of life results.

Notes

1 The Brazilian state development bank (BNDES), for example, provides subsidized loans to large firms. It was particularly useful in driving the stimulus forward and returning the country to high GDP growth after the crisis of 2009. But the stimulus outlived the recovery. Now it accounts for 15 percent of private lending and has a balance sheet as large as the World Bank. The resultant budget deficit of -8.9 percent GDP (Table 2.1), largely from subsidized loans, is high and the taxpayer will pay a high bill in the future, including the possible loss of jobs created by the generous subsidies. The unemployment rate is also high at 12.6 percent (*The Economist*, 2017f1: 64).

2 The standard view is that healthy democracy and high voter turnout go hand in hand. Turnout and contestability (or change of government party composition due to election results) are considered "democratic fitness" indicators. But the link with state delivery of effective results: needed programs and capital works, is even more indirect. Democracy and state effectiveness are not, in our view, directly linked in practice. A more direct link is tax take. For example, Myanmar has one of the lowest tax takes in the world (7.5 percent of GDP compared to 16 percent in Thailand). But it is hard to persuade Burmese to pay more taxes unless they receive better services in return. However, it is also hard to provide more services unless the state collects more taxes!

5 Inability of Both Wealthy and Poor Countries to Reduce Regional Inequalities

Two kinds of destructive nationalism have weakened regimes and their governments and have led to crude and ill-conceived policies in both rich and poor countries.[1] The sources of both ethnic and populist nationalism have been voter dissatisfaction with their economic lot deftly used by demagogues and their supporters against immigrants as scapegoats. Populist demagogues play on the loss of middle-class cultural status and whip up resentment against immigrants who ostensibly threaten their cultures and jobs[2] (Fukuyama, 2017). Fewer demagogues know how to plausibly oppose the job-displacing effects of technology globalization without appearing Luddite. As is known, wealthier countries, spared from populist nationalist upheaval, have solid social safety nets, high world prices for their commodities, and the fiscal space derived from sound policies to deal with regional inequalities and unemployment. The recommendations of da Cunha (1944: xv) for nineteenth century Brazil to follow up cannons with needed public services, investments, and public infrastructure have either been forgotten or not heeded in many cases by modern wealthy states. However, the task of delivering those services and appeasing rural complaints is often more complex than it sounds. Higher levels of public spending are only one option.

For example, until recently Canada was a major wealthy country facing populist nationalist pressures. While oil prices have dropped, leading to high unemployment in its Midwestern heartland, voters have been increasingly frustrated. Western regions feel underrepresented and in French-speaking Quebec, identity politics continue to run deep. In response, the government in Ottawa has used two-thirds of the growth-fueled 2017 budget to reduce the fiscal deficit with more allocated revenues and one-third to spend for social programs, including an emphasis on the working poor. The shift may have to be greater toward social programs and safety nets if the Prime Minister (Justin Trudeau) is to avoid defeat by leftist and rightist populist rivals (BBW, 2017c: 35). If there is no budget shift (more fiscal inputs), or if the spending does not improve incomes and employment (outputs and outcomes), populist nationalists could well claim Canada, along with their victories in

Britain (Brexit) and the U.S. (Trump). Additionally, Germany (Merkel in trouble as centrist CDU and SPD is losing support to hard-line fringe parties worried about immigration and wages); as nationalists support the job their displacement arguments with evidence of immigrant substitution buttressed by cultural threats to local values, practices, and racial composition. Nationalist forces have both caused wealthy country regimes and governments to fall, and produced more problems that even stronger institutions would be unlikely to solve in the short term. Major parties and governments have been slow to respond to these problems with negative effects on regime continuity and policy stability. That is the paradox of strong, modern states in democracies faced by the short-sighted, intense, political forces of populist nationalism.

The target problem and indicator of trouble has been regional inequality. This is a real and actionable problem that has both cultural and institutional causes only some of which can be dealt with by governments in the short run. It is more than an expectations/reality gap, though that gap intensifies the problem and encourages voters toward extreme and simplistic short-term policy solutions. The issues of income inequality,[3] lack of wage growth, and employment effects of immigration are real problems magnified by social media, by and for demagogues and their populist followers. They are the product of policy failures to anticipate changing skill demands and industry needs, advancing automation technology, an overall expectations/reality gap driven by consumption, and the broad urban–rural cultural differences themselves. But even had policies anticipated these regional income and wage growth gaps, better policies could have remedied only parts of the problem. For example, wage growth is logically a product of: (a) currency values (overvalued exchange rates favor other country labor forces); (b) degree of automation (the growth of robots and mechanization by employers to cut longer-term labor costs); and (c) the availability of skilled labor (tight labor market increases average wages). Realistically, national public policies could affect only the level of skilled labor through educational and training access programs. Policies could also dissuade automation but would still have to face competition with international firms and their automated production. Wage growth could also, in theory, reduce inequality by raising worker incomes and reducing the capital income of the wealthy. But for states facing short-term pressures, these solutions amount to only probable gains in the long-term.

Early twentieth century economic theory suggested that regional and national inequalities would even out as richer places would invest in poorer places with more potential (*The Economist*, 2017k: 21). Convergence worked like this until around 1980, when trade and investment patterns globalized and created major fissures for which policy responses were unprepared. Fissures and divergences have been perpetuated and worsened by the effects of scale and networks which drive growth, innovation, and demand for professionals in selected urban places, as everywhere else (i.e. hinterlands) seem to have been further left behind. Such divergences have happened within countries under unitary or federalist structures as well as between those governed by confederations such as the E.U. The problem is illustrated in sample countries in Table 2.2 with higher scores indicating greater regional inequality. For example, extreme U.K. (0.83) regional inequalities between northern conurbations such as East Lancashire, which is one of the most deprived areas, and affluent Milton Keynes could be vastly improved by transport interconnectivity. While it takes 3 hours to travel by train from East Lancashire to booming Leeds, 45 miles away, it takes 35 minutes from Milton Keynes to London! These kinds of actionable and soluble problems (long ignored) have been especially damaging to already weak governments dominated by ethnic parties in which decreasing regional inequalities is viewed narrowly as spending for rival groups and sects. The political effects of these forces have combined to put adherents in office, fracturing support for main political parties and making it harder to counter the forces driving regional inequality and divergence. Many traditional nationalists have simply wanted solutions to long-standing problems such as transport inaccessibility.

While political economy theory failed to encourage governments to adopt innovative policy responses to the problems of growing regional inequality, international donors applying public financial management (PFM) performance criteria since the early 1990s also failed to respond to problems known as allocational inefficiencies. In a replay of the late nineteenth- to early twentieth-century historic clash between rich oligarchies and working classes or peasant majorities (Fukuyama, 2014: 439), the result has been a collective failure to respond effectively to the problems of left-behinds in both theory and practice. Low scores for poorer countries, such as Ethiopia and Liberia, suggest that tragically the inequality itself is spread across the country. Only in wealthier countries, does the split between urban cosmopolitanism and rural provincial poverty and joblessness start to play out over generations (e.g. Russia 0.73 and Brazil 0.56). The modern conflicts over resource allocation (public budgetary and private investment) have added cultural value differences (urban cosmopolitan vs. provincial rural) to income and employment inequality as driving forces of populist nationalism. In practice, PFM standards of allocational efficiency (AE) and technical efficiency (TE) are only indirectly linked to governmental effectiveness and policy results. It is often argued that medium-term budget frameworks (MTBFs) have the most direct influence on AE (Brumby and Hemming, 2013: 221) because they focus on strategic allocation. But that presumes sufficient analytic capability and incentives to use such data for decision-making, which are missing ingredients in the fiscal architecture of most countries.

Inefficient expenditure results are the product not just of failure to scrutinize government expenditures but also of international donor financing of investment projects that may create substantial and long-term recurrent costs (Tommasi, 2013: 169). Aid effects on governance will be covered in more detail below. Here, one notable feature is that aid projects are often donor-driven rather than derived from responses to local problems. The more common problem with AE is that it is viewed narrowly as spending for budget shares and functions—an input focus. Discerning the proper amount of allocative efficiency is difficult in theory and practice. The theory runs into the problem identified years ago by V.O. Key (1940) of deciding how to allocate funds between program A vs. B? Marginal utilities are difficult to calculate and use as decision rules because it is nearly impossible to compare interpersonal utility preferences for programs, such as between education and health. Responding with policies can raise almost intractable attribution problems of linking budget to outputs and results outcomes. To be relevant to expenditure planning, AE has to focus on more defined problems using more specific criteria. The reprogramming and reallocation of expenditures should be mainly within sector programs to increase efficiency and effectiveness for citizens most directly affected, e.g. health. Such budgetary allocation exercises driven by empirical data and need can more easily overcome the problem that regime expenditure allocations are often driven in poorer countries by ethnicity, sect, and tribe which have variable impacts on regions and income classes. Viewed as a means to outputs and outcomes, targeted expenditure reallocations within programs at the micro-sectoral level may be able to deal with these deeper inequity problems.

Tracing allocational inefficiencies and inequalities to public spending is plagued by complex methodological problems which can be overcome in part by focusing then on particular contexts and budget sectors. Since attribution is difficult, more easily measurable results have been obtained at the micro-operational level, often by sub-national governments. For example, faced with the problem of spending more for fire services and rising deaths by fires in specific areas of the city, in 2005 Milwaukee shifted the main performance metric from increased response times (outputs/efficiency) to the reduction of fire deaths (effectiveness/outcome). Analysis of the linkage turned up the sub-problem of failure to inspect and correct faulty household fire alarms. The fiscal result was lower expenditures for equipment to reduce response times (budget savings) and reprogramming of part of the savings to inspections (City of Milwaukee, 2005). In sum, better AE results were achieved through policy analysis driven by budget performance measurement. A further example is from Rwanda, which rediscovered that big budgets have not guaranteed good outcomes. Health care officials learned that the HPV virus, which causes cervical cancer in women as well as cancers of the neck and head, could be treated effectively by vaccine. They began a national program of vaccination in 2011, diagnosing, and measuring results in order to reduce cervical cancer and prevent/eradicate it by 2020. Other countries are far less systematic with vaccinations, despite the many preventable deaths that this relatively cheap and available method could remedy (*The Economist*, 2017l: 11). Consistent with the criteria of AE, in these cases, it is how the money is spent rather than how much of it there is.

That is because how the money is spent depends also on the unintended consequences of planned policies and expenditures. Even the most effective governments define problems poorly and fail to anticipate unintended results. "Unintended consequences" is often used to indicate the near-impossibility of anticipating problems. But messy or "ill-structured" problems can be manageable with the assistance of sector specialists and accurate forecasting methodologies (Guess and Farnham, 2011: 38). Many "unanticipated" problems are such because generalists never thought of them. Sector specialists would ask the right questions instead and deem them well within the realm of solution by better expenditure programming. For example, jobs and industries are needed in left-behind regions to provide welfare and to prevent demagogues from taking advantage of policy failures. In poor countries, this often means electricity generation and access by both rural populations and potential investors who would employ them. The traditional focus has been on more generation to serve cities where most people live and to connect rural regions to these grids. The tragic irony is that in many African countries, electricity generation and access is not equal to use or consumption because users cannot pay urban generation costs/prices for transmission and distribution of current. Including illegal hook-ups to the grid, producing more power does little if people are unwilling or unable to pay for it. Price ceiling policies dissuade investors and resultant subsidies are wasteful and do not stimulate investments in modernizing the transmission and distribution links in the grid. An appropriate but complex policy solution would be to deregulate prices and develop renewable regional energy sources. These would have lower average cost transmission and distribution costs than urban energy generation facilities (*The Economist*, 2017l1: 41). Effective states developing modern energy policies based on sound economics and break-even cost analyses could design such policies if uninfluenced by special interest pleas of ethnic, tribal, religious, and sectarian groups. Nevertheless, aid programs and projects have in fact focused on designing such policy solutions for contexts in which extraneous demands can be managed.

Technical efficiency (TE) is tightly connected to AE in theory and practice. Failures to maintain roads, water supply systems, and urban transit systems lead to infrastructure deterioration and often require premature replacement financed by more debt. That leads to loss of jobs, income, and productivity by region and income class, leading to more allocational inefficiency. Spending from public budgets for O&M in most countries is crowded out by pension, salary and debt service obligations, leaving very little for the rest of current service needs. That is, the technical inefficiency reflects AE at the micro-level. For example, micro-level procurement rules affect both current services and capital spending at the macro level. The days of "force account" or command purchasing (from state manufacturers by and for ministries) largely ended with the Soviet Union but remains for small works, emergencies, or where amounts of work cannot be specified in advance (Schiavo-Campo, 2017: 209). In market economies, the issue remains how to strengthen competitive bidding and how to effectively sole source particular purchasing needs without inducing further corruption. Weak procurement bidding and contracting systems affect AE and TE and via leakage and corrupt bidding. Complex procurement rules and weak bidding systems, together with weak internal controls over corruption (e.g. false invoices) wastes capital funds, and diminishes infrastructure contributions to growth despite often higher appropriations for capital projects. The resultant losses in efficiency can then threaten overall AE as well as national fiscal discipline.

Technical inefficiencies are more fixable than AE problems since reallocation of sectoral budget shares or even adding more funds may not reduce operational spending inefficiencies that contribute to regional inequalities. TE problems have the advantage of smaller scale and more precise problem boundaries. They are structured rather than messy problems. TE can be increased in the short term, with concomitant benefits to AE and fiscal discipline, through such means as dedicated maintenance funds; use of maintenance norms (e.g. 5 percent of the annual current budget); stronger Government Financial Management Information Systems (GFMISs) that require real-time reporting of all expenses monitored by strong internal audit institutions; block grants to subnational governments that allow certain maintenance expenses to be capitalized; and insurance funds. For instance, since 2007, Caribbean Community or CARICOM members in the Caribbean and Central America have contributed to a disaster insurance fund. This spreads the risk of disasters from frequent hurricanes, floods, and even earthquakes across all members in that region. Spreading the risks has kept insurance premiums affordable and the fund has allocated $69m so far (*The Economist*, 2017m: 30). The system is called "sovereign parametric insurance" because payouts depend on parametric "triggers" to release the funds, e.g. wind speed, rainfall, and magnitude of tremors. This works quite well to reward members and punish those who fail to keep up their policies (e.g. Bahamas missed a $32m payout in 2016 after Hurricane Matthew) (*The Economist*, 2017m: 31). The problem is that since the funds flow into member treasuries, it may encourage moral hazards such as reckless decisions on building codes and corrupt spending on shoddy reconstruction. Whatever their source, the funds depend on institutional strength and integrity for effectiveness. That means stronger internal controls and audit systems for which there is, so far, little evidence in CARICOM members.

Thus, if designed properly, then remedial policies and programs can reduce allocational and associated technical inefficiencies—though not necessarily the ability of populists to make a permanent issue of them. For, when is enough equality or growth really achieved? Such questions have always been grist for populist political movements and causes. Nevertheless, reduction of regional inequalities combined with greater overall income and employment growth should give regimes and governments sufficient space to make more effective policies that meet national needs. This suggests a perennial struggle to generate sustained local and regional development is needed. There have been many successes; but also many failures. Though successes would likely be still opposed by populists, the gains should strengthen state legitimacy and longevity for incumbent officer holders.[4] At least six approaches have been taken by governments, alone or in partnership with firms. The sixth approach attempts to reduce ethno-nationalist and populist influences via leveraging external aid to create effective government institutions. But, despite the common populist platform to reduce corruption, such groups usually are demanding more power more than effective government. The last approach will be covered in the following chapters of this book.

First, the strategy of investment subsidies and tax incentives to encourage private firms to locate jobs locally has been used for many decades. Many of them have been allocated by wealthier country governments to jump-start economies in declining or left-behind regions, areas, and cities. The idea is to better the lives of those marginalized and uprooted by globalization. But despite their obvious public and political appeal, their actual impacts are often questioned. A package of tax credits, workforce training and a $1.4m subsidized government loan to a paper bag firm to move to Scranton, PA in 2017, for example, produced only 38 jobs (*The Economist*, 2017k: 23). Because economic incentives often include tax exemptions for up to 15 years (sales, property, and state taxes), local residents must often pay increased taxes to cover resultant costs of extra services. For example, Amazon's multiple agreements for free land and tax credits with Columbus, OH to invest $1b in three data centers were made in exchange for creating jobs in the range of 10–120 full-time and 300 part-time jobs. Because such transactions often lack transparency, it is hard to determine the actual cost per job of these kinds of incentive packages (BBW, 2017b: 23). In short, the communities may actually lose from incentive packages that result in higher cost fiscal and service impacts which require higher tax rates on what amounts to an even smaller local base (i.e. from land taken off the rolls and property tax exemptions).

Second, enterprise zones with tax incentives and hiring subsidies have also been used in many countries. In order to finance economic activity in target zones, states employ multiple devices. For example, many countries use development banks at the national or local levels to finance cost-beneficial projects. BNDB in Brazil, for instance, has been in operation for over 50 years. The general scheme is to provide low interest loans to the more creditworthy local and county governments. That requires full or quasi-sub-national political independence and fiscal autonomy together with independent jurisdictional and project ratings by outside agencies. This system has worked in Romania and Brazil, however it has not worked in Nigeria because its federation is more formal than substantive. In order for this system to work, the existence of a municipal credit-bond market, where investors have confidence in the economic and financial worth of the project to be financed as well as issuer capability to pay its debts, is required. Both Brazil and Romania have those; Nigeria does not. Enterprise zones, betterment districts and tax-increment financing districts function well where such conditions prevail. For example, in the U.S., about 75 percent of state-local debt is guaranteed only by project revenues, via revenue bonds. Bond payments are not guaranteed by the full faith and credit of the issuing government (via general obligation or GO bonds) so issues demand a higher risk premium (more costly to issue but with better yields for investors). Such bonds are used for self-supporting projects that generate their own revenues, such as transit lines, and water-sewer systems; they are also issued by public authorities and enterprises to pay off bonds from bridges, power projects and highways (Mikesell, 2014: 637).

Similarly, tax increment financing districts (TIFs), betterment districts for economic development, business improvements, and industrial parks are self-sustaining development districts designed to finance designated facilities (e.g. street lights, sidewalks, sewers, housing) with repayments from increases in property tax increments. Increases in assessed valuation of district property are expected to bring in more revenues used to pay for debt service costs. For example, roughly 9 percent of the Milwaukee capital improvements plan (CIP) for 2003 was financed through TIFs. The TIFs are considered self-sustaining and are funded through the issuance of GO bonds. The issuer (Milwaukee) sets aside increments in property tax increases to retire the debt contracted by the city or special authority (City of Milwaukee, 2003: 10).

A more complex variant of the above district or city financing approach combines bonds and private financing and are called infrastructure trusts: Cities such as Chicago with its Chicago Infrastructure Trust (CIT), have established these as conduits for multiple sources of funding to use for local infrastructure needs. Similar to MDBs, the CIT provides bond financing collateral and capital grants. CITs enable the city to raise funds from international investors, charities, and pension funds not interested in investing in municipal bonds for tax reasons because they have little tax liability in the first place. It means that projects with lower CIP rankings but clear benefits can go ahead sooner. The assets remain in city hands and under city management, that is, this is not privatization. Chicago is involved so far in $200m of the $7b infrastructure investments planned for 2013–2016 (*The Economist*, 2013a: 14).

Third, incentive packages are often combined into rural or local economic grants. E.U. structural funds to produce "convergence" of living standards are an example of this. But a difficulty of enterprise zones financed in this way has been that they often appear successful but are actually drawing jobs and investments away from other cities or parts of the country in subnational regions or provinces. The French *zones franches urbaines* have had this difficulty, suggesting either a trade-off or net loss for all the incentives that have been provided to investors (*The Economist*, 2017k: 23). The point is that they likely would have invested anyway. But they simply waited for the best locale to try and outsell its nearby rivals for tax revenues and development benefits. In other cases, the benefits do not continue without the incentives. Two British regions received such grants but in 2006, when one of the regions lost grant access, its output and employment gains declined (2017k: 23).

A variant of the structural fund approach is called equalization transfers (ETs), used in such countries as Canada and many other OECD countries. The goal is to create a transfer union by equalizing sub-national capacity in order to provide a standard set of services given: (a) regional differences in costs, (b) revenue bases, and (c) revenue generation efforts. In Canada there is a vertical flow of funds from Ottawa to the provinces based on a common formula of revenue/capita and other factors. The goal there has been to improve horizontal equity to meet minimum service standards by British Columbia, Alberta, Ontario, Quebec, and Nova Scotia, etc. That is, the fiscal transfers are not between provinces but to them from the central government in Ottawa.

But, the ETs are typically based on input measures such as subnational government revenue per capita and flow to local finance departments where funds could be, and often are, misallocated to salaries at best. At worst, they can be siphoned off by corrupt officials. In short, cultures, regional problems, and governance weaknesses are severe constraints to the achievement of better AE or reduced horizontal inequities by these financing strategies. More generic analytic problems, such as improper definition of policy problems, lead populists to focus on populist solutions (overpaid leaders) instead of bad management; lack of industrial productivity and a bi-modal enterprise structure (found in England and elsewhere such as India), meaning a handful of high-performers function well at the top and the rest at the bottom are mostly zombie firms for which grants or loans make little difference. That impedes growth and job creation about which equalization transfers or even different budget shares can do very little other than to provide a broader social safety net of services and infrastructure.

Fourth, government policies try to leverage the first three efforts to create networks of firms and suppliers that can raise incomes and employment in specific locations. "Clusters" are hard to build as the many locales and countries that have tried to recreate Silicon Valley have discovered. But sustained coordination with incentives by effective governments can make a difference. The effort made by Columbus OH just noted is coordinated but probably a money loser for taxpayers that will not see much income or employment increases. By contrast, the efforts of South Carolina in the early 1990s provided incentives for a BMW factory that the state government linked with local universities for worker training and use of their existing expertise in automotive research. The investment generated a large network of suppliers and other auto firms (e.g. Swedish Volvo and Chinese Geely) and improved transport links to other neighboring states. While real income for the state has increased along with population growth, the level of manufacturing employment is actually lower than in the 1990s (*The Economist*, 2017k: 23). The chicken–egg locational problem of finding the right ingredients (workers, infrastructure, and suppliers) can be dealt with if the government has the initial capacity to identify and at least treat these problems in coordinated fashion with the potential investor. The state of South Carolina had that and created effective clusters.

Fifth, given the hit-miss problem of seeding clusters that have positive multiplier effects on incomes and employment, the better long-term option is to increase the attractiveness of laggard regions by spreading tech-literacy and know-how. In principle, this should improve the investment climate that is a necessary precondition for growth and sustained development. The models have been the nineteenth-century U.S. land-grant university system of agricultural and mechanical colleges set up by the federal government; and the 1949 German *Fraunhofer* system of networks of applied research institutions to improve technologies in partnership with firms which receive their funding from federal and local governments (*The Economist*, 2017k: 25). The Germans also have the well-respected apprenticeship system (like Switzerland and Austria) for high-school students to be recruited to firms paid for by federal-local governments. The U.S. also has thousands of junior or community colleges spread across its 50 states that offer multiple technical or vocational majors often in conjunction with the needs of local firms, such as automotive technology and aviation mechanics. Such models can easily be expanded and replicated around the world. The latest (2018) U.K. budget supports more funds for diffusion of technological innovation through more funds for math and science teachers and assistance for older workers. But the U.K. allocated 15 percent less in real terms than was spent for employment and science and technology education in 2010 (*The Economist*, 2017b1, 51).

A more serious constraint to confronting regional inequality in wealthier countries is the severe housing constraint on productivity. Wealthy countries such as the U.K. contain a few internationally advanced and productive companies and many small and medium firms that are quite unproductive. A malfunctioning housing market can constrain productivity growth by making it hard for people to move where they can be most productive (*The Economist*, 2017b1, 51). Very high housing prices and absence of affordable rental properties for younger professionals in many U.S. cities, such as in the San Francisco Bay Area, make it difficult for needed labor supply to meet demand. Proposals to increase housing supply run up against current property owners whose homes have gained substantial value. Lower productivity diminishes much-needed public revenues which drives up deficits and debt levels. Long-standing and obvious proposals in the U.K., such as eliminating the green belt around London to allow housing development, repeatedly are voted down. Other proposals, such as eliminating the stamp duty on homebuyers, which discourages moving, are also voted down as a threat to public revenues. In short, absence of bold policymaking in wealthy countries (both unitary and federalist) constrains the supply of housing which keeps productivity from growing in the vast majority of firms.

Notes

1 Nationalism and nationalistic solidarity can be good qualities to build up national consciousness when states are weak, and also to remember past history. For example, in describing Bela Bartok, it has been said that: "Like other nationalist composers in other lands, Bartok believed that the future of a distinctive Hungarian music lay in recovering its authentic past before the modern world swept it away". (Bedell, 2018: 23). Nationalists seek to recover and emphasize the authentic pasts of their countries. This is harmless and educational until the exercise becomes a tool of repression, blame, and hostility against ethnicities and races for past crimes dredged up by the distorted investigations of amateur historians. As one Macedonian official put it to me, "What I learned about our history in University was a lie". From there, the path to Greater Macedonia, Greater Albania, Greater Bulgaria etc. led to permanent border conflicts and demagogic accusations against domestic immigrants from neighboring Balkan countries.

2 Fukuyama traces the causes of the current rise of populist nationalism to: (1) economics: losses of low-skilled jobs from globalization while benefits flow to urban educated elites; (2) politics: checks and balances of liberal democracies paralyze governments and make them ineffective; and (3) cultural: loss of middle-class cultural status creates resentment against elites and minority immigrants (2017).

3 Wealth inequality has been a constant in capitalist economies for centuries (Piketty, 2014) and, based on newer evidence, dating back 2500 years to the rise of settled agriculture and farming over nomadic lifestyles (*The Economist*, 2017c1: 68). The perennial question has been what can better governance and public policies do about it?

4 This commonsense proposition has been confirmed in practice, for example, by observing participatory budgeting and subsequent voter behavior. The International Center for Human Development in Armenia worked with municipal groups to develop capital projects that were later built, which increased both taxpayer participation and support for local government officials. Participation in design and selection of projects increased voter stakes in government, which increased their support for those who governed (ICHD, 2006).

6   Governing Structures

Even without ethnic and populist nationalist forces that destabilize states, challenges to creating effective governments would still exist. For there are many complex problems in developing institutional rules and processes and establishing sensible structures with which to organize planning and implementation of public services, programs, and projects. Effective states do not simply happen from special evolutionary processes. There is no one best way. States, for instance, must be staffed from objective personnel recruitment criteria and capacity-building systems. Staff ministry roles and responsibilities must be linked to particular functions like health; line units must have authority and discretion to manage services and programs; accountability and responsibilities must be clarified and enforced for best performance by knowledgeable supervisory overseers (officials in all public sectors face the problem of governing and managing for multiple masters); norms and regulations must reflect the core activities of each sector and budgetary function; inefficiencies need to be identified regularly by independent internal audit and inspector general officials within ministries and placed on agendas for remedial action with public knowledge; and many services, programs, and infrastructure projects should be outsourced to private contractors but supervised and regulated by public sector officials with professional competence in each area. Because of their financial and budgetary importance, effective states will have the technical and financial capacity to evaluate contract bids, negotiate contracts, and monitor implementation performance as well as the authority to take corrective action in order to protect the public interest in probity and value for money. Parliamentary supreme audit institutions (SAIs) should conduct parallel program and policy evaluations along with executive branch internal audit units to achieve positive redundancies. Most of these requirements apply to central governments.

Federations and unitary systems financing local units with massive fiscal transfers need to have effective sub-national units as well. Such intergovernmental relations are all part of any consolidated state. In order for fiscal transfers and subsidies to produce maximum results,

they must be allocated according to transparent formulae criteria as part of calendar-driven budget processes by central governments. Unitary systems allocate transfer funds to deconcentrated units of their central governments; federations allocate them to independent sub-national tiers of their governments. The critical decision-making phases of these processes must be transparent and open to public participation and comment. Even if such structural and professional criteria are extant in the parliaments and the executive branches of central and sub-national governments, regimes may still work against them and weaken their own states through patronage-driven electoral systems to keep themselves in power. Power politics often overrides institutional strengths. President Museveni, for example, has created many patronage districts in Uganda to pay voters for populist support of his decades of rule. Payments are in the form of targeted income transfers, district public works, and public-sector jobs, which his regime controls outside formal state authority. Transfers to these districts have worked to drain otherwise profession-ally made public budgets that have maintained aggregate fiscal discipline. Regime reliance on informal patronage systems also weakens states by allowing the shadowy and often violent sources of power to grow more important than state power and to weaken governmental legitimacy.

As in many poorer countries, the state in Myanmar, for example, is a mere formality and has little authority or power in comparison with the army which is independent of the state and exercises real power. In order to appear legitimate under such constrained circumstances the formal civilian state defers important decisions via committee creation which provides the illusion of policymaking and implementation. In short, the right context must exist or be created to beat the odds and produce effective states. The Ukrainian state is controlled by a fragmented regime consisting of rival oligarchs. The state has been largely destroyed by oli-garchic corruption and patronage systems; their power can be measured by the size of their private armies and TV stations. The only viable counter-threat to such institutional desiccation has been the creation of the National Anti-Corruption Bureau (NABU) that was created by pressure from Western aid donors as well as the IMF and trained by the FBI (*The Economist*, 2017i1: 51).

Is it simply that wealthier states are more effective because they can afford more professional human resources, analytic methods, and man-agement systems? We have seen that some poorer states, such as Botswana and Costa Rica, can beat the odds with will and capacity. One manages its ample resources with many benefits and few curses to quality of life or governmental effectiveness. The other has few natural resources, other than tropical forests and tourism, and has managed both for substantial developmental benefits. Nevertheless, we are seeing that wealthier states, such as the U.K., U.S. and Spain are becoming more ineffective through failures in their electoral and representative systems. Centrist parties in countries such as Germany have lost ground to populist parties of the extreme left and right. So income alone is no longer the distinguishing feature of effective governance. Political cultures receptive to the rule of law, and to traditions of professional and competent states, can also be found in poorer MENA countries such as Tunisia and Jordan.[1] The domestic policy and overseas aid question is how to create and sustain these contexts in other countries with fewer or perhaps different advantages? The differences between poor and rich country budgeting and policymaking are more than just wealth and income. Wealth means institutional redundancy and professionalism (Caiden and Wildavsky, 1974) which is a function of values and practices in the political culture as well as income. Their important insight is that institutional wealth can exist in poor countries (e.g. micro-sectoral successes in health, education, and social services) and institutional poverty can exist within wealthy countries (e.g. bankrupt cities, ineffective services, corrupt project implementation).

Differences in income are likely less than political structure, then, to comprehensively explain the differences between governmental effectiveness and ineffectiveness. For example, wealthy countries also have patronage-ridden cities as well as corrupt sub-national units of government. Rarely are whole states overwhelmed by special interests or patronage systems. There have been historical exceptions in the U.S. where corrupt central regimes and cities have both distorted policies and budgets. Note that central governments in the U.S. and other OECD countries still provide uneconomic subsidies to construct coal and nuclear energy generation facilities despite ample evidence of their waste, but high special interest political benefit. Similarly, city government policies are distorted by politically connected firms and unions seeking generous favors and financial gains through public contracts. Though not technically corrupt, they are distortionary and inefficient, resulting usually in high-cost projects that may not produce value for money. They contribute in part to loss of public expenditure control by producing budget allocations to the least cost-effective options (Guess, 2015: 176–177). For example, New York City is constructing the most expensive mile of subway track in the world. The entire procurement and contracting process is politically permeable, allowing contractors and unions to intrude with repeated government approvals to inflate capital costs. This produces excessive project contractor staffing, minimal competition for bids, and generous contracts that reward often unneeded jobs at $1000/day (Rosenthal, 2017).

Wealthy countries, federation or unitary, should be able to change policy and operational rules and governance structures (e.g. reassigning fiscal roles and responsibilities) in the short term and without serious constraints. While the New York City case illustrates suggests even that proposition may not be true in practice, most poor countries have rule and governance structures often for reasons dating back to the colonial histories of not only their colonial rulers but to their major legal systems (i.e. common and civil law) as well. We have described some of the complex colonial histories of particular African countries. Once governing structures have been adopted, which are often centralized unitary systems or in rarer occasions federations, they must develop methods, systems and processes to conduct necessary policymaking, administrative and management functions. The design of these systems and processes often flows from both colonial history and the grants/loans of international donors offering them as best modern practices. As they should, legal systems facilitate and constrain public management to some extent in every country. Public administration experts from around the world frequently offer models of their often home-country methods and processes for adaptation to local routines.

For example, manual and computerized systems of accounting, auditing, budgeting, and evaluation are now widespread and both developing and transitional countries have adopted them with local modifications. Modern computerized and web-based sub-systems of personnel, purchasing, and contracting are also widely known and have been adapted for local use. Other core sub-systems of a modern state, such as judicial administration, are well-known and tested systems for processing cases and strengthening civil procedures. For instance, Mexico is considered a democratic federation. Yet 93 percent of the country has not been covered until now by an adversarial system of criminal justice (*The Americas*, 2016). That means defendants have been arrested, jailed and tried according to an inquisitorial system that merges law enforcement and criminal investigation roles, weakening civil protections, and increasing the probability that the wrong person will be convicted. How can this institutional deficiency in rule of law be reconciled with its democratic status? When state performances are reviewed and reforms suggested, various kinds of functional review and state modernization methods are available to clarify policymaking and administrative roles to improve implementation and overall performance of programs and services. There are fewer disagreements on functional methods and systems than about the structures in which they operate, and the will and capacity of host country regimes to support and implement them. It is not uncommon for functional methods and systems (and equipment) to be adopted but not used properly or at all. Governmental effectiveness remains low despite inputs of new modern systems.

Thus, formal and legal structures require accompanying regulatory and administrative rules and institutional processes for making and implementing them. Ruling elites and regimes attempt directly and indirectly to ensure that rules and processes are consistent with their values. Persistence of these rules and processes results in the governing values and practices that, over time, become the political culture. Features of a political culture are malleable in the shorter run at the operational level. That is where micro-level governmental initiatives can have the most effect on needs and improve overall state performance. Properly designed and implemented overseas aid can make a difference by providing modern values and practices at this level (tools and systems) to develop modern states. Larger changes in the political structures require much more time and sustained efforts by donors and counterpart regimes, which must persist and remain supportive.

An important component of the governance problem and aid design issue is evidence that federation is the most successful political structure with which to respond to multi-level, sectoral issues. The theory is that multiple autonomous tiers of government can do this better than unitary or deconcentrated political structures. Competitive federalism, for example, where sub-national units such as states compete to induce investments by improving infrastructure and permit approvals, can increase state incomes and employment and lessen dependence on aid—either external or domestic via transfers and subsidies. But to work, competitive federalism requires a strong central government that unifies central regulations (i.e. normative centralization) and allows sub-national units political and fiscal autonomy (i.e. operational decentralization). The Indian federation is currently attempting to implement its version of competitive federalism under Prime Minister Narendra Modi, for example, through such efforts as a national goods and services tax to replace the myriad provincial levies. We have also seen that an incomplete federation, such as in the U.K., can eventually lead to existential governance problems. Full federations, such as Malaysia, in relatively poor countries can make a large difference to effective governance. But creation of quasi-federalist programs and systems within unitary systems, as in Indonesian fiscal decentralization and Rwandan health care decentralization (and the examples from Costa Rica and Taiwan), can make an important difference to quality of life. Full federations in wealthier countries, such as the U.S. and Brazil, can serve as an institutional defense against destructive populist nationalism. Conversely, confederations such as the historic U.S. Articles of Confederation and the existing E.U. cannot make or enforce the necessary hard budget, policy, and security-defense choices to effectively sustain operations.

Thus, full federation would be the solution to effective governance in an ideal world. Federalism or federation is considered to be a process structured by a set of institutions in which states or subnational units are represented in central government policymaking (Rodden, 2006: 30, 31, 36). Of course, necessary legal institutions and political structures need to be in place to ensure subnational autonomy and representation, that is, actual subnational fiscal and political autonomy and election systems that reflect their preferences/needs. Federation then is more than just a process, otherwise they would be merely formal federations and substantive confederations. Though not all democracies are federal systems or federations, they can be associated in the long-term with democracy and growth. The essence is substantive subnational representation, often measured by public spending through transfers, programs, subsidies, and direct expenditures. The exceptions often reveal quasi-federalist institutions or traits operating within unitary systems. Taiwan and Costa Rica are examples. In Taiwan, democracy began at the local level in the 1920s and spread to the central government in the 1947 Constitution that created a republican form of government with strong checks and balances. It is considered to have "traits" of federalism. As indicated, the federalism issue in Taiwan is often confused with that of being a potentially devolved province of the PRC (which is a unitary government). Costa Rica is a small country that has been a strong representative democracy since 1948. Its small scale allows it to combine federation traits in its unitary form of government: local fiscal and political autonomy and elected mayors to provide an overall inclusive government.

The argument is that federations are best able to respond to voter needs and fiscal spillovers because of the flexibility, resiliency, and redundancy of the multi-tiered governance structure. Fiscal federalist structures can stabilize regimes and political shocks to the central government by spreading country institutional risks to lower tiers. But federations paradoxically require strong central governments to work. Weak central governments and unsupportive regimes in federations can also magnify problems of policy failures to control and provide discretion to lower tiers. They can become major centers of corruption, or worse, as seen in Catalonia, secessionist movements. In short, design of fiscal and political federalism requires detailed attention to the assignment of fiscal and management roles and responsibilities. Assignments and reassignments must be based somewhat on theory but mostly on results—the actual practices of the multi-tiered governmental system. Subsidiarity in the form of responsiveness and accountability must be balanced against the need for overall efficiency for national fiscal and political benefit. Such balances are not achieved simply by promulgating laws and drafting constitutions. Their results in programs, services and projects by region as well as nationally must be re-evaluated by legitimate institutions. Authoritarian-unitary governments can also redefine and reallocate intergovernmental roles and responsibilities to increase their responsiveness to citizens.

A critical link between structure, financing, and governance is through the design and allocation of fiscal transfers. Effective governments have sufficient sub-national assignments of fiscal and political authority to deliver programs and services consistent with local needs. Transfers have three purposes, to (1) equalize vertically (improving revenue adequacy of sub-national units); (2) equalize horizontally (for interjurisdictional distribution); and (3) minimize interjurisdictional spillovers (externalities) (Yilmaz, *et.al.*, 2012: 118). Failures in the design and allocation of transfers can lead directly to the regional, class, and sect inequities which create severe pressures on regimes and governments. Their failure to reassign roles and shift transfer allocations are common problems that lead to populist nationalist pressures. These have alternately brought down governments, induced them to respond with greater military force against opponents, or in some cases brought about positive policy responses. In some cases it is the federalist systems, with frozen inter-governmental roles and responsibilities, that have created pressures for change by their voters to be more responsive.[2] Federation regimes may be served by unrepresentative electoral systems which, by design, over-represent rural areas at the expense of highly populated urban areas. Their roles may be frozen in the first place because of antiquarian laws or elected regime incompetence. In both cases, incomplete or imperfect federations are functioning to allow systems to muddle through without major political or structural changes.

In general then, either federation or quasi-federation structures are best equipped to respond to complex social and policy challenges, including changes of political regime. They are better at limiting governments and provide more policy and management flexibility. Criteria for effective or "good" governance mostly coalesce around these standards: (1) rule of law protections (meaning the portfolios of rules, institutions, and traditions that measure this concept) for firms and individuals by independent judicial branches; (2) responsiveness to the needs of minority groups, sects and opinions; (3) national unity via jurisdictional coverage of boundaries and economic rules treating nations as unions; (4) regional–local autonomy representation via fiscal transfers and fiscal decentralization (aka allocational efficiency or AE); (5) strong, legitimate national state, or central governments; and (6) delivery of services, programs, and capital projects that meet needs.

The reality is that in most transitional and developing countries, and not a few European countries, states are inefficient and ineffective. Especially their central governments are often bloated and unable to deliver most services and programs effectively, or implement a capital works project without corruption, delays, and poor results.[3] Such states are closed organizations, incentivized by the internal care of their employees rather than for service to citizens, taxpayers, or service users. Supervision of officials is guided by rigid, outworn codes that are practically irrelevant to improving service delivery performance. Where countries must rely on one large central government to deliver programs via deconcentrated units, the outputs and outcomes are almost invariably poor. Federations increase the chances of better results by delegating authority to separate and independent sub-national units. Federation by definition offers more incentives and autonomy to make competitive and entrepreneurial decisions and policies. That should lead to greater public sector efficiency and cost-effectiveness. This institutional redundancy should produce greater satisfaction with both services and the state, which gains in deeper legitimacy.

Are there examples of federation withstanding extremist pressures and maintaining effectiveness and institutional integrity better than unitary or authoritarian states? Can they sustain that success or are there limits? There are obvious examples of successful countries, such as democratic and federal Venezuela, being brought down over decades of political rancor and dysfunctional populist economic policies. The federal system established by the 1999 Constitution making the "Bolivarian Republic of Venezuela a decentralized federal state" provided no sub-national tax authority and left municipalities and states dependent on central transfers in practice for financing. This meant it was a false or incomplete federation (of 22 federal states, 2 federal territories and 1 federal district in Caracas) and unitary in practice. This system has been distorted further in the past two decades by populist nationalists who have turned the central government into a centralized, ineffective authoritarian state.

Venezuela is still a relatively wealthy country, governed by a series of misguided, dysfunctional regimes dating from the late 1990s that for 20 years have enforced unsound policies with entirely predictable results. The regimes of Hugo Chavez and Nicolas Maduro provide a textbook's worth of economic principles and the predictable penalties for ignoring them. By ignoring policy lessons learned from past political economy and institutional problems in countries such as Argentina, Ecuador, Peru, Brazil, and Mexico, Venezuelan regime practices remind one of Dickens' Circumlocution Office in *Little Dorrit* where the operating maxim was: "how it should not be done" (1967). As Venezuelan Ricardo Haussmann explained (2017: 33):

> There are no excuses for Venezuela's catastrophic decline. It is the consequence of the adoption of policies that have been known by the world, by everybody, forever, as leading nowhere. Whether it's multiple exchange rates, lack of fiscal discipline, expropriation, uncertainty over property rights, a lax monetary policy, price controls, we know that these things devastate a society.

Such destructive populist regimes follow a script of hollowing out states, repressing civil societies, and relying on (usually dated, confused, and inapplicable) ideological expertise for policy designs. Costly populist actions have destroyed cultural and economic wealth and have not built on decades of institutional strengthening that made Venezuela once the wealthiest country in the region. Venezuela has been subsisting on its stock of accumulated wealth from many decades of sound governance and economic policies. In 1977, the Venezuelan per capita GDP was $15,581, among the highest in Latin America. Per capita income remained at $15,100 in 2015 but that figure and the high HDI score are illusory. The *flow* of economic and social welfare policy benefits, ended more than a decade ago along with the end of the most recent commodity boom. Once Latin America's richest country, 82 percent of households now live in poverty compared to 48 percent in 1998 when Hugo Chavez came to power. The rise in poverty follows Venezuela's biggest ever oil windfall which provided more than $1t in revenues to the regime (*The Economist*, 2017n1: 29). Every indicator of fiscal and governmental performance has dropped dramatically since 1996: the deficit is now 39.9 percent of GDP, debt is low because GDP has dropped but debt service payments are unsustainable; the governmental effectiveness score has dropped from 25.3 percent to 10.5 percent; corruption has worsened from an already low 23 to 17 in the same period; and fiscal transparency has dropped from 35 to 8, one of the lowest scores in the world.

Why did the federal structure in Venezuela collapse if federation is a superior form of political structure? The answer is that it was not a full federation to begin with. That often explains other federation failures as well. In Venezuela, fiscal and tax authority was retained at the center, and left sub-national units reliant for current and capital funds on central transfers. While there have been 200 years of federalist legislation and constitution-drafting, none of the provisions actually created a devolved state with fiscal and independent sub-national political authority. Gains that had been made toward evolution to full federation began to be reversed by the 1999 Constitution of Hugo Chavez. For instance, the 1999 Constitution Article 164.7 provided nothing other than stamp duties that would serve as sources of sub-national finance. Article 168 stated that the organization and management of municipalities was still subject to national authority (Guerrero, 2007: 25). That effectively deconcentrated sub-national authority form the center, as in standard unitary states, and left sub-national governance at the whim of the central government regime. Fiscal decentralization was a myth folded into the empty formalities of a "decentralized federal state".

As noted above, Pakistan is also a formal federation (Rodden, 2006: 39). But the state neither fully controls its territory with its security forces nor does it cover the country with social services. Government remains ineffective and plagued by its legal and practical status as a theocracy. Despite a vigorous civil society, including the media as countervailing forces to the state, it never developed the secular political Islamic tradition of, for instance, "Kemalism" in Turkey, which valiantly persists today as a stabilizing secular and political force (White, 2015: 17). Besides Venezuela and Pakistan, another federation in Yugoslavia also fell apart under the strains of ethno-nationalist and populist nationalist pressures in the late 1990s. As discussed above, the demagoguery of Slobodan Milosevic stoked ancient religious and ethnic identify conflicts in a country of provincial borders that contained multiple ethnicities and religions. What seemed to work for 50 years was successfully manipulated by competing nationalists into major internecine and sectarian conflicts that resulted in the break-up of the federation followed by the Balkan Wars of the late 1990s and early 2000s. Many of the sectarian conflicts had, of course, persisted locally for decades within the clear context that the Serbian sense of grievance was the strongest and that it would be a driving force behind any break-up of the federation. The delicate institutional balance that kept the federation functional was the political genius of a Croat, Josip Broz Tito, who successfully played ethnicities and nationalities off to maintain the peace and keep the federation legitimate and effective. The leadership vacuum created by his death in 1980 created many opportunities for demagogues and nationalists to destroy his successful institution-building. They did so rather quickly which suggests again that even functioning federations often rely on slim reeds such as the balancing genius of one leader. The breakup also suggests that even positive institutional redundancies can only withstand external and internal nationalist shocks for so long.

The question then is: how could full federalist systems in places such as Venezuela or Pakistan have been so easily hollowed out by militant populists and produced the resultant levels of societal breakdown and governmental dysfunction as in places such as the former Yugoslavia? In principle, institutional desiccation and rot caused by sustained populism should take longer to contaminate more complex systems. Institutional sunk costs should also provide sunk benefits that persist. Full federalism consists of fiscal and political power networks, relations, repetitive transactions, supply chains, and stable expectations built up over long periods of time as forms of sunk benefits. Such values and practices become part of the political culture (as they have in Costa Rican democracy since 1948) and are or should be hard to change. Strong sub-national power blocs become part of the national institutional architecture: almost like dealing with separate nations on a vertical scale. But even the strongest blocs can be hollowed out and values/practices changed over time. The political–sociological and historical questions become as with Venezuela: how did it all happen? Few modern examples exist of full federalist deterioration. The Yugoslav example suggests that the system buys time to become functional again, either through the ballot box, innovative regional programs, or revised fiscal transfer formulae and fairer revenue-sharing schemes that appease sectarian conflicts, and halt domination by one ethnicity to restore balance. If none of this works and conflict spreads, outside intervention, as the UN and NATO in Yugoslavia, is necessary to reduce or eliminate the scale and intensity of the conflict and bring back some form of peace.

To date, there are no precise comparative examples of institutional and political desiccation followed by renewal attributable to federation. The "how to" policy guidebook on how to prevent federalist deterioration and stimulate renewal has not yet been written. The U.K. is seemingly in a process of desiccation and will need a renewal; it is also not a full federation as noted. The Yugoslav federation split up into separate countries, some of which are both in the E.U. and Eurozone. Spain may lose a province but was a unitary system to begin with. As the major federation under institutional threats, the U.S., despite its size and level of development, may be a better case comparison of the dynamics that produce viable options and useful solutions for stimulating pushback and positive political renewal.

The Trump variant of populist or reverse ethno-nationalism differs slightly from other movements in Europe, for example, Alternative for Germany (rightist anti-immigrant), Five Star Movement (M5S) (anti-establishment), Golden Dawn (Neo-Nazi), Nordic Resistance Movement (Finnish Neo-Nazi), and Podemos (leftist austerity). Trump gained power through skillful use of social media and understanding of the need to maximize the votes of his base in an electoral system favoring rural areas with gerrymandered districts. It did so without spending vast sums of cash on traditional media ads and coverage. The method was to stimulate fear and resentment not only of immigrants and minorities but between the urban cosmopolitan and what the base derided as "politically correct elitists" and his followers of rural, provincial purists and hard-working patriots. His base and its opponents are roughly the same contestants for power and office in Europe.

Also similar to trends in Europe is the fact that the Trump faction prevailed from the moral exhaustion of the two main parties: what the Democrats argued were the "immoral identity politics" of the GOP and what the Trump base believes are the "identity socialists" of the Democrats leading to the Democratic weak policies and economics that leave America and his base behind. These have been roughly the lead ideologies on offer for more moderate voters of both parties who noted that the pressing policy problems of health care, public debt, educational failures, and criminal justice were denied, ignored, and were not on the agenda of candidates from either party (Gerson, 2017). The two major parties played out these competing versions of identity politics with the result that the latter GOP "in-your-face" narrative of ethnic fear, simplistic though it was, became more compelling to its electoral base (but not the majority of voters). For example, the belief that an actual (as opposed to virtual) high border wall would be built to simply keep out Mexican immigrants was tangible and is fiercely supported by Trump followers.

The American variant of populist nationalism is revealed by the Trump base of the left-behind, less-educated elements of the white working class, which supports four platform efforts: (1) the need for anti-immigration measures to maintain cultural differences. From security fears and rejection of cultural differences, the base favors deportation of unregistered immigrants and bans on Muslim immigrants; (2) an anti-federal or central government agenda. The seeks "freedom" from environmental and health regulations and entangling international military treaties and trade agreements that prevent America from "being first" or regaining prominence in such smokestack industries as coal and steel that have for decades affected its geographic and demographic voting base; (3) the base seeks to discredit established governmental and media institutions, such as long-respected federal institutions as the FBI, CIA, State Department, EPA and the CBO. The vacuum has been partly filled by news from own-sourced news outlets favoring the Trump agenda and its supporters, such as Breibart News; and (4) the base favors to wealthy voters with major business and income tax breaks, supported by deregulation of their activities to stimulate more wealth. Growing policy contradictions between this agenda and the Trump base are evident, such as policies favoring the wealthy, reduction of health care coverage for the working classes, reduction in immigration affecting a tight labor force that is short of skilled labor, and denial of long-standing conservative causes such as the control of public deficit and debt levels. Standard populist actions against government have included: hollowing out the courts with rightist and loyalist judges; regularly appointing departmental (ministry) heads opposed to the mission of their agencies, such as environmental protection, health and human services, overseas development aid and diplomacy, multilateral and largely free trade agreements; and maintenance of budgetary discipline and sound fiscal management.

The current Trumpian presidential base agenda is transformative in that it contradicts hundreds of years of U.S. political and legal understandings and evolutionary rules and practices that have led to a modern democratic state. The question then for state-building and federalism, is how has the system withstood these strong, multi-pronged threats since 2016 and what has been the pushback? The impact of policy plans and accomplishments, such as tax cuts and immigration restrictions, as yet has not made much difference to the national fiscal position (i.e. no S&P downgrades yet) or to commercial production requiring skilled labor. The measurable economic impact of this four-pronged agenda is still not there, other than buoyant investor spirits and financial sector euphoria at rising wealth opportunities. For instance, on-shoring of the significant corporate income kept abroad as the result of the new tax law will now occur via sales in their U.S. Treasury bonds that will be distributed to their shareholders in the form of dividends and royalties. The wealthiest will gain even more wealth.

The governmental impact and popular pushback against the institutional and philosophical distortions from the Trump faction has been occurring on several fronts: (1) voting behavior, (2) civil society organizations, and (3) federation institutions. The first major test will be the congressional midterm elections in 2018. Opinions vary on the probable outcome, but evidence is gathering that there could be major GOP losses and pushback from opposition Democratic Party voters will produce a landslide. Second, a major theme of the Trump regime has been to discredit the mainstream press as "fake news" (most of which opposed his election) and to broadcast alternative news through its outlets and social media to its base of intense zealots. The issue for federalism is the resilience of civil society institutions, such as the media, in the face of both governmental (from new politically pliant appointees) and non-governmental threats (such as evangelic and partisan organizations from its hard right base). The anti-elitist and fake news gambits worked to gain power in the 2016 election. While 70 percent of trump supporters still believe that the "press is the enemy of the people", only 15 percent of non-supporters do. According to Silverman (2017), since 2016 there has been a 23 percent surge in trust and confidence in the press by Democrats and 15 percent by respondents from both parties. This suggests that the "fake news" charge of Trump supporters is wearing thin among overall voters and that a backlash has begun.

Third, the impact on federation institutions from the GOP anti-government agenda was already clear and preceded Trump. Even his followers are beginning to experience the impact of this agenda at federal, state, and local levels in a growing number of policy areas. For example, the federalist system failed to define the water quality problem in Flint (Michigan) in 2014 and remedy it despite clear legal requirements that actions be taken. It began with the decision by GOP Governor Rick Snyder's appointed Emergency Manager to save money by allowing the City of Flint to switch from its treated-water supplies from Detroit to untreated water from the Flint River. State officials failed to follow laws required ensuring that corrosion-control additives were in the new water supply. Federal EPA officials knew of the claims by activists and the corrosion problem but claimed their hands were tied by interagency rules (Bernstein and Dennis, 2016: A6). The institutional and policy failure exposed thousands of children to toxic lead in their drinking water for 18 months. One could argue that a tighter, more unitary and authoritarian chain of command from the EPA could have identified and resolved the problem more quickly. In the U.S. federation, the Constitutional Supremacy Clause exists for just such cases where, because of the high probability of negative externalities or spillovers (from water pollution) and evident jurisdictional fragmentation, efficient and effective governmental responsiveness would require a response with high economies of scale and very low subsidiarity (i.e. centralized). As in the similar cases of social assistance payments, the most efficient level of regulation and service delivery are central governments (state and federal). EPA was already authorized to act under the Safe Drinking Water Act and U.S. Constitution but failed to do so and deferred unreasonably to the state. However, the causes of the problem were state and local decisions and inaction. In this conflict, note that the alarm was initially sounded by civil society activists (Michigan ACLU) not governmental institutions responsible for environmental protection.

Conversely, one could also argue that it was a failure of governing not government: "(Governor) Snyder undertook an arrogant public policy experiment, underpinned by the ideological assumption that the 'experience set of corporate-style managers was superior to the checks and balances of democracy. This is why Flint happened" (Milbank, 2016).

The Republican governor (elected five years before Trump in 2011) spoke in the new-wave privatization consultant's language of "deliverables", "outcomes", "customers" and "reinvention" of the state to make government business-friendly. He sought to replace federal vertical and horizontal checks with managers experienced in a simpler context (not accountable to multiple masters) and incentivized for profitability (by selling discrete products). While the contexts are incomparable, focusing on technical problems with narrow technical solutions would seem to precisely fit the experience set of private sector managers, which could anticipate serious profitability and shareholder problems from failure to deal quickly and quietly with the obvious technical problem (i.e. untreated water). Private managers do in fact perform these decisive analytic activities all the time. Nevertheless, despite its corporate status and experience, Volkswagen failed to make such obvious calculations before devising overrides to pollution measurement and hiding actual air quality performance data until the public (i.e. customers) found out.

Federations such as the U.S. ultimately must deal with the daily tensions and weaknesses exposed by problems affecting accountability and authority at all levels. On the contrary, threats to institutional integrity and dangers of wider accountability contamination from ideological appointees (such as Governor Snyder) often lead to unexpected systemic strengths provided initially by the federation political structure devised in the 1790 U.S. Constitution. Given the willingness of the independent judiciary to grant standing to sue, for instance, state level attorney-generals have been able to block presidential decrees and orders. The combined weakness of Congress as a check on the executive and the assertion of power by sub-national judiciaries have given new life to the federation. Though policy matters should be adjudicated by the elected branches, the problem has been that Congress has abdicated responsibility. The vacuum has been filled in part by states attorney generals. James Madison ensured in Federalist Paper #10 that one cannot always assume the existence of "enlightened statesmen" and that ambition was needed to counter ambition. Institutionalists would need to counter populists in the future (Krauthammer, 2017).

While James Madison referred to horizontal institutional checks, the Constitution, by reserving power to the states, also created a vertical system of checks necessary for maintaining flexibility and legitimacy. Article I distinguished "enumerated" congressional powers such as regulation of commerce, issue of currency and making fiscal policy for the federal government, including "necessary and proper" actions to bring them into effect, and "reserved" powers (e.g. education) to the states (in the 10th Amendment). The expansion of state-level judicial decision activity could then be termed an "organic response of a constitutional system in which the traditional barriers to overreach have atrophied and a new check-and-balance emerges…" This is a "reassuring sign of the creativity and suppleness of the American Constitution, of its amphibian capacity to grow a new limb when an old one atrophies" (Krauthammer, 2017). It is also an argument for full federalism as the best political structure to withstand existential political crises.

Federations are hard to create, often designed poorly, implemented partially, and are plagued by weakness at the needed central or federal level. Sub-national institutions may be weakened by lack of financial independence. They are often lacking in constitutional protections or rules in organic laws that prevent sub-national taxation by central governments. Rules need to be in place to protect sub-national finances and to ensure they can mobilize substantial own-source funds. Vertical separation of powers and balances must be maintained to ensure that the sub-national units of federations have substantive content and not just formal independence. States are actually represented through devolved local autonomy and central spending in their behalf. The U.S. Constitution and Supreme Court decisions provide for intergovernmental tax immunity. The \$4t state–local bond market also depends on the continued immunity of their borrowing instruments (e.g. municipal bonds) from federal taxation. Local borrowing authority decreases dependence on central transfers and encourages the maintenance of stronger local financial conditions to meet rating agency criteria. By contrast, authoritarian systems and regimes inhibit the development of non-governmental mediating institutions. Authoritarian institutions offer uniform solutions to complex problems requiring nuanced design, ostensibly fitting varying ethnic and regional needs with 'one size fits all' policies. They back up their solutions with force which reduces legitimacy and makes effective governing harder. Unitary governments work at smaller scales but tend to be unable to serve more complex and challenging contexts. Confederations work well on paper and function properly until the first large problem arises. Then they are unable to forge consensus among their member states and manage conflicts—either at the ethno-national or macro-micro-policy sectoral levels.[4]

Thus, the problem of how to strengthen governments through technical assistance and local capacity-building that are over-centralized and unresponsive to citizens has been a perennial problem for both domestic and overseas aid policymakers. Both sets of policymakers must (or should) move from policy plans to allocation of actual budget shares and specific micro-sectoral programs and projects to achieve their aid objectives. For instance, years of civil war followed Argentina's independence from Spain in 1816. The struggle over governing structures and processes divided up between Unitarians who sought a strong central government

in the largest city, Buenos Aires, and *Federalists* who wanted safeguards on the authoritarian tendencies of central authorities and strong leaders to benefit the provinces. In practice, the clash of academic governance definitions deteriorated quickly into a struggle for control of the nation. The clash was between provincial caudillos led by Estanislao Lopez in the Littoral who labelled themselves Federalists, and groups called *Unitarios* led by the first governor Juan Manuel de Rosas which wanted national unity led by the City of Buenos Aires.

Here again, the real conflict was over control of revenues from the Buenos Aires customhouse. The provinces wanted protection for their industries against cheap imports from Europe. But Buenos Aires and the Unitarios controlled the tollgates and kept the money rightly regarded by the provinces for their own "national" purposes (Herring, 1972: 704). Federalists had pledged to create a Federal Commission as early as 1831 to organize the nation on a federal basis in the future (1972: 706) but were as loath as the Unitarios to make any political or economic concessions to the provinces (1972: 704). In fact, Rosas and his Unitarios wanted a weak confederation dominated by Buenos Aires, i.e. himself. The battle was really over shades of centralization. This paradoxical situation of national–provincial tensions supported less by leaders with clear political ideas than provincial caudillos (warlords operating from their *estancias*) seeking to amass personal power, still continues today despite finally evolving into a legal federation as recent as 1994 (163 years later!). Only in 1994 were municipal governments and the City of Buenos Aires granted legal and fiscal autonomy by the National Constitutional Convention, which created four levels of government.

The episode in Argentinian political history could be condensed into the perennial and modern struggle between those who fear external threats and want to preserve national identity (e.g. any reconquest by former colonial powers such as Spain; ongoing E.U. strictures in Europe; waves of uncontrolled immigrants to Europe from North Africa; persistent military border threats; and third-columnists from somewhere abroad), and those who seek better quality of national life and economic growth through more legitimate and responsive domestic institutions. The latter groups are interested in societal development and democracy. They are typically practical and support measures that will deliver better services and smarter regulations that encourage growth and prosperity. From the latter social democratic perspective, financial and political authority should be apportioned to institutions at different levels of government and safeguards should be built in to check probable abuses of authority in order to amass power (ironically recreating the very colonialist authoritarian systems that ruled from afar). Conflicts such as those in Argentina are often historically confusing since the supporters of the opposing positions are fragmented and often conflict with each other as much as their adversaries. Nevertheless, the populist nationalist vs. democracy and governance agenda differences are clear.

Historic conflicts with similar fault lines can be identified in the ex-colonial countries of Africa, Middle East, Asia, and the rest of Latin America. With few exceptions, the starting points have been authoritarian dictatorships operated from large capital cities that dispense public services from central ministries. Regime political control and security is tightly exercised and safeguarded by its national police and armies through deconcentrated district bases and barracks located around the country. Within these major regions, particular countries have made efforts to evolve into federations and produce better governance. The catalysts for change have often been institutional models and technical expertise from the ex-colonial powers that have attempted to learn lessons from the mistakes of their periods of colonial rule. These lessons have been diffused through international aid and donor institutions such as the World Bank, regional donors such as IADB, and bilateral aid agencies such as USAID and DFID (or UKAID). With few exceptions, those that have absorbed this advice and funding have strengthened their governing structures while those that have not often degenerated into failed states. There are often good reasons for failure to absorb and effectively use donor advice: geopolitical conflicts (i.e. territorial issues) and cultural constraints (e.g. especially in health care and education). But such constraints are real and those countries with stronger federal systems, or which have developed federalism by stealth at the operational and program levels for particular budgetary functions, are better able to overcome these constraints and prosper.

The challenge has been to build stronger governing institutions that can respond effectively to fiscal and political problems despite the many constraints faced by developing and transitional economies. That Argentina remains over-centralized despite federation structures suggests at least four propositions that will recur in case studies of other unitary, confederation, and federalist systems. First, concerns mount that political systems are rigged in favor of elites and are incapable of responding to the concerns of ordinary people. Second, even federal systems can be hollowed out by distorted electoral systems and ruling parties that favor ruling elites in capital cities. Federations often ameliorate these tendencies that are more pronounced in unitary states and confederations. Third, over-centralization (measured commonly by vertical fiscal imbalances) is still possible within federal systems. Fourth, it is a difficult and long-term slog to move from single-level centralized unitary governmental control to multi-level decentralized federations. Aid can help.

Needed to reduce the fragmentation, chaos, and destruction unleashed by ethno-nationalist and populist nationalist pressures are stronger state institutions. This can be facilitated by efforts to design federations rather than govern through autocratic and authoritarian, centralized states.

Populists often ensure that democratic institutions are weakened and that federation structures are off the agenda for future reform. More importantly, countries considering federation as a structural option, such as Yemen, Iraq, Venezuela, and even the U.K. have had little experience or tolerance for the institutional tensions and ambiguities which federation requires. The U.S. framers had experience with both a failed confederation and early links to European unitary and authoritarian governments. They were able to credibly put forth in a written Constitution the federation option which provided enough benefits to partisans and representatives of the time to be approved. The federal rules of the game had to be transparent, known, and the consequences reasonably anticipated before Constitutional approval. The members of the Constitutional Congress also had to be interested in a long-term blueprint that avoided the structural weaknesses of past governance models.

As noted from our review, populist successes in many countries such as Venezuela have taken over states, created macroeconomic problems with populist policies, and halted efforts to deal with problems of inefficient allocations of resources to micro-sectoral areas affecting regions, ethnicities, classes, or sects. The cycle has weakened states further in a vicious circle. Especially in poor countries, group demands combine expression of real unmet needs (poverty, unemployment, and poor health and education services) and revenge for past governmental repression with efforts to gain power for leaders and represented groups. Means used to achieve these ends range from social media and peaceful protests to violence. Failures to meet these needs and manage tensions are evident in the growing spate of governmental legitimacy crises. Around the globe, responsible institutions have not responded effectively to these group-level demands. The issue for poor countries is how government can gain the capacity to prevent ethnic groups and sects from controlling government for its own ends at the expense of other sects and regions. For wealthy countries, the issue is how to prevent demagogues and populist movements from mobilizing opinions and votes against the minorities representing these sects and tribes in their home countries that are the source of either current or future immigrants. They must also consider reforming defects in their electoral systems that allow traditional populists to direct spending and programs to their supporters for votes.[5]

Notes

1 Tunisia is considered a success story of the 2010 Arab Spring and is classified as "free" by Freedom House. The conclusion that it "will probably democratize by 2020" was reached by Richard Cincotta, based on a political demography hypothesis or method of his, known as "age-structural" theory. When a country reaches near replacement fertility rates, it reaches the "intermediate age-structural phase" (aged 26–35) and has a high propensity to protest. As

Iran is now also at the intermediate stage it, like Turkey is ripe for democratization (Bershidsky, 2018: 11). Contrary to the assertion that this demographic thesis makes democratization and state effectiveness efforts irrelevant, given the potential for protest for expanded rights, the Government of Tunisia and aid donors should step up efforts to make their institutions more responsive and accountable before either disruptive revolution or pointless civil war occurs, leading to possible military takeover. The people appear to have growing power and importance to the regime. But the religious and security establishment wields the ultimate power in Iran.

2 Failure to reassign and/or strengthen sub-national budgetary, political, and management roles for particular services such as urban transport leaves "silos" in place that interfere with the flow of hierarchical orders, empirical information, and learning. Vertical and horizontal silos block command structures and accountability channels and can destroy the positive effects of federations. For example, in theory the NYC MTA is responsible to the state governor and city mayor for operating bus and subway systems. In theory, this intergovernmental accountability structure should work better than a confederation of jurisdictions funded by voluntary contributions (i.e. Washington "Metro" or WMATA). In practice, the NYC MTA has deteriorated from a lack of funding and failure to enforce rules necessary to maintain performance standards. From June 2009–2010, there were 530,000 reported subway "delays". Delays are caused by signaling system malfunctions, electrical fires, train equipment failures, crew errors, and other problems. Management needs to know the precise cause to fix the problem. Yet, records indicated that 80 percent were lumped into the vague category "supplemental schedule" (Rosenthal *et.al.*, 2017: 29). Other management documents indicate that the most common cause of delays is "overcrowding". Since overcrowding usually results from delayed train arrivals, the cause is being confused with the effect. From such, almost deliberate, ploys and gimmicks to avoid responsibility and accountability, management has been unable to target the actual delay causes which still remain an administrative mystery. In short, accountability and responsiveness are not necessarily improved by federations. Performance has to be examined by sector and roles reassigned accordingly. As Caiden and Wildavsky (1974) noted, whether in wealthy or poor countries, institutional poverty and lack of complex redundancy can destabilize budgeting, service delivery, and performance. Despite the relative wealth of NYC MTA in the context of state and local resources, the system has not performed well because institutional advantages and fiscal wealth were allowed to diminish. Sector and system failures such as this indicate that internal audit and inspector general institutions are not performing their designated analytic and oversight functions.

3 A co-worker once described Belarus ministries in the 1990s to me as bulky and full of grim-faced officials reciting tractor production statistics. Former Soviet states mostly fit this depressing, Kafkaesque description of the government machine. Since then, European states, and transitional and developing country governments have modernized to provide needed outputs and outcomes. But most have not, and are still closed institutions, hermetically sealed off from the public and from any substantive accountability for their performance.

4 It is argued for example that an Israeli, Jordanian, Palestinian confederation would work better than a two-state solution to the perennial conflict there.

The argument is that a stable confederation is consistent with equality, symmetry, economic viability and recognition of basic rights asserted by each of the parties (Hirsch, 2017: 20). But the problem with confederation stability, from the Iroquois League of Five Nations to the E.U., is how to maintain stability? A 3-state confederation is unlikely to provide stable effective governance any more than a 2-state confederation. Stability and effectiveness require a legitimate central authority built into the structure to resolve disputes, that is, a federation. This is also a stumbling bloc to the reunification of Cyprus. Since the 1974 invasion by Turkey after a Greek Cypriot coup, the country has remained split, with the north recognized only by Turkey. In 2004, a UN reunification plan was put to a referendum. The Greek south voted in favor; the Turkish north voted against and the country remains split, just as Israel–Palestine and other places with intractable conflicts derived from deep sectarian hatreds. Despite the incentives for both sides of substantial E.U. funds there is little chance of any more than the creation of a loose confederation along ethnic lines (i.e. what already exists).

5 What is the draw for demagogues and populists? Why is it often so easy for them to mobilize opinion and support for nationalist–nativist movements to stoke sectarian conflict? Populists draw upon multiple bases of support. First, poverty, jobless, and misfortunes often limited to regions and classes provide grist for blaming others even if these conditions have been endemic for decades. The others are now often immigrants from different cultures. Second, perceived victims often lack skills, education, and the ability or willingness to move. They now believe they have been left behind and someone is to blame. Third, nativists are often unopposed by nimble opposition leaders or parties that are there to counter their simple solutions. Opposition parties often rely on the obvious benefits of modern democratic institutions and cosmopolitan values that are not obvious to large swathes of countries that believe or can be made to believe that they have been left behind. So, for many British, urban cosmopolitanism, globalization and free movement of people mean cultural differences and competition for resources at schools and hospitals which also divides British along well-established class lines. Such divisions exist in many countries with urban–rural divides and differential effects of technology and globalization. This fuels populism and the opportunism of demagogues. Nigel Farage, then of the UK Independence Party (UKIP), drove then Prime Minister Cameron to offer the referendum to those dismissed by him as "fruitcakes, loonies and closet racists". But UKIP mobilized these older, non-graduate, lower social order people with grievances and they won. Finally, the electoral system can provide demagogues with an advantage by favoring rural regions. If France used the U.S. electoral college system, for instance, Marine Le Pen would have won more of France's 18 regions than Emmanuel Macron (8 vs. 6 and came in higher in 4 others). Cosmopolitan Clinton won the populous urban regions just as Macron but it made no difference given the electoral system.

7 Response to Governance Challenges
The Problem of Aid Design and Implementation

Introduction

To repeat the question posed earlier, how can domestic country and overseas aid policymakers break the vicious cycles of states weakened by ethno-populist nationalism as well as the common impulses of many regimes to use the state as the source of financing for traditional populist measures to keep them in power? For, weak states make bad policies and bad policies perpetuate weak states. For the most part, as discussed, macroeconomic policy problems and such threats to regime stability have been eliminated except for rogue political regimes that ignore the obvious comparative lessons of faulty economic and financial policies.

The three tools to influence state growth and development have been: trade, investment and aid. Trade has always been viewed as a major force that would break the cycle of state weakness. From mercantilist trade policies, colonies were exploited and their weak states perpetuated in the name of providing metropolitan colonial powers with raw materials such as timber and minerals for their benefit. African countries, for example, sold more of their raw materials to their former colonial masters than they traded with each other. African countries currently trade twice as much with Europe as with each other. Colonial leaders and generations of successors learned from this and could see the contradictions of one-way trade and the notion that exports were good and imports bad. Liberal trade, by contrast, encouraged the mutual reduction of import tariffs for the benefit of all parties. But regulatory obstacles and non-tariff barriers remain and have prevented trade liberalization. Policies based on faulty economics still rely on import tariffs. They have often been in the name of import substitution to protect nascent industries that can work for a time but must be removed in the future at some point that never happens because of political pressures for such lucrative subsidy entitlements.[1] Countries also impose export tariffs and protect local agricultural products from competition in the name of pro-poverty policies. These work against both the poor and trade in lower priced goods that could, with domestic policy support, spur local producers to become more nimble and efficient. Poorer countries suffer the most from these flawed policies because they lack the options of wealthier complex countries with multiple sectors and trading partners.

Going forward, all three sources of growth and development financing will ultimately be replaced by domestic country resources. Aid fatigue and trade protectionism have reduced the already small contribution of those sources and will continue to diminish their role further in the future. Of about $8t in needed development financing, only about $1t can be obtained from private investment (domestic and foreign), gross ODA (less than $200b), and short and long term debt financing (Rozner, 2018a). That means domestic country resources need to be mobilized. Aid needs to be allocated and targeted to micro-sectoral level programs and projects to strengthen revenue collection and administration systems. This must be part of the continuing effort to strengthen country public financial management (PFM) systems. Efficient and corruption-free revenue systems need to be strengthened to increase taxpayer trust in paying and satisfaction that revenues are spent for needed projects and services, such as health and education. Participatory capital budgeting, as will be discussed in Chapter 8 (ICHD, 2006) is one means of linking revenue revenues with specific project spending to increase taxpayer satisfaction. By increasing incentives for tax compliance and raising tax revenue GDP ratios, ODA can help make states in transitional and developing countries resilient enough to withstand populist nationalist and ethno-nationalist threats, while linking state revenues with budget expenditures for services and programs that benefit stakeholders and citizens. Recent ODA efforts to mobilize domestic resources are decribed further in later chapters.

The four threats to political regimes and governmental effectiveness indicated in Figure 0.1 are interactive and not independent of each other. They may also not be distinct, such as ethno-populist nationalist leaders and movements and the traditional populism of many political parties and regimes in both rich and poor countries. In principle, aid must serve the country regime in power regardless of its ideological make-up and policy purposes. Assistance is designed to be used for the benefit of all country people, not just governments or particular sects. This means the term "threat" can be highly political in itself. Minimizing threats to regime stability and preventing failed states to some may for others be simply preventing damage to an already failing system rigged for the few. The latter would be the view of traditional–radical populists such as Jeremy Corbyn's Labor Party in Britain. They propose such standard populist policies as stiffer taxes for companies and the rich, nationalization of industries, autarchic industrial production, protectionist trade, and fiscal profligacy in behalf of followers which would, consistent with mainstream economic research, be disastrous for most people in most countries. Aid agencies would need to breakdown each policy into components and try and improve the design and implementation of the least damaging, such as public utilities and national railways, which can and have been made to work with incentivized public management as well as by private ownership. Hollowing out respected institutions, such as Venezuela's state oil company (PDSVA) and replacing engineers with unskilled cronies of the Chavez and Maduro regimes is the wrong way to implement even traditional populist policies. Eventually, the political costs of fiscal profligacy will be higher than those of fiscal austerity for such regimes. Aid fiscal adjustment programs can provide empirical evidence of impact, which the regimes will then either defiantly ignore or accept as the price of new loans and continued participation in global credit markets. Such problems as these represent the paradoxical nature of aid work in difficult settings.

Overseas aid may play a part in building states; but some of its programs can discredit regimes in host countries as well. One oft-repeated example of state weakening is the USAID P.L. 480 program. By providing U.S. agricultural commodities to poor countries for emergency and non-emergency needs, the program floods local markets, lowering local farmer incomes and reducing state tax revenues that otherwise could have been earned from a stronger agricultural sector. This weakens state capacities to finance its own broader needs through local budgets. In addition, faulty industrial and trade policies can create macroeconomic instabilities which threaten regimes by increasing unemployment and stirring up ethno-nationalism. In Guyana, for instance, the ruling coalition, which relies on African-descent voters, is threatened by having to lay off many of the mostly Indian descent sugar workers. Most Caribbean region sugar industries have higher average costs than more mechanized operations in Australia, Brazil, and even Belize. Countries like Guyana exported sugar to the E.U., which had country quotas and guaranteed prices. These were abolished in 2005, depressing local export prices and sales. Belize gains 25 percent of export earnings from sugar and now produces high-value white sugar from modernizing and mechanizing its processing factories. The proposed CARICOM remedy of a common 40 percent import tariff for sugar imported from outside its member confederation will likely only depress outputs, employment, incomes, and profits further (*The Economist*, 2017k1: 32). Caribbean regimes should provide fiscal and economic incentives to modernize their sugar industries.

The proposed Continental Free Trade Area (CFTA) composed of 15 African countries is one attempt to escape the colonial legacy of mercantilism by cutting tariffs on 90 percent of products and igniting Africa's stalled industrialization (*The Economist*, 2017j1: 70). Increased inter-country trade can expand markets for member countries, leading to greater competition, investment, and expanded industrialization. Such initiatives as CFTA can serve as frameworks to enact other reforms to improve local trade climates, such as enforcing modern customs processing and control systems to increase efficiency, transaction costs, and reduce corruption. But improved trade depends on strong, effective states that can process trading transactions without delays and corruption. The introduction of computerized, real-time customs systems, usually through aid programs, suffer from the same problems as GFMISs in that they are (deliberately) not fully installed and allow corruption from such practices as keeping transactions off the books or allowing false invoices to be processed and paid.

Foreign direct investment, as a byproduct of trade, is also viewed as another alternative to aid and a potential resource for state improvement. But improving investment climates is difficult in poorer countries. Modern, consistently enforced rules again require strong states and supportive regimes. Temptations are especially strong to shelve rules and look the other way in behalf of large natural resource investors that make some elites in poor countries very wealthy. For, many countries are dependent on large natural resource investors (providing grist for the "curse" theory) that develop and thrive on patronage relations. Mining and timber firm investments have created and perpetuated kleptocratic regimes in many countries, both rich and poor. Instead of a transparent and stable set of investment rules, investors find regimes favoring certain investors that threaten others which dissuades them from making needed major investments for the long term. Those that do are high risk-takers that behave in buccaneering capitalist fashion to make short-term profits rather than make any local long-term investments that could contribute to development in the host country.

Thus, it falls to overseas aid in support of trade and investment, to break the cycle of weak states and policies. The insertion point is overseas aid from bilateral and multilateral donors, and NGOs often linked to private foundations or charities. All aid requires a supportive state; none can work under the radar for long and pretend that its development work is independent of host governments (as some NGOs have done in such countries as Haiti). Aid can work from the outside by providing rewards for compliance with conditions and norms and punishments for failure to meet conditions. Aid has long suffered from multi-pronged criticism that it is a waste of funds and stimulates local corruption. Specific examples can be cited of such problems but in general the criticisms are wide of the mark. While aid is often considered a constraint, it has achieved important gains at the operational level in particular sectors of many countries. Aid programs and projects have reinforced quasi-federalist features of otherwise bad governance contexts. Though these gains are often ignored in donor efforts to hype macro-benefits in order to gain more funds from their member governments, the projects and programs have benefited many people in all parts of the world. Nevertheless, aid effectiveness is diminished by strategic and operational defects that make it both a threat to itself and to the common objective of facilitating state effectiveness overseas. To those we now turn.

Aid as Constraint and Opportunity

Specifically, given the reliance of most transitional and developing countries on overseas aid to finance their budgets and macroeconomic stabilization efforts, the fourth challenge to the effectiveness of states is whether aid (both overseas to host countries and in-country programs and transfers for domestic purposes to reduce regional inequality) is: (1) well-designed: the aid agencies (or domestic regimes) use in-country and comparative experience to design their programs; (2) allocated sensibly: the aid agencies allocate funds to the highest need programs and projects (as opposed to populist-driven); and (3) managed well in host countries: the aid field projects are managed and supervised to get the most results (outputs and outcomes) during implementation for the budgeted funds (Figure 0.1). Since the aid in the field is often not well-managed or supervised, or poorly designed and allocated in the first place, it often serves as an additional constraint. Whereas wealthier countries need to make better policies to improve regional equalization and induce stronger growth, poorer countries, in addition to better utilizing their own policy and fiscal professionals, need to leverage overseas aid to supplement their own resources in order to stimulate regional and local development. That seems like common sense. But there has to be demand for the aid as well as any investment, public or private. Mere supply of public investment infrastructure is usually insufficient in the long-term if the demand was lacking in the first place (e.g. political projects). Supporting private investments need to be in place, which mean feasible and profitable investments. State subsidies as incentives can then cover part of the package with a greater likelihood of income and employment multipliers.

States often supply aid where there is insufficient demand for it by other than a narrow slice of beneficiaries. In China, the massive public accumulation and investment in targeted sectors with state enterprises to fill in for private investors and stimulate their interest has been inefficient but so far effective for GDP growth. This was partly the Stalinist model modified by China to become state capitalism. But whatever the aid mix only by enough improvements in the economic climate to stimulate private investments can laggard regions in countries like China move forward. In addition to development for its own sake, growth and regional and local development are needed to reduce the influence of ethnic and populist forces that weaken governments and make it even harder to attain socio-economic development. Regimes with foresight and interest in modern democratic governance recognize the devastating consequences of leaving some of its regions behind through neglected service coverage and scarce provision of transfers and subsidies. Most regimes unfortunately do not.

Overseas aid, intentionally by design or unintentionally, works on the institutions and cultures of host countries to try and stimulate growth and more effective government. By improving institutional capacity to make smarter rules and regulations, aid may even promote more trade and investment which adds to both growth and public revenues. USAID and DFID, for example, have targeted substantial amounts of their aid to improving the management and finances of public sector institutions at the center, for sub-national governments, and intergovernmental relations. Depending on the aid sub-sector, country, and type of project, to the extent the aid targets sectors, such as health, education, and economic growth, and fiscal and economic policymaking institutions, it works well. But much of U.S. aid is targeted globally to democracy and governance and larger causes such as human rights and good governance (13 percent of USAID's 2013 fiscal year (FY) allocations). Those are proper long-term goals and strategic objectives. But they may not be the best use of funds to strengthen states now in the face of severe threats to their legitimacy and very existence. In varying degrees by region then, states face the four noted threats from ethnic and populist nationalism (and combinations of them with traditional populism), macroeconomic instability and poorly designed aid programs. In this second section of the book, we examine the problems created by (1) poorly targeted aid design, (2) corruption and waste in allocation, and (3) misguided and often arbitrary project oversight. The question is how has aid been used to respond to each of the four threats in these regions for wealthier and poor countries?

Because of in-country constraints to effective governance, and to the delivery of aid externally by donor rules and practices, attribution of any gains to state effectiveness due to external aid or internal budget policy reallocation of resources is quite difficult. Are there examples of success? Yes, many at the micro-systems level. The focus of this book will be on overseas development assistance (ODA globally or DA from USAID) since the bulk of state modernization, and state sectoral programs such as education and health and public financial management reform programs, are planned and financed through that category. ODA is intended to stimulate the economic development and welfare of recipient countries. ODA (U.S. spending mainly by USAID is called DA) effectiveness is evaluated by separate donors, e.g. World Bank by its Independent Evaluation Group (IEG); USAID by its Bureau of Policy Planning and Learning office,[2] and from budgetary outlay reports submitted annually to Congress;[3] other donors have similar institutions responsible for generating evaluation reports on programs and projects. Some are more independent than others. The IEG has a long history of very critical reviews that are used by Bank project planning staff as well as independent writers critical of World Bank aid; USAID's institution is less independent. Due to cost and scarcity of personnel to perform aid evaluations, most are on a case-by-case basis and lack any longitudinal data by type of project and program on their outputs and outcomes. But a more serious problem for designing and implementing specific, coherent, and high-impact country programs is that there are no evaluations of aid for all donors by country. That makes rational country programming of all aid difficult. By contrast, U.S. military assistance is not evaluated at all nor is there an annual report to Congress on its effectiveness. Other types of overseas aid (in the USG budget account #150 but not classified as DA) are budget support (Economic Support Fund) for economic stabilization and humanitarian aid which the U.S. provides directly, as well as a contributor to international NGOs, charities and multilateral organizations such as the UN. Regardless of label, the combined effects of the three main types of aid (DA, military, and humanitarian) should be coordinated in-country to stabilize the climate and improve conditions for trade, investment, growth, and development.

The US Overseas Assistance Program

> History is written by the victors, they say, but it seems to me that history is written above all by those who weren't there, which may be the same thing. I had a hunger: to look into the faces of those who *are* there, hear their stories, eat with them, learn new words.
>
> (Kassabova, 2017: xviii)

Most aid field workers are motivated by the same hunger to understand the real lives of the men and women with whom they interact daily. To them, they are more than "clients", "aid recipients", or metrics for performance ratings. Aid field workers and other related line officials at the project level are the ones who are there and cross borders between and within countries routinely. Unfortunately, the stories they hear and insights gained are rarely put in reports or used by policymakers in donor countries. Often their insights are traded in pubs and restaurants to other aid workers and in that sense do make a difference in practice. The fact is, such anthropological observations are rarely asked for or published by overseers or even evaluators for wider publics. If this were to be so, aid design and delivery might even improve.[4]

Given that the U.S. spends more in absolute terms on ODA than any OECD country, it is useful to focus on its processes and results. The U.S. spends roughly $20b/year on international aid and affairs which amounts to about 14 percent of all ODA (Tarnoff, 2015: 11). It is distributed by a politically driven Congress across programs and projects that were mostly designed and preapproved by permanent local missions. Since it is bilateral, the link with governments is potentially less than host country multilateral aid. Host country projects from multilateral donors tend to be implemented through units within ministries (project implementation units or PIUs) giving them immediate and daily impact on government operations and greater potential for transferring to the rest of government and for scaling-up. Instead, bilateral projects tend to be overseen by their donors. Project COPs report to multiple masters, one of which is the local donor mission. Moreover, local donor missions are deconcentrated units of central aid agencies and therefore at least indirectly in charge of project management and operations. But bilateral aid impact may be greater as project budgets are typically larger and in-country delivery time periods are longer. In short, U.S. ODA is similar in process and result to other large country and institutional donors. Smaller countries, such as Switzerland, fund and deliver focused aid projects, through its Swiss Agency for Development and Cooperation (SDC), that are very effective for poverty reduction and sustainability on a small scale, for example, rural cheese-making training and facilities in countries such as Ecuador to provide skills and employment.[5]

The modern-day U.S. concept of international development assistance took shape after World War II ended in 1945. George C. Marshall, the Secretary of State from 1947 to 1949 provided significant financial and technical assistance to Europe after the war. Known as the Marshall Plan, this was a successful effort that allowed Europe to rebuild its infrastructure, strengthen its economy, and stabilize the region. It is argued that international aid reflects (and in some instances drives) U.S. foreign policy. The lines between U.S. foreign aid, trade, and broader policy are blurred.[6] Building on the success of the Marshall Plan, then President Truman proposed an international development assistance program in 1949. The 1950 Point Four Program focused on two goals: (1) creating markets for the United States by reducing poverty and increasing production in developing countries, and (2) diminishing the threat of communism by helping countries prosper under capitalism. From 1952 to 1961, programs supporting technical assistance and capital projects continued as the primary form of U.S. aid, and were a key component of U.S. foreign policy. During this time, USG leaders established various precursor organizations to USAID, including the Mutual Security Agency, Foreign Operations Administration, and the International Cooperation Administration.

In 1961, then President Kennedy signed the Foreign Assistance Act into law and created the U.S. Agency for International Development (USAID) by executive order. Once USAID became operational, international development assistance opportunities grew dramatically. The time during the Kennedy and Johnson administrations became known as the "decade of development". In the 1970s, the USAID began to shift its focus away from technical and capital assistance programs to more specific country needs. In this period, U.S. development assistance stressed a "basic human needs" approach, which focused on functional or sectoral programs in (1) food and nutrition, (2) population planning, (3) health, (4) education, and (5) human resources development.

By the 1980s, U.S. foreign assistance broadened and deepened its concerns to currency stabilization and strengthening financial systems to improve growth. It also promoted market-based principles to restructure developing countries' policies and institutions. During this decade, USAID reaffirmed its commitment to broad-based economic growth, emphasizing increasing poor country employment and income opportunities through the revitalization of agriculture and the expansion of domestic markets. Also in this decade, development activities were increasingly channeled through private voluntary organizations (PVOs), and aid shifted from individual projects to portfolios of projects within larger sectoral programs, such as health care.

In the 1990s, USAID's top priority became sustainable development, or helping countries improve their own quality of life. During this decade, USAID tailored development assistance programs to country economic conditions, which meant that: (a) developing countries received an integrated package of assistance, (b) transitional countries received help in times of crisis, and (c) countries with limited USAID presence would receive support through non-governmental organizations (NGOs). USAID also played a lead role in planning and implementing programs following the fall of the Berlin Wall in 1989. This was the beginning of USAID programs that overtly attempted to establish functioning democracies with open, market-oriented economic systems and responsive social safety nets.

During the 2000s, USAID evolved further with foreign assistance, with many calling for further reform of how the agency conducted its business. With the advent of the Afghanistan and Iraq wars, USAID was called on to help those two countries rebuild government, infrastructure, civil society, and basic services such as health care and education. The Agency began rebuilding with an eye to getting the most value for money out of its funding allocations. It also began an aggressive campaign to reach out to new partner organizations—including the private sector and foundations—in order to extend the reach of its foreign assistance.

The U.S. Agency for International Development (USAID) plans and administers the country's *bilateral* development assistance program. Other bilateral aid agencies provide DA or what is known internationally as ODA through their foreign aid institutions, such as: Britain's (DFID), Australia's (AusAID), Canada's (CIDA) and Sweden's (SIDA). The U.S. program is delivered through USAID via the Department of State parent organization. As an example of the rough annual allocation patterns, the components of State Department's $55b FY 2011 program were: (1) direct economic and development aid (DA) ($23b); (2) DOS—embassies and Foreign Service ($11b), (3) military aid ($11b); (4) international organizations ($7b), and (5) USAID operations including food aid ($3b). DA projects fall within the current functional program categories of: health care, agriculture, education, economic stabilization and public finance, infrastructure, natural resources, and democracy and governance.

Broadly, there are three types of aid: (1) military, (2) humanitarian (such as UNHCR) and (3) development (DA). As indicated, the U.S. provides the largest amount of development assistance (with grant projects for the longest periods) of any Development Assistance Club (DAC) member. While the $23b economic and development assistance proportion of the FY 2013 U.S. aid budget is the largest amount of any country, it represents perhaps the smallest percentage of donor country GDP (only 0.2 percent) or roughly that of Japan (JICA) which provides only $11.0b mostly in what are known as "tied aid" projects—funds in exchange for supplier contracts with home country firms. The highest ODA percentage of GDP is provided by Norway (1.1 percent), or roughly $4.6b, by its NORAD agency. As indicated, most USAID DA consists of unconditional grants rather than loans. Policy conditions may be attached by Congress and operational requirements must be met before DA is approved, such as functioning internal controls and reporting practices consistent with USAID requirements for sound financial control.

By contrast, *multilateral* aid organizations such as the IMF provide balance of payments assistance, bail-out contributions and conditional aid (loans in exchange for meeting reform conditions) such as a recent $2b loan to Jordan in exchange for cuts in fuel subsidies and numbers of civil service positions. IMF does not plan or administer ODA but many of the World Bank's programs and projects fall into the category of ODA. That other multilateral and regional aid agencies allocate funds for country projects can limit the ability of the USAID program to exert leverage where needed to achieve its development objectives, especially where other programs work at cross purposes. For instance, Chinese infrastructure loans and lease purchases of farmland in countries such as Congo would work against efforts to develop higher yields and greater secondary in-country agro-industrial processing. Investments by Kuwait in Cambodia for similar neo-mercantilist purposes has resulted in pasture expansion and increases in deforestation that work against the objectives of USAID programs for better forestry and natural resources management. This underscores the need for comprehensive country evaluations of all aid sources and types.

The flow of ODA can be thought of using the energy metaphor of generation, transmission, and distribution of electricity. Aid is generated by national budgets or international donor budgets. These are like the thermal plants powered mainly by coal, oil, or nuclear sources to generate electricity. After programs are designed, they are transmitted to countries via multiple contractual mechanisms in the form of grants or loans at below-market rates. Like electricity transmission lines, they consist of high and low capacity systems depending on the expected supply and demand for use when it is distributed. Specifically then, aid flows can be viewed through a policy metaphor similar to electricity of (1) the *generation* of program and projects takes place through national–international budgets of bilateral-multilateral aid agencies; (2) project grants and loans are *transmitted* and allocated via contractual arrangements; and (3) aid funds are the electricity which is *distributed* via local systems, for example, NGOs, government ministries, and local governments through such mechanisms as conditional transfers to individuals or grants to institutions for specific USAID programmatic purposes.

Continuing with the flow of electricity metaphor, the U.S. aid program requires large fiscal electricity lines to transmit the largest amounts of aid for usually longer (2–5 years) projects consisting of a portfolio of technical assistance, training, and equipment. As will be noted, depending on the type of demand and the willingness of the supplier (USAID, Treasury and Congress), project aid is administered through mechanisms that can rely either on donor management systems or some combination of recipient financial management systems. That is, the aid can be devolved, something like small-scale renewable energy suppliers feeding small grids rather than rely on centralized generation. Finally, the electricity is distributed among households. Meters are used to gauge demand; economic and demographic statistics measure income and results of use in order to set prices, provide maintenance and quality control. Similarly, aid is distributed within countries using locally designed mechanisms for local purposes. The Brazilian conditional cash transfer system is an example of aid distributed to individual families. The cash incentivizes compliance with national norms for health and education. Local departments monitor compliance and performance results. This book focuses on the generation–transmission and distributional linkages for international aid to improve governance and build democratic political systems.

All OECD countries provide ODA; the focus here is on U.S. ODA or DA. Tarnoff (2015: 11) details USAID's allocation within both the International Affairs (#150) function and the overall U.S. budget. It is roughly 33 percent of the former (#150) and 1.4 percent of the latter (total spending). But DA is a smaller amount than all USAID spending; it amounts to only 3 percent of the USAID budget (about $3b), which suggests that its impact is actually much more limited in changing regimes and stimulating governmental effectiveness. Because resources budgeted are simply too small, DA alone cannot create stable, effective states. Figures 7.1, 7.2, 7.3, and Table 7.1 below detail the breakdown of USAID spending:

Note that these are resource input figures and indicate nothing about the output efficiencies or program–project impacts and outcomes of aid. Such results should be measured and related to inputs by proper independent evaluations as noted above. Despite the small scale, USAID DA programs and projects can make, and have made, important differences to state-building, growth, democracy, and development. That is, DA

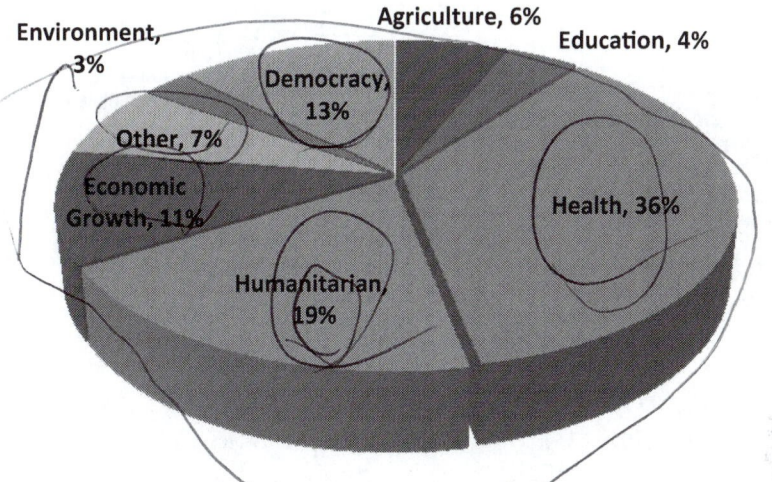

Figure 7.1 USAID Implemented Funding by Sector FY 2013

Source: Tarnoff (2015: 19); USAID, U.S. Overseas Loans and Grants, https://eads. usaid.gov/gbk/ and CRS calculations.

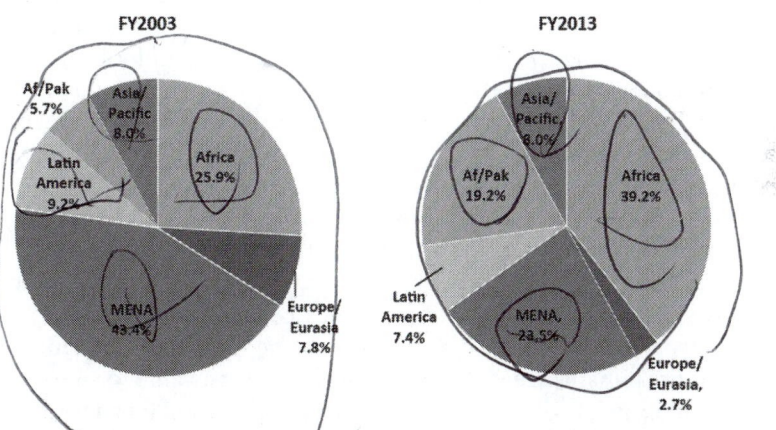

Figure 7.2 USAID Implemented Funding by Region FY 2003 and FY 2013

Note: Af/Pak = Afghanistan/Pakistan; MENA = Middle East and North Africa.

Source: Tarnoff (2015: 17); Based on obligations attributable to regions. USAID, U.S. Overseas Loans and Grants https://eads.usaid.gov/gbk/ and CRS calculations.

is translated from programs down into project grants (and some soft loans) for such needs as: schools, clinics and hospitals, roads, water-sewer systems and improved election administration systems. The importance of incentivizing aid is that larger, targeted sums of money are involved and they need to be spent wisely. Measured as a percentage of GDP, the

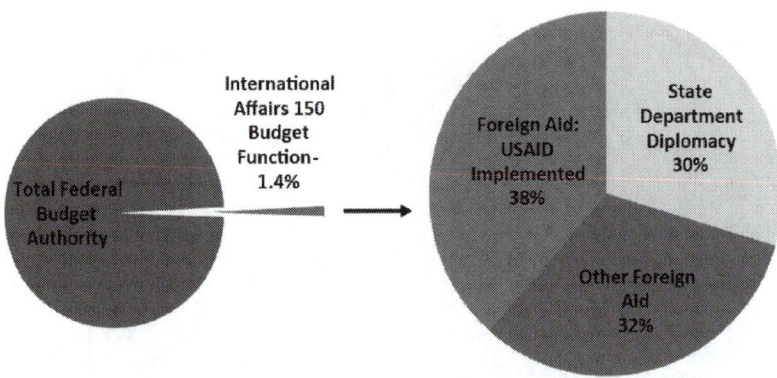

Figure 7.3 USAID Portion of Federal Budget and 150 Functions FY 2015
Source: Tarnoff (2015: 14); OMB Historical Budget Tables FY2015 and CRS calculations.

U.S. provides one of the lowest levels of ODA (about 0.03 percent in 2005), mainly because the U.S. GDP is so much larger than any OECD country. Denmark ODA spending was the highest of OECD members at 0.08 percent of GDP (*The Economist*, 2005). By contrast, measured in total ODA spending, the U.S. was the highest ($27.5b) of all OECD countries in 2005. Denmark ODA spending was only $2.1b in 2005 (*The Economist*, 2005). Administered mostly by USAID, U.S. ODA consists of the longest projects (3–5 years); the largest projects ($5m–$100m), and projects which usually have the highest local employer impact (i.e. local consultants and sub-contractors). The bulk of USAID projects are executed in the field by local staff and NGOs that also hire local staff and purchase local supplies. Though in U.S. fiscal terms, the outflow of U.S. aid is small, the inflow of U.S. aid funds is large for most country budgets. This means that their capacity to manage these funds is critical for U.S. aid fiscal management objectives to (a) achieve value for money by internal efficiencies which can be helped by devolving aid management to recipient country MOFs and treasuries, and (b) eventually phase out the aid program for particular countries. Skilled and trained staff need to be able to carry on with project-type activities in their later careers in the public, private, or non-profit sectors.

In general, all ODA is channeled to countries according to specific targeted purposes using one or more of three mechanisms: (1) general or sectoral budget support to the national budget through the treasury account. Co-funding from the national budget may occur and there is no earmarking of funds (other than to the sector); (2) basket or pooled funding. This is called cost-sharing and consists of joint funding by a number of development partners through a common bank account. It

Table 7.1 USAID Appropriations FY 2012–FY 2016 Request (Tarnoff, 2015: 11)

	FY2012	FY2013	FY2014	FY2015 est[a]	FY2016 req.
USAID Program Total (est.)	**16,780.5**	**17,349.0**	**16,545.5**	**19,163.0**	**11.117.7**
Core Programs:					
Global Health Programs—USAID	2,629.8	2,626.1	2,773.9	3,096.0	2,755.0
Development Assistance (DA)	2,520.0	2,717.7	2,507.0	2,507.0	2,999.7
International Disaster Assistance (IDA)	1,095.0	1,550.4	1,801.0	3,331.3	1,741.0
Transition Intiatives (TI)	93.7	68.8	57.6	67.0	67.6
Complex Crises Fund (CCF)	50.0	53.0	40.0	20.0	30.0
Development Credit Auth Subsidy [Possible Transfer from other Accts]	[40.0]	[40.0]	[40.0]	[40.0]	[40.0]
P.L. 480 Food for Peace Title II (USDA Apps)	1,466.0	1,359.4	1,466.0	1,466.0	1,400.0
Shared Programs:[b]					
Global Health Programs—State Dept: USAID Portion (est.)	2,738.0	3,470.0	3,572.1	3,572.1	3,418.4
	(5,542.9)	(5,439.8)	(5,670.0)	(5,670.0)	(5,426.0)
Economic Support Fund (ESF): USAID Portion (est.)	5,716.4	5,456.8	4,268.0	5,048.6	5,706.0
	(6,146.7)	(5,867.5)	(4,589.2)	(5,428.6)	(6,135.3)
Assistance for Europe: Eurasia & Central Asia (AEECA): USAID Portion (actual)	424.8	0.0	0.0	0.0	0.0
	(626.7)				
	46.8	46.8	60.0	55.0	0.0
Democracy Fund: USAID Portion (actual)	(114.8)	(109.0)	(130.5)	(130.5)	
USAID Administration Total	**1,536.3**	**1,458.7**	**1,321.1**	**1,434.1**	**1,700.5**
USAID Operating Expenses	1,347.3	1,279.3	1,140.2	1,235.3	1,425.0
USAID Capital Investment Fund	129.7	123.1	117.9	130.8	203.3
Development Credit Authority Admin	8.3	7.9	8.0	8.1	9.2
USAID Inspector General	51.0	48.4	55.0	59.9	63.0
TOTAL: USAID Program & Administration (est.)	**18,316.8**	**18,807.7**	**17,866.6**	**20,597.1**	**19,818.2**

Source: Tarnoff (2015: 11); U.S. Department of State budget documents and CRS calculations.
Notes: Totals include Overseas Contingency Operations (OCO) and transfers. FY2013 amounts include post-sequester and across-the-board rescission. Of FY2015 CCF $50 million appropriated total, $30 million was managed by States.
a. FY2015 totals include Ebola emergency funding.
b. Shared Programs: Amounts shown on top are estimated USAID-implemented portion of account. Amounts shown in parentheses are account totals as appropriated. USAID portions of Global Health-State for FY2012–2013 are estimates based on USAID reporting: FY2014–2015 is based on FY2010–2013 average proportion (63 percent). USAID ESF portion is based on USAID estimate of historic average of about 93 percent, but the actual percentage may vary widely from year to year. AEECA amount of actual USAID portion reported by Europe/Eurasia Coordinator. Democracy Fund amount is actual allocation to USAID.

requires common rules for all partners; and (3) and project-funding which consists of individual development interventions for specific object-ives within a broader program framework. While donors use different acronyms for their tools, they can be divided into the above three general categories. The three types of mechanisms that are used by USAID which correspond roughly to those used by other donors. The two major issues for aid design for stimulating host country governmental effectiveness are (1) the amount of funding by mechanism and (2) its effectiveness in channeling aid for intended results.

USAID programs/projects are disbursed primarily by grant instruments that allow varying degrees of discretion to country officials, that is, MOF, and sectoral ministries. About 90 percent is still disbursed through *direct budget support/task orders* (DBS) that are almost totally managed by USAID. This is termed *centralized aid*. About 10 percent of U.S. DA is disbursed through *implementation letters* (ILs) and *fixed amount reimbursements* (FARs and expanded FARs). These provide for cost-sharing in exchange for achieving performance targets. They rely more on country PFM systems for disbursement and control. That means more *decentralized aid*.

While the terms "assistance project" and "development project" might be used indiscriminately, it helps in understanding USAID's work to distin-guish between: (1) the development projects of local (i.e. country) govern-ment agencies and NGOs, such as their projects to improve public health services or schools for a particular beneficiary group, and (2) USAID's assistance projects, which support local development projects. The key to successful assistance is how well it fits the needs of local development projects, while the key to a successful development project is the institu-tional capacity of the local government agencies and NGOs, including the professional ability of their staff members.

When a local development project's assistance needs have been identi-fied, USAID arranges the agreed assistance through funding agreements with implementing organizations, often referred to by USAID staff as "implementing partners". Private firm and non-profits bid for these projects. For example, *Practical Concepts in Development* (PCD), the implementing organization in our case (Appendix), is discussed below.[7] A variety of different kinds of funding agreements can be used by USAID to support implementing partners. Also, USAID sometimes finances sev-eral different implementers to provide a number of different inputs to a single development project. To illustrate, a multifaceted assistance effort supporting a single development project could include the following four types of funding agreements: (1) budget-support grants to a government agency (2) contracts with a firm for support to USAID, (3) grants to a local NGO serving the beneficiary group, and (4) grants to an inter-national NGO to strengthen the operations of the local NGO. These are set out more specifically as follows:

(1) *Budget Support Agreements to Government Host Country Agencies.* These take the form of a letter from USAID's Mission Director, countersigned by the recipient agency, explaining the agency's objectives, the amount of USAID's financial commitment, the specific expenditures to be financed by USAID's grant, and other operational aspects of the agreement. USAID's technical office assigns a staff member (U.S. or local) to oversee progress in the agency's implementation. USAID's financial management office transfers funds to the agency, in tranches as needed. Audit under this kind of government-to-government (G2G) financial assistance is usually performed by the host government's own audit agency. USAID then may sign technical assistance contracts with government agencies. As a government agency is usually specialized in services to its beneficiary population (medical services, for example), its staff may not be equipped to undertake investments called for in the agency's program, such as construction, acquisition of equipment, or management of training and study tours. The government agency might therefore request USAID's assistance in these areas, and USAID could respond by contracting with a firm to supply the services or technical assistance requested.

USAID's technical office collaborates with the government agency and stakeholders in drafting the specifications for what is needed (generally referred to as a "Statement of Work" for the contract) and in conducting market research for available sources and potential bidders. USAID's Contracting Officer would then advertise for bids, manage the selection of a contractor from among the competing bidders, sign the contract, and assign a technical office staff member as the Contracting Officer's Representative to oversee the performance under the contract. (If the work load permits, this staff member might be the same person who oversees USAID's financial assistance to the government agency). The contractor supplies technical assistance directly to the government agency, so that, in monitoring contractor performance, USAID relies substantially on the agency's evaluation of the contractor's work.

(2) *Contracts with a Private Firm.* The result of project bidding processes may be award of a contract to a private firm to implement USAID's Terms of Reference (TOR) in the particular country or set of countries. Private firms earn profits performing development work for USAID and other donors but their primary purpose is to make profits for owner groups and they are therefore taxable. Governments earn surpluses (as in budget surpluses or deficits) while NGOs and private firms earn profits. NGOs (e.g. foundations, charitable organizations, associations, social welfare and religious organizations) earn profits and use them for the benefit of aid clients. NGOs need to earn profits to provide and expand services to clients (Finkler, 2010: 19). But since that is the primary purpose, they are not liable for corporate

income taxation. Thus, free space provided in an NGO-operated clinic for private doctors would likely be a taxable activity. There are roughly 2500 NGOs in OECD countries; 250,000 in developing and transitional countries. Private international development firms, such as Development Alternatives, Incorporated (DAI) and Chemonics International, operate in the field just like NGOs but are taxable in their home country. Both DAI and Chemonics, for example, are U.S. firms based in Bethesda, Maryland and Washington, D.C. respectively.

(3) *Grants to Strengthen NGOs.* USAID may provide grants to non-governmental organizations that are, like their government counterparts, usually already engaged in service provision in areas where USAID wants to assist, and they often have unique abilities that complement public programs. Therefore, USAID technical office staff might set aside a budget and, with the help of the mission's contracting office, publish a solicitation for applications from NGOs for financial assistance to their programs. One or several grants could be made to select NGOs by the contracting office's "Agreement Officer". Similar to the case of a contract, a USAID technical office staff member would be assigned as the Agreement Officer's Representative to monitor progress in the NGOs' implementation and to arrange for external evaluations. USAID grants require recipient NGOs to contract for external audits.

As some local NGOs may be small and young organizations with no prior experience in receiving awards from USAID, the USAID mission's financial management office conducts a careful review of grant applicants' administrative systems to ensure that they are capable of managing USG funds. Where necessary, USAID can devote part of the grant to the NGO's internal organizational strengthening to help the NGO qualify for USAID's financing and build the capacity of the organization in the process. Thus, USAID provides grants to strengthen an NGO so that it can deliver services needed by USAID. International NGOs have their own development projects and capabilities. If USAID and its counterparts determine that development objectives can best be met by supporting an NGO project, the relevant USAID technical office will draft a program description and the contracting office will issue a request for applications to solicit responses from the international NGO community. The process is used if grants to local NGOs would not be able to achieve the USAID Mission's objectives or if local NGO capacity is not yet sufficient. Disbursement of the portion of USAID's grant financing the NGO's project would follow completion of the NGO's internal organizational development.

(4) *Grants from Unsolicited NGO Proposals to International NGOs.* NGOs frequently make unsolicited proposals to USAID, requesting funding for their own planned assistance activities. Where NGOs or business enterprises are dedicating a substantial amount of non-USG

resources to their projects, they can receive USAID funding through "Global Development Alliance" grants, provided that the non-USG resources are at least equal in value to USAID's grant. In general, USAID provides financial assistance (grants) to support other organizations' programs when those programs correspond to the areas that USAID wants to support, while USAID uses contracts to procure products or services requested by the leaders of local development projects.

The Rationale for Overseas Aid

The economic rationale for aid to poor countries has long been the provision of capital or funds to treasuries unable to finance their own programs and projects. Perennial political economy critiques of aid have come from the left and right and are well known. The left argues that aid creates imperialist dependency and constrains governments from otherwise appropriate development choices. The historically archaic quality of the radical leftist critique of aid is revealed in its presumption of host country state capacity to plan and execute development programs and projects (Wood, 1980: 5). To imagine that the commonly entrenched and bloated bureaucracies of the Third World are pent-up sources of human energy awaiting release is simply contrary to experience (Guess, 1987: 67). Despite the many aid project follies that can be cited, the real problem in most poorer countries beset by ethnic and populist nationalism is precisely how to create effective states—through overseas aid or mobilization of domestic political will. The rightist critique has consistently argued that aid creates and maintains corrupt regimes and deep supporting cultures. It recommends aid cutoffs altogether or at least substantial decreases in ODA in order to let private investment and trade pick up the slack. As an alternative, the right has also pushed for the replacement of ODA to governments to aid for NGOs or non-state actors or institutional gimmicks to move around USAID, such as the Millennium Challenge Account (MCA), which disburses aid to democratic trajectory countries.

Worldwide cuts to ODA have pushed trade and investment by default to replace aid and the results have been encouraging. But weak states still constrain trade and investment from achieving hoped-for results. Politicized state corruption controls, and weak rules of law for contracts, bankruptcy, civil rights, and commercial transactions all impede private investment effectiveness. The private sector is relatively powerless to change much of this except in countries with accountable and responsive states and a spate of professional candidates for office. The different critical perspectives of aid have been summarized in Guess (1987) and remain largely unchanged up to the present day, except for the argument that ODA design and allocation is over-centralized. This suggests that a structural change in aid allocation could improve its effectiveness. The arguments are that centralized aid works against aid results in that it diminishes local stakes in local outcomes, and prevents more nuanced local aid targeting that could provide better results. Decentralized aid could also be modified or reprogrammed more quickly and flexibly than at present through large aid bureaucracies such as USAID and World Bank. Thus, country PFM systems should be strengthened to administer overseas aid which would be regularly assessed for fiduciary risks.

The rationale for aid devolution is based on the tested premise of learning by doing. Capacity is not built by supply of skills that are often unused. Rather, skills are learned by creating an immediate demand for them which is what administration of overseas aid would do for country officials. Thus, the argument for aid PFM devolution is twofold. First, it can provide host countries with a larger stake in the outcomes of aid allocations. Not infrequently, aid projects are designed, financed, and managed by donor country institutions, firms, NGOs, and consultants. The local stake is then minimal which provides disincentives for local commitment to manage the projects for results or to support the projects after the donor aid is discontinued. This creates the twofold problem of (a) a lack of control over fund disbursement and (b) failure to achieve stated purposes of the grant program—the services are not delivered. In the field this translates into: schools without teachers; hospitals without staff or medicine; and public transit systems that are not maintained for effective operations. Devolution seeks to engage country officials and civil society organizations in the process, building stakes that will improve results. Second, devolved aid can be adapted more readily to local needs and allows more flexibility to make course corrections where necessary to achieve project aid objectives. Some have written on decentralization of aid financing, such as Hirschman (1971: 216) and more recently by USAID (2014) itself. But there is not much empirical literature testing the results of centralized vs. decentralized aid management.

In order to devolve aid, donors need to know the risk of financial loss and potential misallocation of resources. In order to provide this information, aid donors use frameworks and methods to assess country- and sector-level fiduciary risks relating to public financial management. Because they synthesize these many sources into comprehensible scores and indices, the best-known PFM fiduciary risk assessments are Public Expenditure and Financial Accountability (PEFA) Assessments (www. pefa.org) and Country Public Institutional Assessments (CPIAs) (www. worldbank.org). PEFA is one of three elements in PFM reform agreed by development partners in the OECD-DAC group. It focuses on technical PFM but not allocative efficiency, poverty-reduction or performance of the economy (Guess and Ma, 2015). Donors rely on public financial management system risk assessments in order to decrease the risks of loss and to maximize returns for their aid allocations. More recently, OECD countries formalized the intent to devolve aid in the 2005 Paris Declaration on Aid Effectiveness (OECD, 2005) and the OECD-inspired 2008 Accra

Action Agenda (which builds on the Paris Declaration). Those agreements committed members to (1) use country systems better and (2) harmonize their risks and procedures with other donors. They were to do both of these without attracting unacceptable levels of additional risk. To assess fiduciary risks, in the last decades donors have intensified the use of PFM evaluation tools such as PEFA and USAID's PFM risk assessment framework or RAF (Guess and Husted, 2011).

At the operational level, to strengthen country PFM systems and devolve aid, Allan makes a strong case for integrating all project aid (ODA bilateral and multilateral) with country systems (William Allan in Allen *et al.*, 2013: 540). While he focuses on which systems, why, and how they might be integrated, the overall objective would be to provide information on how all aid affects particular countries. This is a major weakness of aid country programming that is performed on a donor by donor basis. Allan notes that the current status of parallel in-country aid planning, budgeting, and transaction processing systems is costly and often impedes PFM reform. Learning opportunities for fiscal reporting and financial control over multiple projects from multiple donors are lost to countries that suffer from the very PFM weakness that the aid should be trying to strengthen. External and uncoordinated accountability to multiple donors (with country "aid management units" or AMUs trying to satisfy individual donor approval and reporting requirements) takes precedence over "dual accountability" systems that, in his view, could provide incentives to country PFM institutions. Such incentives could result in less competition among donors for PFM projects, help with coordination where there is overlap, and reduce the tendency of countries to substitute aid funds for their own budgetary commitment to PFM reform. More importantly, increasing the proportion of aid on budget (for both recurrent and capital investment funds) and using country systems would strengthen country transaction processing and improve fiscal and financial control.

Like others (e.g. USAID, 2014), Allan believes that increasing the amount of aid run through country accounting and reporting systems should be a primary emphasis in donor lending (Allan, 2013: 548). He notes that foreign financing and domestic financing are separated and disconnected from country accounting and treasury systems (2013: 546). This leads to perpetuation of PFM institutional weakness. AMUs, for instance, could record third-party contractor payment transactions from donor accounts as part of local fiscal accounts. But they don't. AMUs typically fail to set up ancillary accounting systems integrated with country systems and merely report (with delays) statistics, disbursements, and debt service from donor reports. Line ministries in many countries have few reporting obligations to AMUs that would enable them to reconcile PIU and donor records. By contrast, countries such as Colombia and Bolivia have obliged donors to process aid transactions, including investment loans through their GFMISs (2013: 548).

Currently, the three types of USAID allocation mechanisms are:

1. *Host Country Managed Mechanisms*: these are used where the host country has the capacity to manage the activity and take fiscal transparency and anti-corruption efforts seriously (e.g. Fixed Amount Reimbursements or FARs and Implementation Letters or ILs).
2. *USAID-Managed Mechanisms*: these are used where substantial USAID involvement is required (e.g. cooperative agreements) but where local capacity is weak; contractors are responsive to USAID objectives; and USAID lacks a major local presence (e.g. Grants and Cooperative Agreements often through project implementing units or PIUs in country). These include general budget support (GBS) that often includes policy targets.
3. *Third Party Managed Mechanisms*: used where other donor or public international organizations have capability and are willing to manage pooled funds.

Each of these mechanisms has strengths and weaknesses as well as particular conditions under which they should be used. Multilateral and bilateral donors may use a blend of these mechanisms and still be consistent with the Paris Accords. For example, DFID (UK) often allocates funds to sectors via sector-wide support (SWAP agreements) using both sectoral support through national treasuries and basket or pooled funding.

Some rough measures of the comparative degree of aid devolution are:

(1) Percentage of aid for country using national PFM systems (US 15 percent; UK 53 percent; World Bank 36 percent; Norway 56 percent). Norway as noted also spends the highest OECD amount on ODA as a percentage of its GDP (1.1 percent).
(2) Percentage of aid disbursed for government sector (US 30 percent; UK 45 percent; WB (62 percent); Norway 57 percent).
(3) Percentage of aid for procurement using country procurement systems (US 11 percent; UK 51 percent; WB 30 percent; Norway 66 percent).

What these figures suggest is that, despite USAID developing a framework for "aid localization" (Tarnoff, 2015: 43) and conducting PFMRAF reviews in multiple countries, most of U.S. ODA is still donor-managed and controlled. About 96 percent of USAID funding (ODA or official development assistance) is provided through direct budget support and grants (such as IQCs and task orders of the second type of mechanism above). These mechanisms devolve very little of PFM management to local authorities. To increase local stakes in aid and to provide more targeted aid that can be more flexibly modified to meet changing needs, the intent is to increase USAID ODA allocations to 50 percent by other mechanisms such as FARs and ILs (type one mechanism above) (Guess and Husted, 2011: 10).

Notes

1 Identifying the "faulty economics" underlying policies may not be so simple. For example, Recep Erdogan warned the Turkish central bank not to raise interest rates (to 12.75 percent) because of his theory that higher interest rates cause inflation. This flies in the face of standard monetary theory that official rates need to be raised to control price and cost inflation that sap incomes. His belief is based in part on playing to his nationalist political base (defending against the international interest rate lobby of financiers and bankers and powers that want to drive up rates, damage the Turkish economy, and rid the country of his authoritarian regime) and partially on an economic theory (the structuralist school in the Latin American 1960s to 1970s argued that raising borrowing costs for local firms added to the bottlenecks that drove up prices, prevented firms from receiving needed credit and thereby prevented local production). The theory suggested meant monopoly structures in the banking and financial sectors prevented access to the credit needed to increase production resulting in higher local prices (Champion, 2017: 39). The Structuralist insight was that monopoly structures (but local not necessarily international as they argued) needed to be eliminated and regulated in order to stimulate competition. That has happened in Latin American countries but not Turkey. The more retrograde insight was that regimes should push for economic autarky with less reliance on international capital and goods. That would be a hard sell for an indebted country like Turkey that needs access to credit itself based on creditworthiness and at borrowing costs partially determined by the ratings of international credit agencies.

2 The USAID Bureau of Policy Planning and Learning submits annual evaluation reports to Congress on aid performance results compiled from implementing contractors in the field and from "scoping trips" using external academics for greater objectivity and rigor (USAID, 2013).

3 The original *Greenbook* report to Congress known for over 50 years as *U.S. Overseas Loans and Grants: Obligations and Loan Authorizations* was superseded in 2012 and renamed the *Foreign Assistance Dashboard*. It now covers 21 USG agencies with an aid portfolio including USAID. While the aim is to make reporting on foreign assistance more transparent, the data templates are all budgetary inputs for projects/programs and only plans in the future to "make performance metrics and documents available" (USOMB, 2012: 7).

4 *Border* is a stylish, energetic and unique work of poignant insights from travels and interviews with the people in the Southeast Balkan border regions. Other quality works like this include: *Danubia: A Personal History of the Hapsburg Empire* by Simon Winder (New York: Picador, 2015). But of course these are works by professional authors and not aid workers! My own: *Foreign Aid Safari: Journeys in International Development* (London: Athena Press, 2005) was a collection of formative personal aid experiences. They mostly revealed the author's inexperience, surprises, ironies, and mistakes committed in facing new cultural practices in several regions of the world.

5 www.eda.admin.ch/deza/en/home/activities-projects/figures-statistics.html
6 George M. Guess (1987) *The Politics of United States Foreign Aid* (New York: St. Martin's Press), p. 1, (republished by Routledge Development Library edition, Vol. 7, 2011).
7 George M. Guess and Dennis DeSantis (2016) *Managing Development Projects in High Risk Environments: The Case of Pakistan.*

8 Aid as Stimulus for Democracy and Governmental Effectiveness

Introduction

Much has been written on overseas democracy-building via aid, a lot of which is quite critical. Nevertheless, a strong political economy case can be made that aid, particularly U.S. aid, has strengthened the foundational elements of open societies and markets, of political democracies, and market economies. For example, many projects over the past several decades have clearly strengthened election systems, civil society organizations such as media and charities, labor unions and political parties, local governments, and public sector budgeting, accounting and auditing and taxation systems for greater accountability and financial capacity. But have fully functioning democracies, such as Costa Rica or Taiwan ever been created through aid? The short answer is no. Nevertheless, following are some intriguing and still debatable examples.

South Korea

Asian countries perform at widely different levels, such as South Korea and Singapore vs. Myanmar and North Korea. But their almost uniformly strong states have been noted as a common feature which has led to growth and development or political and economic disaster. On the positive front, South Korea since the war in 1950 has often been credited with aid-driven economic and political success. South Korea like other regional countries has strong institutions but used this to become an authoritarian state with a relatively weak judicial system allowing rulers to skirt the law when it fit them (Fukuyama, 2014: 291). The "Third Wave" of democracy began in South Korea in the 1970s (2014: 400). This included the spread of formal democratic processes and procedures, such as local participatory budgeting (from Brazil), horizontal (inter-branch) and vertical (federation) checks and balances, and free-fair elections (2014: 521). To enforce them required determined political will directing strong institutions. Many Asian countries such as Korea and Taiwan have both. But in the 1970s, Korea was still emerging from the aftermath of the 1950s war. Strongman Syngman Rhee used U.S. aid to finance his patronage system in order to stay in power. Rhee's successor, Park Chung Hee centralized planning, budgeting, and oversight in a central state bureaucracy which reported directly to him. He also centralized economic policymaking, cultivating an alliance between big business and the military to consolidate his power. He nationalized banks and approved state credit to the family owned conglomerates or "chaebols" that became the main growth mechanism (Corning, 2011: 3). The chaebols borrowed to finance heavy industrialization and growth but also added significantly to national public debt.

Dating from postwar to the present, South Korea had been a large recipient of ODA from the U.S., Japan and the E.U. The U.S. aid flowed in between the 1950s and the early 1970s and was then matched by other donors in amounts (Marx and Soares, 2013: figure 1). It was a good aid recipient and managed the ODA inflows well for social and economic development. It is one of the few countries that received ODA which later was to become a significant ODA donor itself. But the main Korean drivers were macroeconomic stabilization and trade policies leading to the growth that facilitated political and economic opening. The economic aid for military and geopolitical reasons preceded the wider ODA, which facilitated social and political development efforts.

But macroeconomic problems surfaced, requiring financing which Korea did not have. Specifically, the first IMF rescue program for Korea followed the 1979 oil crisis and failure of rice crops. The resultant austerity package required more borrowing to finance budget cuts. Pressure grew in the late 1980s for both economic liberalization (opening the financial sector to investment) and political opening (the first election was 1997) (Corning, 2011: 4). A second IMF austerity package in 1997 in the wake of the Asian meltdown focused on cutting more budget expenditures, raising taxes and interest rates, ending excessive state borrowing and weakening the monopoly status of chaebol in the economy. But the badly designed and ill-targeted IMF program resulted in Korean currency devaluation (decreasing reserves further as the state tried to maintain its value), banking system paralysis, scarcity of dollars and refusals to honor letters of credit needed for trade financing (Corning, 2011: 6), a further drop in exports, increases in the current account deficit, higher interest rates and reduced economic growth. By 1999, macroeconomic stability had increased, growth resumed, unemployment dropped (10 percent to 2 percent), reserves increased and the won regained value (Corning, 2011: 9).

The second IMF program is another example of aid that can actually worsen state integrity and policy effectiveness. For, the IMF program of multi-pronged structural reform decreased economic growth, caused panic, and led to fierce political backlash. In short, the IMF program targeted the wrong problem: monopoly structures and the public finances as opposed to weak loan origination from state banks and opaque business–government financial and political relations. Austerity was less-needed than focused and scaled financial sector reform targeted to the outcome of more creditworthy lending. As evidence, the IMF backed off on conditions attached to its $57b loan package in 1998 (Corning, 2011: 11). Nevertheless, defenders of the IMF program argued that the short-term austerity shock produced results. The IMF could use this approach in regions such as Asia and Eastern Europe (e.g. Poland) given the tradition of reticent suffering from both fear of further failures and growing confidence in mainstream economic policies to improve conditions. The "shock" approach works less well in Latin America, with its short cultural fuse and long tradition of hitting the streets against the IMF (e.g. Ecuador in the 1980s to 1990s) and cultural practice of both rapid and violent social mobilization against regimes in current distaste.

Since the U.S. aid in South Korea in particular was not specifically targeted to democracy, a major result of early aid was to shore up the dictatorial regime of Syngman Rhee, whose policies contributed to neither economic nor political liberalization. Later U.S. allocations of ODA did lead to economic and political opening and to its graduation to donor status. Moreover, it could be argued that it was the failure of domestic bureaucratic authoritarian economic policies that led to both domestic and international pressures for opening the financial sector and beginning the process of political liberalization with elections in 1997. In short, ODA financed what was already an ongoing transformation of the political system. It could be said in this Asian case that earlier focus of all aid (military and U.S. DA) should have included a component for democracy and improved governance.

Taiwan

Taiwan was discussed earlier as a case of locally driven quasi-federation democracy. The role of U.S. aid in its growth and development has been essential. In the 15-year period in which the bulk of U.S. aid was provided (1951–1965), the assistance was greater than $1b and amounted to 43 percent of investment and 90 percent of the flow of external capital and donations to Taiwan (Chang, 1965). The aid consisted of two kinds: "primitive aid" (initially grants of labor, equipment, technology, and materials) to particular sectors: transport, agriculture, infrastructure, industry, human resources, and "derivative" aid. Aid to the agricultural sector supported the Sino-American Joint Commission on Rural Reconstruction (JCRR) land reform program which was modeled on the Marshall Plan of providing individual land tenure security, sufficient credit, widespread technical assistance and extension, agro-industrial processing technologies, and marketing strategies. "Derivative" aid augmented and multiplied the effect of primitive aid by depositing funds in Tai currency from sales of U.S. aid goods into a fund at the Central Bank, which the Government of Taiwan allocated to its core priorities (similar to the mechanism used by the U.S. Food for Peace program in its target countries). From 1957 on, U.S. aid consisted of low-interest, long-maturity loans. The aid premise was to stimulate industrialization and growth via large inputs of capital and technology for economic liberalization that would then support political liberalization. The aid was considered essential to Taiwanese economic and later political "take-off". Given the careful use of U.S. aid by the Taiwanese government, it has been called the "most successful example among LDCs of applying U.S. aid (Zhang, 1994).

The case of Taiwan is significant for aid planning and development in other countries (at least in Asia) for several reasons. First, the aid was not directly targeted to creation of democracy and better governance. Rather, it focused on supplying sectors with civil necessities and raw materials. The aid consisted of material, capital equipment and advice on its use for growth and development. Final decisions on micro allocations were largely left up to the Government of Taiwan. Second, Taiwan had the advantage of an existing strong state in the Asian tradition, that is, a legitimate one did not need to be built from scratch. This state could be relied on to allocate the aid properly for local needs and it did. Third, the economic and development aid was linked to geopolitical security considerations with mainland China that still exist today. The core objective was economic growth and development in a market economy with strong guidance from the state. This was achieved. In 2016, it ranked very high in human development (0.882); governmental effectiveness (88.0); and per capita GDP ($22,561). The U.S. contributed targeted aid for economic development and only later nudged the system toward elections, rule of law and widespread participation to ensure accountability.[1] As indicated, the thrust for democracy came from the sub-national levels of government. Successful local reforms were scaled up to the national level. Unlike SSA and MENA countries, in Taiwan and Asia generally, there was no legitimacy vacuum waiting to be filled by sects, tribes, and ethnicities that could generate instability and threats to political regimes.

Costa Rica

This is an example of decentralized democratic development that demonstrates that humans are agents who can control their destinies even as material conditions shape their choices (Fukuyama, 2014: 270). The very name Costa "Rica" was always a joke in that it had no natural resources and whose main population was in the mountains cut off from the rest of Central America. It was quite poor. Through a series of "happy historical accidents" it escaped the Latin American "birth defect" and began with a "clean slate" (2014: 271). The population was relatively homogeneous, consisting of original Spanish colonialists, many of whom stayed on there with their families. Farming was mainly in small plots rather than the regional pattern of large plantations which produced class and ethnic differences (e.g. oligarchies in Argentina, Peru, and Mexico). There were coffee and banana grower oligarchies in Costa Rica that had controlled politics through the nineteenth century (Skidmore and Smith, 2004). But the geographic isolation and common agro-cultural feature produced a people that are noticeably more practical or transactional, perspicacious, and diplomatic than their neighbors. Whether Socialist, Communist, or centrist, most leaders were far more enlightened and moderate than the standard Latin American mold at the time.

Events involving a group of liberal leaders led by Jose Figueres in 1948 changed the course of its political and economic history. A leftist coup led by Rafael Angel Calderon attempted to depose the winner of the election Otilio Ulate Blanco, and stay in power (Booth, 1998). Following a brief civil war led by Figueres in the "revolution of 1948", he became president of a "junta" for one year (1948–1949) and then handed power back to the legitimate winner Ulate. At the end of Ulate's term, he was voted in as constitutional president for the term 1953–1958. The institutional pattern was set for legitimate elections and power contestability between the liberals, conservatives, and far leftist parties that still persists today. Even nineteenth-century dictators such as Tomas Guardia were more enlightened in their focus on education and efforts to control oligarchic influences over regime policy (Fukuyama, 2014: 274).

Several initiatives by Jose Figueres and successor presidents began a qualitative reset of Costa Rican institutions and policies to give it a different development path than other Latin American countries. For example, he set the stage for the abolition of the army (1949); the establishment of an independent election management body (TSE); mandated budget shares for health and education; and extended the vote to women. Costa Rican policies such as rural teaching requirements for educational fellows and "barefoot doctors" which must serve in rural clinics for several years as part of their resident training were copied later by such politically different countries as authoritarian Cuba. The values and practices of 70 years of democratic development have been baked into the political culture, reinforcing future choices that strengthen state institutions.

The results are evident: very high quality of life (0.773), high per capita income ($9714), and high governmental effectiveness (67 percent). High spending on social services and safety nets has produced higher budget deficits (-5.2 percent) and despite ample agricultural and commercial diversification efforts for many years, higher unemployment (9.7 percent). Structural reform to make the state more effective here is not required. Costa Rica is a unitary system which works well to cover a small geographic area with services to municipalities with deconcentrated powers from the central government. A federation would likely add the costs of operating multiple levels of government to the budget, diminishing the available funds for mandated social programs, infrastructure, and pensions. Federation is an optimal solution for complex, larger countries with significant regional, ethnic, or sectarian demands. This is not the context here. Nor has overseas aid been an important factor. U.S. aid (DA) has assisted farmers and social services for many decades. But even indirectly, as in Taiwan above, in no sense did this aid "cause" the democratic developments in Costa Rica. The aid programs reinforced institutional and cultural values and practices that had been set in place by leaders and regimes long before the first project.

Thailand

Development aid also can have little effect on effective government and stability where the regime is tightly controlled by a king or absolute monarch backed by the army and an anti-democratic middle class. Such is the case of Thailand that has all the traditional ingredients of effective governance: middle class, strong Asian state, strong commercial banking system, and thriving tourism. Policy is made and enforced by the army to prevent more coups and instability. Lending support for the China model of authoritarian development superiority to democracy, Thailand's HDI and governmental effectiveness ratings are very high and roughly the same as those of Costa Rica: 0.74 and 0.67 respectively. It is not a functioning democracy nor has ODA had much effect either on stimulating or retarding that result.

Venezuela

Venezuela, as discussed earlier in Chapter 6, backpedaled from being a wealthier democratic society to the authoritarian chaos at present over several decades of turmoil and instability. Venezuela developed on commodity exports (oil) and became the model of a successful Latin American federation. But the institutional underpinnings were weak, allowing partisan pressures driven by populist nationalism to gain control of the regime. Costa Rica's tradition of moderation and resource-poor development from good policy choices to maximize its own agriculture, forestry and hydro-electric resources provided the needed foundational balance for its political culture to bake in these values and practices and for the political system to persist. None of this happened in Venezuela. DA had nothing to do with the rise or fall of Venezuela; nor as we have seen did it have any major contributing role in the political and state development of Costa Rica.

In short, ODA has been unable to create functioning democracies. It has created democratic sub-systems and strengthened elements of civil societies that laid the foundations for future evolution to democratic states. A severe institutional constraint, as indicated, is that many poorer country states consist of ethnic and sectarian controlled ministries which virtually assure allocational inefficiencies and persistent policy mistakes. With institutions hollowed out by patronage appointments, the state and most societal transactions are corrupted. Pliant regime members benefit from all this; they proudly support such states to further their own narrowly focused operational systems. The only way out of such vicious cycles is for ODA to cultivate reformist members of future regimes that can and will purge the state of contaminating elements and reform its core systems to prevent corruption. In most cases, that is a long shot.

Military Aid and Democracy

A discussion of aid effects on country governance and prospects for democracy should include all aid, civilian and military. Military aid is designed like civilian aid with conditions attached for needed reforms to meet donor norms. Such norms usually reflect standard industry or international best practices. What then of conditional military aid? The U.S. gained experience in the aftermath of WWII with joint military (Civil Affairs) and civilian (Marshall Plan) aid to Europe in order to reconstruct governmental institutions and to replace destroyed infrastructure. This experience carried over to the provision of economic aid to Taiwan emphasizing the capital investment and equipment needed to rebuild the country. Both examples built on traditions of strong states, which allowed the U.S. planners to provide assistance which host countries allocated efficiently and effectively. Rebuilding wealthier-country institutions and states is an easier task than building effective states from scratch. The latter task requires nuanced knowledge of local cultural and social values and the practices of local political actors. Aid planners are perennially accused of "not knowing how" under these conditions. Civil Affairs units after WWII in Europe and in Taiwan were nevertheless able to rebuild strong states and to stimulate economic regrowth quite well. This likely led to overconfidence by the aid community in its ability to achieve economic growth and political liberalism in entirely different contexts.

As an example of the uses and misuses of U.S. military aid, U.S. Marines intervened in the Dominican Republic both in 1916 and in 1965 in an attempt to quell conflicts from violent political coups, fraudulent elections, and armed conflict between rebel groups, some of whom were pro-government. By 1965, the U.S. had a lengthy record of Latin and Central American military interventions to quell civil unrest, e.g. Guatemala in 1954. The U.S. support of what was termed Operation Cleanup (*limpieza*) in the Dominican Republic (1965) was designed to restore order, hold elections and to withdraw (Herring, 1972: 455). Such strategic policy interventions ignored the need to build a strong, legitimate local state that could govern inclusively and respond to regional and ethnic needs without countries returning to civil war. Such civilian aid elements were not considered as part of these foreign policy-driven military aid programs in any country. A result of this state-building oversight and failure in the Dominican Republic after the intervention in 1916 sanctioned by President Wilson was the thirty year brutal dictatorship of Rafael Trujillo (*El Jefe*) from 1930–1961.[2] In 1965, the Marines returned again. Thus, military policy was designed to produce quick returns and support a strong leader that could hold the country together without direct and lengthy U.S. involvement. That simplistic strategy did not work and led to years of policy failure in Latin America and more recently in MENA and SSA countries.

By the late 1970s, U.S. policymakers began learning the value of building on existing institutions (even the military) and making marginal interventions by civilian authorities to host country counterparts in order to support elections, civil society, and sectoral programs in agriculture, health, and education. That approach worked better and Latin America has developed and turned democratic without any overt U.S. support in most countries. The positive lessons learned from years of failure, however, seemed to have been forgotten in more recent U.S. efforts to use military aid (Security Assistance or SA) to stabilize particularly poorer MENA states in wars generated and sustained by religious and ethnic nationalism. Even under the best of conditions, the main lesson is that military aid in training and equipment to host country military partners alone does not produce democracy or effective governance.

The recent cases of Iraq, Afghanistan, and Yemen reveal many of the constraints on using hard power to achieve the soft ends of strong, legitimate, and effective states. It also reveals the difficulty of building from outside assistance a core state function: provision of security for its citizens. If the host state is to be effective, the design and implementation of the assistance provided to it must also be effective. To avoid direct involvement in overseas conflicts by committing politically toxic ground troops, the premise of SA is to create autonomous partners who "act like the U.S. military" (Reynolds, 2017). As expected, SA is how the U.S. provides security in war-torn places with failed or fragile states. SA is the main tool to deal with the devastating effects of populist and religious ethno-nationalism on states and their citizens. Like DA, SA requires strong partners who trust each other. Since 2000, for example, the U.S. provided \$274b in security assistance (SA) to "build partner capacities". But, in 2014, both the Afghan and Iraqi armies withdrew from conflicts and abandoned their U.S.-provided weapons and equipment to the Taliban and ISIS respectively. How did this happen with SA? Pentagon-commissioned studies from RAND and independently by CRS and GAO concluded that the SA program had not targeted recipients of training effectively. Instead, the program had relied on the standard relationship between DOD and host country military "partners" which is usually short-term and hardware-focused, and, as indicated and in contrast with DA, was not evaluated regularly nor were any results reported to Congress. In fact, according to Reynolds (2017), none of these problems have been dealt with or remedied in any of the SA country recipients.

More importantly, SA overseers often deny that such failures reveal an actionable problem. As the Islamic State seized control of another airbase, the Iraqi army fled and deserted from what one officer described as a "lack of leadership", the then-Director of U.S. Intelligence suggested that predicting the "will to fight" of the Iraqi army is an "imponderable" and that underestimating enemy strength and ally weakness is "always a problem" (*Washington Post*, 2014, 2014a). So far, the United States has spent $25 billion to equip and train the Iraqi army. How could the intelligence community not notice this deterioration in capability for four years? It is clear that soldiers anywhere will only fight and die for professional leaders whom they respect. That includes respect for the state and regime which deployed them. Lack of leadership is actually not an imponderable but an obvious indicator and predictor of military performance. DOD knew that from 2010 to 2014, Prime Minister Nouri al-Maliki was openly replacing professional military leaders with inexperienced cronies and political hacks, for example, by replacing respected Sunni generals with Shia leaders who lacked military experience. This corroded the effectiveness of U.S. military aid to Iraq at all levels. So the question is, why is disbursement of U.S. military aid to Iraq and other countries not conditional on its likely professional management and use by host country leaders? It begs the question of why Congress regularly monitors and receives performance reports from USAID and other independent evaluators on the use of DA but not on the use of military aid (SA).

The MENA events point to two problems noted by both DOD analysts and CRS-GAO: (1) bureaucratic complexity leading to diffuse responsibility for results and (2) lack of cultural rapport. The SA program is formally DOS responsibility which develops frameworks for each country but actually develops them at the discretion of DOD which chooses the program details. DOD executes the training and equipment allocations for DOS. Moreover, the SA responsibilities are diffused over dozens of functional and regional bureaus within both DOD, DOS and between them (Reynolds, 2017). Some of the SA is performed by CIA and Special Forces and is hard to trace for program accountability or budget purposes. Moreover, finding reliable partners in a place such as Iraq is nearly impossible in that most of them have been formed (or reformed) recently and have no track record either as fighters or public servants of the state. As in the case of DA, trainers often "parachute" in and out delivering their terms of reference to trainees who often have questionable professional qualification. But unlike DA programs and projects where corruption scandals are frequently uncovered and project terminations are regularly issued, SA participants (i.e. often contractors) in the processes of recruitment, field performance, and leadership quality are not evaluated by one U.S. institution and acted upon to correct problems. In DA, recruitment of qualified personnel with exceptional staff management and/or technical line past performance is thoroughly reviewed before, during and after contracts are awarded. As revealed by the case study in the Appendix, even with such a fine-tuned process, there are still major DA personnel performance problems at the project level!

That leads to the second SA problem of cultural rapport. Just the basics of whether Afghan and Iraq trainees are literate enough to read weapons training manuals and how differently belligerents might behave if they were sedentary (Shia usually live in villages) instead of ambulatory (which describes Sunni Bedouin tribes) are not viewed by DOD as serious challenges to be confronted before committing SA funds. Reynolds (2017) notes that Oreo Cookies spends large sums to identify the unique factors in each of its disparate markets in order to tailor the product and to make changes in its recipe for maximum sales. It responds to the diversity of local demands. By contrast, SA provides one type of "Oreo cookie" for everyone: training and equipment of partners. DA planners spend lots of time finding staff members that have experience in particular political cultures in order to try and achieve rapport with locals during project execution. SA planners appear to ignore the specific values and practices that, in a combat setting, will affect which rules are made and how they are enforced (or what tactics they will use and how they might use surprising moves to enforce them).

The risks of using the hard SA approach as opposed to either DA or non-unilateral involvement altogether are illustrated elsewhere by the case of Yemen. Here, a weak state and long-standing tribal and sectarian conflict has heaped devastation upon poverty. The seeds of today's fighting go back to the battles of the 1960s in which a civil war in the south and an insurgency against British colonial forces in the north produced two Yemeni states. Leaders in the north turned to the authority of Islamic clerics for legitimacy; those in the more secular south to Marxism, aligning themselves with the USSR. After failures in the 1970s and 1980s to find an acceptable constitution for one country, a civil war in the north erupted among the Shias between the dictator Ali Abdulah Saleh's forces and other Shias disaffected with his rule. The Houthis are a radical offshoot of disaffected Shias. Pro-government Saleh forces fought Houthis between 2004 and 2010, after which the dictator stepped down in 2012 and was replaced by his Vice-President Abo Rabbo Mansour Hadl. To make leadership more complex in this mosaic of betrayal and intrigue, former Yemeni dictator Saleh was murdered by the Houthis in December 2017 for trying to make a deal with the Saudi coalition fighting the Houthis.

In this "period of hope", a federal system and parliament split between northern–southern representatives was proposed. But the growing power of Islah, an Islamist party affiliated with the Egyptian Muslim Brotherhood, produced more resentment. As conflict increased again, the Houthis broke a UN-brokered power-sharing deal and attacked the capital Sana'a. The Houthis gained power but had no plan or competence in providing services to Yemeni—they didn't know how to actually govern (*The Economist*, 2017: 20). This is a problem since Yemen has suffered the biggest cholera outbreak in modern history (from bad water); the harshest famine in the world for decades; and the world's worst humanitarian crisis (21 million of 28 million people displaced and needing help) (2017: 19).

Into this violent mix entered the Saudi Arabians in 2015, regional champions of Sunni to do battle with proxy power and rival Iran in Yemen. This campaign has been a fiasco and has merely added to the ongoing devastation of Yemen. But supported by U.S. (with SA) and British logistics and equipment, the "coalition" provides equipment and training and relies on regional Sunni neighbors such as UAE and the Saudi to fly the planes and drop the bombs. But targets have included the cranes of Sana'a port. The port is needed for humanitarian supplies and fuel for water-pump stations. But replacement cranes from the U.S. have been blocked by Gulf coalition members. Despite U.S. precision-guided munitions and advice on targets, many civilian targets are being hit with large numbers of civilian deaths. That points to a major problem with SA: control of its use and maintaining control of the overall command. The U.S. finds again that it retains ultimate political responsibility despite delegating operational authority to the "partners". This loss of control over both the principal (Saudi Arabia) and other members acting as agents weakens further the use and administration of SA. It is not an effective tool of foreign or military policy and produces far more costs than benefits. The chances of peace from SA and emergence of an effective state in Yemen as elsewhere are very low.

If U.S. SA cannot produce effective states and especially constitutional democracies and if strategic-level DA is a costly distraction in many cases for host countries, why should micro-sectoral DA be able to produce effective states or democracies? Have the micro-projects led to greater governmental effectiveness? Put another way, has DA spending and support for projects focused and scaled to specific outcomes led to wider demands for responsiveness, accountability, and performance? The short answer to these questions is that directly it has not. But indirectly, DA projects and programs have strengthened governmental systems improving governance and enhancing prospects for deeper democratic reforms. Many have failed for the reasons to be discussed below. Nevertheless, micro-sectoral overseas non-humanitarian civilian aid efforts have produced many gains in poorer, weak-state contexts to which effective governments can later be attributed. Support for these kinds of projects is the way forward if aid is to enhance state effectiveness over the medium to long-term.

For example, donors such as: IMF (as part of program conditionality), USAID, World Bank, Asian Development Bank (ADB), Inter-American Development Bank (IDB), and the Swiss Aid Agency provide technical assistance, computerized public financial management (PFM) modules and training to many host countries in the multiple areas of PFM, for example, treasury, procurement, budgeting, and accounting. Stronger PFM systems at central, sub-national and eventually whole of government levels allow policymakers to make better fiscal and economic policy choices which will contribute to macroeconomic stability. Sound macroeconomic policies facilitate budgetary stability which improves governmental delivery of services, programs and capital projects by narrowing the range between planned and actual outlays and physical results. Properly installed and utilized, PFM systems can enhance public spending efficiency. Most important for reducing the threats to governmental effectiveness from macroeconomic instability and regional populist and ethno-nationalist forces, better PFM can improve both AE by focusing spending on the most valued programs and projects, and TE by meeting program objectives at least cost (Hemming, 2013: 20). MTEFs have been the tool of choice for linking budget allocations to multi-year fiscal and economic projections in order to obtain stability, growth, and spending efficiency.

In specific PFM areas, public budgeting systems and process have been a focus as the central incentive mechanism of the political system. They perform an inherently political function by both providing information from which to determine the allocation of resources among competing stakeholder claims and by providing analytic methods to assess the sustainability of available financial means vs. proposed programmatic ends. Improved PFM systems and data cannot ensure that, for instance, costly water subsidies will not be provided to Israeli or Saudi farmers to grow bananas or that prices can be raised enough to reduce water consumption in Jordan before its population suffers from thirst. But, several budget formats besides MTEFs have been introduced in many countries at the central and local levels to clarify the options for such choices and point to preferred recommendations (Guess and Husted, 2017: 43–45). Their effectiveness depends on top-level regime support from prime ministers and mayors. Participatory budgeting, for example, was developed in Porto Alegre, Brazil nearly 30 years ago (1989) as a vehicle to present citizen demands for programs and projects of civic importance. Because it legitimizes the governing regime as well as satisfying citizen needs and even increases incentives to pay taxes, that budgetary method has spread to more than 50 countries, often with ODA support. Older systems such as Performance Budgeting have been used around the world to link spending inputs to actual outputs to gauge spending efficiency for each service. Efforts to link inputs to outcomes to gauge spending effectiveness through such systems as Program Budgeting have been less successful (or formally installed and not used) because of the difficulty of attributing specific public spending to wider outcomes (e.g. health spending and infant mortality) and because legislative political points are scored by district and not by budget program or cost center. By contrast, objects of expenditures in traditional budget formats are discrete and tradable for political allocations. That accounts for their staying power in most governments.

PFM aid focused first on enhancing fiscal databases, since without valid and reliable data, estimates of receipts and outlays are useless for estimating deficits, debts and estimating budget size and composition to deal with external economic problems (e.g. drops in oil and other commodity prices). Thus, aid concentrated on clarifying budget classifications to ensure that few overlaps existed between line-items that would allow burying expenditures and using gimmicks to charge the wrong accounts (e.g. capitalizing operating expenditures to reduce deficits and finance them as capital items with debt). Assistance also concentrated on the larger problem of off-budget expenditures made by many countries to hide outlays for political projects, SOEs and payments to clans, friends and family. Classification and coverage work, such as that carried out by IMF for several years following the transition of the FSU (1989–1994) to international standards for fiscal and monetary policies, is often unnoticed but has been crucial for enforcing fiscal discipline and macroeconomic stability. Such stability still persists in most regions dating from that period and enforced by IMF conditionality or other donors using the enhanced data from prior IMF reforms of country classification and coverage systems.

PFM expertise has also focused on the weaknesses of internal audit and control systems as well as gaps in procurement system controls which lead to fiscal leakage, waste, and serious corruption problems in many countries. Such problems waste funds for social safety nets, socioeconomic sectors and growth. Strengthening them thus indirectly strengthens governance and democracy. As noted from case discussions, particularly in SSA countries, state-building is more than simply adding professionals to formal-legal governmental structures on organization charts. Powerful family clans control many regimes linked to sects and tribes that provide patronage and strangle attempts at the substantive reform of systems and processes that would enhance effectiveness. Such state *clientism* exists in virtually all regions. The chain of command is often not vertical as indicated on charts but diagonal and horizontal, particularly in the Byzantine systems of Asia and Central Asia. In such countries, nuanced and locally well-known parallel structures and chains of command exist. The man (usually) at the top of the pyramid may be powerless to enforce even his own decisions. One approach to power-mapping and understanding resource flows is to use types of political anthropology to sort out the real power networks and attempt to influence them.[3] Long-term field consultants often use these methods quite effectively. But as regimes change, so do networks and influence flows in different patterns. One must then update the informal organization chart to figure out new patronage relations in order to target ODA most effectively.

The second approach is to use simplifying systems. By unifying all outlays and revenue inputs into real time treasury single accounts (TSA) and strengthening core procurement and personnel systems that absorb most treasury funds, unauthorized and unaccounted for (and off-budget) spending can be controlled. Internal control systems in personnel and procurement, for example, are policed regularly for breaches by autonomous internal audit units reporting around ministry superiors to units in the executive (Controllers-General) and parliament (Supreme Audit Institutions). Such audit efforts, checking links between personnel rosters, budgeting, and treasury payments systems often turn up evidence for the "ghost workers" (no-shows whose salary is still collected by that person or someone else) (Stevens, 1994a: 115), that plagues many transitional and developing countries. Better data and real time TSAs also allow improved measurement of fiscal deficits and public debt levels for macroeconomic discipline and sustainability of public finances. PFM assistance has for decades worked to strengthen these sub-systems, including TSAs. Installation and use of such standardized and simplified systems can be achieved more quickly than the anthropological approach. But the simplified systems seek to produce fiscal transparency and thus can be dangerous for practitioners. Through use of these systems and institutions they will now be controlling corruption at its very source. Internal audit units, even in the U.S., are often deliberately weakened to avoid such embarrassment and eventual prosecution.

Internal control and audit systems are also important for capital assistance. DA loans and grants have long been used to provide infrastructure to countries for highways, ports, railways, and water-sewer facilities. A substantial portion of U.S. aid to Taiwan was straightforward infrastructure to spur growth. The funds were allocated efficiently and effectively by the existing strong and competent state. By contrast, most aid recipients lack strong states, leading to fund allocation to high-visibility political projects; leakage of capital budget funds through corruption of bidding processes; misappropriation of funds during construction; and failure to maintain resultant works leading to more wastage of funds and the need for premature replacement of assets. That means that the capital assistance does not produce the expected economic growth and political stability. Compromised bidding processes are perhaps the largest sources of corruption in all countries, both rich and poor.

PFM assistance often attempts to control the direction and use of state capital allocations in order to ensure better plan consistency for purposes of achieving AE. This can take several forms. First, DA can assist mainly by providing better data and analytic information and background advice on its use for budget allocations; it cannot force proper host country state choices. Thus, GFMIS capital budgeting modules are often included in the design of general ledger systems along with a procurement module for this purpose even though core systems only usually include such modules as accounting, budgeting, treasury, debt, and cash management. For evaluation of Financial Management Information System (FMIS) projects, they often report whether the central government actually plans and monitors public investment projects through the new FMIS system and whether public investment programming (PIP) and management capabilities have been improved through use of the FMIS. Such performance results measures are part of the GFMIS aid project design and are included in system implementation contracts (Dener *et al.* 2011: 133). In practice, falsified invoices can weaken any control system and cannot be identified alone by computerized systems; actual auditors must find them (like bank examiners) and that is where the incentive to avoid personal risk constrains all FMISs and control systems. But FMISs can detect unauthorized commitments in cases where available budget funds are lacking. In such cases, the treasury system will automatically refuse payment. Despite these human flaws, aid-funded FMISs are operating in most countries around the world to facilitate fiscal discipline and may be credited with the success of budget control and minimizing deficits in even the poorest countries (Table 2.2). That indirect accomplishment has stabilized more than one regime and facilitated the development of at least the ingredients of democracy, for example, procurement of election administration machines and systems.

Second, to build institutional strength in MOFs and Ministries of Public Works, ODA from multiple donors has focused on installing and ensuring the use of public sector capital budgets (PSCB) for central governments or capital improvements programming systems (CIPSs) used by sub-national governments. The latter have been used for over half a century by U.S. state and local governments to try and avoid uncontrolled debt and uneconomic capital projects. These best practice institutional frameworks should ensure that public assets (defined by useful life + value) be created and maintained sensibly, transparently, and efficiently. The CIP framework, for example, tries to ensure that tools are used by governments to budget, maintain, and affordably finance their capital assets. In the U.S., the CIP consists of (1) the multi-year plan to strengthen and maintain capital stock, and (2) the adopted capital budget for projects and programs. Specifically, there are at least twelve steps in establishing a functioning CIP that DA has for decades been funding and installing around the globe through technical assistance and training (Guess, 2015, chapter 4; Guess and Todor, 2005).

DA has focused on some of the following seven activities to build and strengthen CIPs. First, DA should facilitate in-country discussions in order to identify a lead CIP agency with direct approval authority and control by the prime minister's office or mayor. Large money projects create enormous pressures for workarounds of rules that are costly, inefficient and often unlawful; ideally the lead agency will have authority to integrate the standard MOF and ministry of public works (MOPW) firewalls and associated silos that prevent integrated planning and budgeting in many countries. Second, DA programs should develop capital needs assessments from both technical and user-citizen survey inputs. Often, regulatory solutions or continued rehabilitation at regular intervals is cheaper than building new capital works, especially if annual debt service and addition to overall debt burdens are considered in the calculus. Third, DA should ensure that CIPSs include analyses of both borrower (government) capacity to repay (creditworthiness) and the project effect on this capacity (affordability to pay new levels of debt). The former is measured by standard credit agency and bank creditworthiness analyses; the latter by ratios of debt service to operating revenues and project debt to total debt. Because of the political pressures to approve unneeded projects, such analyses are often not performed in the U.S. and other wealthier countries.

Fourth, as part of ongoing DA efforts to spur fiscal decentralization as a means to democratic development, aid is provided to mainly sub-national governments to develop their own revenue sources. Table 2.1 indicates that such efforts have been successful, in countries such as in Indonesia and Brazil (which did not receive DA for devolution of tax authority). But most poor countries in the SSA region have few revenue sources and little or no discretion over tax rates or bases. Efforts in Latin American and FSU/CEE aid programs have focused on devolving tax authority with more success (e.g. Hungary). Other countries, such as Romania, have used business development districts to assess district beneficiaries and capture property value gains to pay back loans for smaller projects such as street lighting and sidewalks. Countries such as Indonesia have used fiscal transfer receivables as collateral for local capital project matching requirements. Fifth, DA projects should ensure that multi-year plans of projects be derived from objective criteria for both economic feasibility and need as well as for ranking against other projects also supported by stakeholders. DA has provided substantial assistance to develop hard and soft criteria for inclusion in the plan, and ranking, for example, weighting and scoring matrices. These have to be piloted in specific locales and used by them to establish plans that can later be verified or changed if necessary, consistent with changing needs. Sub-national governments in many countries such as Armenia have used the matrices, which combine participatory budgeting and capital planning in one or more citizen-government exercises (ICHD, 2006). In the case of Armenian participatory municipal budgeting, citizen selection of projects and their subsequent gains in quality of life benefits led to the "virtuous cycle" (Levy, 2014) of: higher taxpayer compliance, greater city revenues, and higher public support for and trust in local government political leadership. But, as in many countries with local project and systems successes. it has been harder to scale up this small win to public support for the national government or conversely, the persuade national governments to emulate local successes on a country-wide basis. The scaling up of local reforms in Taiwan to the central government, as noted, has been an important exception.

Sixth, DA has provided assistance in producing final capital budgets from the plan rankings consistent with available revenue derived from revenue forecasts and CIP affordability analyses. This sixth activity is the actual capital plan tied to a hard budget constraint. Seventh, DA has provided assistance on implementing capital budgets. It is here that pressures for unneeded change orders, and payoffs for work unperformed with false invoices, occurs and needs to be identified. To do this, PFM assistance has been common in such areas as purchasing and inventory systems, internal control and audits of bidding systems, and enforcement of procedures to remove completed capital projects from capital budgets and place their O&M on current budgets.

Finally, DA for PFM systems development has focused on fiscal decentralization. Such efforts have been designed to strengthen multiple tiers of government and to build the foundations for decentralized political democracy, and even federation. Often the initiatives come from the host country central governments as in Pakistan, Indonesia, and the Philippines (Guess, 2005a). That is, they were not ideas suggested or mandated by donors. If countries seek assistance in designing and implementing fiscal decentralization programs, aid donors then provide the technical assistance to develop practitioner skills in using systems and enforcing new rules. The importance of fiscal decentralization to state- and democracy-building cannot be overemphasized. Political democracy only works with institutional checks and balances. They need to be vertical between tiers of government as well as horizontal between branches of the central government. The extreme political and fiscal centralization that exists in many transitional and developing countries allows local issues, such as bad transit, sanitation, health, and education services and infrastructure that cause daily suffering to become national issues that are then used by ethnic and nationalist populists to destabilize regimes. These structures make states worse and discredit efforts to build democracy. In war-torn countries such as Kosovo (as in other Balkan countries) where opposing ethnic, religious, historical, and territorial claims degenerate into war, devolution is often seen as a solution by all parties. Kosovo was slightly different than other countries in that, as a formally autonomous member of the Yugoslav federation since 1945, it had a seat on the federal assembly. But by the 1980s, the advancing police state eroded these powers (Ebel and Peteri, 2007: 13). Kosovo was also different in that the governmental response was that it took back local control with parallel institutions that dated back to a long tradition of Kosovar self-management and local governance (2007: 14).

In this area, PFM aid is based on the political economy theory that properly decentralized political structures can provide efficient and responsive levels of services to match need. Drawing from concepts introduced in Oates (1972), Fisher (2007) described the conditions underlying "optimal" governmental decentralization. The "correspondence principle" referred to the condition where public goods and services are appropriately assigned to the lowest level of government where there are no external effects outside that particular level. Macroeconomic stabilization policies, income redistribution, and national defense responsibilities are generally assigned to the highest level of central government because of the nature of the available revenue instruments and/or the possibility for major external effects. Central governments are assigned macroeconomic policies because they require large fiscal and monetary instruments typically not available to subnational governments. Relatively generous income redistribution benefits by subnational governments can encourage the in-migration of lower income individuals into those local areas, and out-migration from the higher-taxed areas with high income residents. Defensive actions by potentially losing jurisdictions could create large externalities spilling over into neighboring districts, which would mean that non-residents of the defended area could benefit from the spending without paying taxes i.e. by 'free-riding'. On the other hand, governmental service responsibilities like police and fire protection, waste management, urban transportation, and education are often assigned to the lowest subnational governments, where the benefits are contained and do not generally spill over to the neighboring governments. The primary benefit associated with the correspondence principle is that the lowest level may employ information to provide amounts of the public good or service that best matches different demands for these goods across a diverse country. Oates's "Decentralization Theorem" was that more efficient "levels of consumption are provided in each jurisdiction than any single, uniform level of consumption maintained across all jurisdictions" (Guess and Husted, 2017: 213).

For aid to put these tested intergovernmental fiscal theories into practice, regimes need to be persuaded to redefine and reassign fiscal roles and responsibilities between tiers of government and to cover financing gaps with transfers and the devolution of additional authority. Fiscal decentralization is designed to reduce two kinds of fiscal imbalance: vertical (because the central government has control of the key revenue sources) and horizontal (differences in spending needs and tax bases between national governments and regions) (Ebel and Peteri, 2007: 122). Fiscal ⸻ for this purpose and aid programs have focused on the ⸻ to maximize revenue generation and spend it to provide ⸻fficient services. In Kosovo, for example, education sector ⸻) are distributed based on a formula that rewards cities for the past year grants. A problem with many governments in many poor countries is that, ironically, they cannot spend funds budgeted because they lack administrative capacity. This is another example of the paradox of wealth amidst institutional poverty (Caiden and Wildavsky, 1974). Kosovar localities that spend full amounts receive the same or additional grants the following year; those that fail to receive less and the funds not distributed go back into the pot or "overall envelope" for distribution the next year (2007: 29). While there are obvious perverse incentives here (to spend the money), there are also incentives to increase administrative efficiency and spend the funds to meet educational program objectives. As noted in the three Asian cases, governments have followed fiscal federalist theory (even if they are not federations) to strengthen sub-national political representation and public finances (Guess, 2005a). At least some of the credit can go to the DA efforts in PFM.

PFM work including fiscal decentralization is funded mainly through the economic growth function while the others are in the named functional sectors. By sectors, in FY 2013 the USAID budget targeted health (36 percent), democracy (13 percent), economic growth (11 percent), agriculture (6 percent), and education (4 percent). Its regional focus is SSA (40 percent), MENA (23.5 percent), and Afghanistan/Pakistan (19.2 percent). USAID's budget is 38 percent of the total *Function 150* for International Affairs, which amounts to about 1.4 percent of total USG budget authority (Tarnoff, 2015: 11). But of the approximately $20b request for USAID, only about $3b or 15 percent was allocated for DA (Tarnoff, 2015: 12). Still, as indicated, small amounts of US government overseas aid can mean large total contributions. The roughly $9.5b provided for health aid in FY 2016 amounted to about 33% of total global spending (of $37.8b) for health aid (Economist, 2018e, p.5).

Despite the fact that the DA contribution to total USAID expenditures is relatively small and that amount is only part of worldwide ODA allocated to countries, aid successes and some setbacks can be identified in particular sectors in different regions and countries. For example, despite extreme ethnic and populist nationalism and destabilizing macroeconomic weaknesses in the SSA, some successes can be noted. One example is in the Rwandan health sector which, along with governmental systems generally, suffered from genocides of the 1990s that decimated the country and destroyed health levels. Since the late 1990s, it has decentralized the financing and management of its health care system. With strong commitment from the central government and support from WHO to make and enforce technical norms and transparency and accountability standards on NGO providers, by 2013 the system reduced TB, HIV and malaria rates by 80 percent and increased life expectancy by 60 percent. Local health care financing earmarked for the sector has been provided by performance-based central transfers that include enforceable norms and performance metrics as incentives for results. Partly as the result of this successful experience, the government has implemented a national health insurance system (*Mutuelles de Sante*) that now covers 80 percent of the population. The result is a replicable model for SSA that can be used to scale up reforms to other sectors and to the central government which has improved its capacity to govern by implementing this program (Aud, 2017).

Next, the 2014 outbreak of Ebola in Liberia, Guinea, Sierra Leone, and Nigeria provided a demonstration of the need for institutional strength and resilience in the face of sudden disaster. All four states lacked universal health care systems and all were faced with a lack of resources. (World Bank, 2004, Chapter 8). For example, shortages in medical personnel were apparent in Liberia, Guinea, Sierra Leone and, to a lesser extent, Nigeria. Each of these countries had thousands of cases that were increasing at an alarming rate, resulting in high rates of death. To combat this outbreak, Liberia had 51 physicians for its entire population of 4.3 million. One result of this health care shortage was that officials in Sierra Leone admitted "defeat" in fighting the progression of the outbreak and urged families to keep the infected people at home. There was also a shortage of basic medical supplies like gloves and gowns. That deficiency meant that the countries experienced Ebola mortality rates two to three times higher than probably would have occurred in more developed countries. The Ebola outbreak is an example of the strain created on the insufficient medical systems found in many underdeveloped countries. Although in large part the result of inadequate sectoral resources diminished by competing budgetary demands, the institutional weaknesses of the delivery systems were not the same in all countries. Some were effective despite a lack of resources. Though the Ebola outbreak started in Guinea, its epidemic destruction was not as acute as in neighboring Liberia and Sierra Leone.

What explains these differences? First, note that the medical infrastructure and access to basic health-related services such as clean water was much higher in Guinea: 83 percent access to water vs. 11 percent in Liberia and 25 percent in Sierra Leone. In addition, the affected countries had received different levels of international assistance from their former colonial overseers: France to Guinea; America to Liberia, and Britain to Sierra Leone. This represented more than financial support in that the funding was linked inextricably to norms, laws, and cultural practices in the health sectors of the respective and more advanced country donors. Finally, weaknesses in state institutions, particularly in Sierra Leone were illustrated by recurring strikes and its inability or unwillingness to: pay health workers hazardous duty pay; prevent bribery to release infected bodies to relatives who wanted a traditional burial (another cultural effect); and control shortages of gloves that ended up on the black market instead of in clinics. Such institutional failures diminished the effectiveness of responses to the Ebola outbreak (*The Economist*, 2014a: 50).

In general, poor countries have made improvements in providing universal health care where states provide (1) clear universal care mandates, and (2) decentralized system designs within overall structures of normative centralization. First, effective poor country health systems have clear government mandates to provide health care to all of its citizens. Ghana is a good example of this. Like other African countries, it had a very high rate of maternal mortality in the early 2000s. In 2004, the state made a critical health policy decision to exempt women from delivery care costs in all health facilities. This effort was initially funded by the World Bank/ IMF debt relief fund initiative, known as the Heavily Indebted Poor Countries (HIPC) Initiative. From health sector success, eventually Ghana scaled up the system to a national health plan that paid for country-wide universal care.

The second explanation for performance differences is that some health care delivery systems have been decentralized and accountable to local populations. Outside of SSA, Cuba is an example of a country with an excellent medical system even though its personal income levels are also low. Its low infant mortality rate ranks at the top end among all developing countries and it also compares favorably with many developed countries. The Cuban health system is characterized by the provision of clear instructions to medical advisors, staff motivation, and, perhaps most important, constant monitoring and evaluations of the system. This has allowed the government to put an emphasis on placing doctors in rural areas (like Costa Rica as noted in Chapter 8), where there had been severe resource deficiencies. The government has established opportunities for public involvement and confidence in the system, by providing health indicators and carrying out routine inspections of health facilities. Although Cuba has not faced a severe outbreak like the Ebola outbreak in West Africa, its tight health care structure makes it better able to sustain such a crisis. Thus, institutions must be properly designed with built-in political and fiscal incentives to deliver health care effectively. The central government role in such crises is to absorb international assistance and ensure that the proper lessons of international practice are being applied (Guess and Husted, 2017: 159).

Another sectoral area of mixed DA results is the agricultural–forestry sector. The U.S. developing country assistance effort began after WWII reconstruction in Europe and Asia with efforts to stimulate growth and development in poor countries, most of which were dependent on primary agricultural products. Subsidy and spending policies were so distorted that many poor countries imported their basic grains for food despite growing rice, corn, and beans. Thus, DA took an early interest in stabilizing food supplies and encouraging agro-industrial production. Some of the oldest development firms implementing USAID projects were originally agricultural operations.[4] Efforts included programs for: small farmer credit, extension, seeds, crop processing and marketing, secondary manufacture of agro-forestry products such as furniture, and specialized exports such as macadamia nuts and tropical hardwood furniture. The aim was to diversify economies away from the mono-crop dependence in which most countries found themselves, reducing risks of being shut out of markets and suffering from the external shocks of lower commodity prices. Projects were eventually quite successful in Latin America and SSA. Earlier projects presumed local ignorance of farming in the face of U.S. technical and experiential superiority. But it soon was revealed that aid advisors were often arrogant and out of touch culturally as well as blind to the local possibilities for agricultural diversity (Paddock and Paddock, 1973).[5] For local political reasons, local regime policies often failed to support project successes with the result that economies remained vulnerable to outside market forces; they did not manage risks by diversifying as any small farmer knew how to do. Some countries in South Asia and SSA have still not diversified despite decades of successful demonstration projects that indicate the benefits of doing so.

Agricultural sector projects also focused on land tenure security for farmers (in order to provide loan collateral) and fiscal incentives to reduce rampant tropical deforestation. From one of the worst deforestation rates in the world in the 1970s, Costa Rica now generates investment funds that are used for forest preservation, tourism and to support social program budgets. Costa Rica and the Philippines, for example, were some of the first countries to use fiscal incentives for small farmer forestry (tax credits and subsidized loans) (Guess, 1991). Bolivia and Costa Rica were some of the first countries to successfully use debt-nature swaps for profit and preservation purposes. The debt-nature model was devised in the 1970s and began in the 1980s. The scheme works on variants of the following steps: an indebted country with tropical forestry resources sells its debt to an international bank (e.g. the World Bank and/or a commercial bank) which resells it at a discount, which leverages cash for the borrower treasury. Implementation of the forest preservation programs is then managed by an NGO.[6] Variants of this model have been successfully used in other poor countries to reduce debt, preserve forests, and generate funds for socio-economic development. Other DA projects included loans to companies to provide small farmer out-grower (supplier) schemes and income–employment opportunities for workers. Latin American countries have diversified significantly: Brazil, Peru, Mexico, and Costa Rica are all standouts.

Remaining failures to take advantage of the knowledge, experience, and benefit of such DA projects often comes down to regime refusal or inability to make the necessary supporting policy and institutional changes. This regime refusal or denial of the benefits of DA for such purposes still remains a large problem that, with only some justification, is often blamed on DA ineffectiveness. In practice, lack of regime support may be nearly impossible to correct with better project design or implementation strategies. Like many who fail to see the DA constraint here, Carothers has argued (2014) that more U.S. policy support is needed to stem the brutality of authoritarian dictatorships and encourage them to develop open political systems rooted in democratic accountability and rule of law. But the notion that more democracy and governance aid programs leads to more democracy is rightly viewed with increasing skepticism by others and especially some USAID officials. One reason may be that program supply does not create country demand (i.e. supply side aid doesn't work).

Carothers also notes that Ukraine did not consolidate rule of law and democracy over the last two decades of aid democracy programs efforts. But the reasons for failure there did not lie in the absence of democracy projects but the failure of the host government to support the many that did exist; nor did the regime allow any political space for civil society organizations to actually grow. As in many countries, there was simply no host country buy-in. This was especially true in the Eastern regions now controlled by Russia. In the Kiev area, where the author worked on local government democracy and health programs, the government was indifferent at best and often hostile by, for example, locking us out of the ministry of finance. As stated, our argument is that more support for U.S. functional aid programs at the operational level is needed to, for instance, build the health infrastructure systems in Liberia, and strengthen public financial management systems in virtually all poor countries to ensure that planned funds for vital services are spent effectively. Of course, regimes can still ignore sectoral project results and ignore the wider benefits from adopting and expanding their practical lessons. But scaled-down projects at least benefit most of their intended users. Larger projects aimed at democracy often result in accumulated promise fatigue from surfeits of virtuous platitudes. As services improve from operational-level aid programs, such as improved health and education, and users demand better service accountability from officials, the ends of democracy and governance programs may then be achieved indirectly (Guess, 2014). The argument then is for a second-best approach to DA to be used for state democracy-building.

Finally, much work at the sectoral aid level has been done in primary–secondary education reform. The provision of primary and secondary education is one of the fundamental governmental functions. Since World War II, educational expenditures have been the fastest-growing area of public spending in OECD countries. Educational importance on national agendas is reflected not just in budgetary outlays. The most important values and interests of a society are represented in education policy (Adolino and Blake, 2011: 321). Defining such basic interests has been a matter of great controversy across the globe. For example, in 2000, representatives from 164 countries met at the World Education Forum in Dakar, Senegal and pledged six education goals to be achieved by 2015, including expanding early childhood education, increasing access to and improving the education for all citizens, particularly for girls and the poor, providing equal access to education, improving literacy by 50 percent, and eliminating education disparities between boys and girls. Two education goals that were to be accomplished by 2015 also appear among the eight UNDP Millennium Development Goals (MDGs).

One was the attainment of universal primary education and the other goal targeted the elimination of gender disparity in all levels of education. A country being receptive to reform depends to some extent on political structure and income levels. In federal systems such as Canada, Australia, and the U.S., systems are more decentralized with delegation for important policy, administrative, and financing decisions to the local level. In unitary systems such as France and Japan, educational decision-making authority is more centralized and most strategic and operational decisions are made at the national level. Nevertheless, in all industrialized countries, the trends have been toward more decentralization of authority to public schools, and various forms of state-supported schools such as charters, that give more authority to local officials (Adolino and Blake, 2011: 322). That trend can be characterized as normative centralization of national and regional standards, and operational decentralization over the methods and tools of learning to local officials.

In the current context of multiple reform options, programs have proliferated across the world between national and local levels. The focus on choice of schools and performance dominates wealthier countries and particular provinces such as the U.S., Alberta (Canada), Chile, the U.K., and Sweden. The Swiss and German approach continues to involve tough centrally set standards; early student performance tracking, with emphasis on teacher pay and quality; and many options for apprenticeships and vocational choice. The Japanese approach is similarly focused on rote learning of facts and emphasis on test performance. But it offers fewer alternatives to those tracked out early. The Anglo-American model differs broadly from this in its effort to provide greater access and repeat opportunities for advancement along more traditional paths. This model focuses on alternative delivery systems, school decentralization, and incentivizing performance with transfers. Within the U.S., cities have experimented with pay for performance (e.g. Dallas and Chicago); school closures for failing performance (e.g. Detroit, NYC, Washington, D.C., Newark, Providence); as well as the expansion of choice approaches through voucher funding, charter schools, and performance transfers based on tougher central standards (e.g. the No Child Left Behind and Race to the Top federal programs). In the U.S. and elsewhere, standoffs with teacher unions have been an important determinant of results. School unions often act as a brake on student results, focusing instead on teacher employment security. This is as true in OECD countries as it is in poorer countries engaged in school reform, for example, Pakistan and Mexico. Often improvement of teacher quality, for example, is impeded by union rules. Teacher quality refers to professional qualifications as well as actual time spent in classrooms. Reformist regimes in such cities as New York, Chicago and Washington, D.C. successfully forced unions to change their rules in favor of teacher pay for performance schemes that exchange more funds for less security. All reforms have been controversial and comparative policy research offers a rich library of best and worst practices for reformers around the world who seek to improve educational performance. Overseas aid designers thus have a substantial body of empirically tested results that can be offered to poorer countries as models for adaption and use.

Educational projects amounted to only about 4 percent of the USAID DA budget for FY 13 which worked out nevertheless to be over a hundred projects in 60 countries. USAID works in 125 countries and has 60 permanent missions (Tarnoff, 2015). These were less "reform" projects than assistance for improving reading skills in crisis and conflict countries. Some 83 percent of funding in FY 13 was targeted to those basic purposes (2015:20). Here again, aid agencies such as USAID can supply well-designed and proven methods and systems but there must be regime demand and buy-in for the projects to be successful and for lessons to benefit the entire sector as well as governmental effectiveness. Often there is not because of instability and chaos or simply from indifference and an expectation that aid agency grants will continue to pay for any improvements.

As in the health sector, education ODA projects are typically solid, well-designed and professionally staffed. Such efforts are made by USAID, World Bank, and ADB projects for example in Myanmar. But all of them have lacked either regime or sectoral ministry (i.e. Ministry of Education) buy-in. As noted in Chapter 2, Myanmar has been ruled by a military junta for decades and is now a "facade democracy" with elections but permanent majority control of parliamentary seats by the army. Populist nationalism has been used for many years by the regime to fight exaggerated "threats" from ethnic and religious minorities. The State Law and Order Restoration Committee (SLORC) did this through the army in the 1990s against Christian and Muslim minorities as well as many of the other 135 ethnic groups. SLORC specialized in finding outrageous political and military security conspiracies against it to justify a state of permanent martial law. Currently, the campaign against the Rohingya Muslims produced 7000 deaths in August 2017 alone. More than 650,000 refugees have fled to Bangladesh.

In such an authoritarian centralized context, it is unsurprising that educational institutions perform poorly. Rote education is an important means of generating quiescent followers for dictatorial regimes everywhere. Aid for Western liberal educational reform under these conditions is low official priority. The centuries-old tradition of monastic education gave Myanmar (Burma) one of the highest literacy rates in Southeast Asia at the time of independence in 1948. In 1962, the army seized power and launched a campaign against foreign influence. In education, schools were nationalized and spending plummeted. It now spends less than 1 percent of GDP on education which is below the 3 percent regional average. The military uses textbooks as tools of indoctrination rather than instruction. Into this context, educational teams and local bureaucrats have attempted liberalization and reform to inject critical thinking and and introduce vocational skills training curricula. But, as in many countries with educational aid projects, the Ministry of Education refuses to listen to outside advice, and reforms have gone nowhere (*The Economist*, 2017g1: 35). Without local demand from regimes, supplies of educational aid can only achieve minimal results.

Realistic Expectations of DA

Even before we examine the planning and operational problems of USAID and DA projects, we noted that the budgetary amounts spent for both are relatively miniscule in terms of both U.S. GDP and the USG budget. USAID receives only 38 percent of total International Affairs #150 account funding, of which only 3 percent is for DA (Tarnoff, 2015: 14). Total U.S. foreign assistance includes: "State Department Diplomacy" and "Other Foreign Aid" or 62 percent of the total. But USAID's more than $3b appropriation is still a lot of funds in nominal terms (given the large size of both U.S. GDPs and budgets) to be allocated for its projects. The $20.6b total in FY 15 meant that the U.S. remained the largest donor of bilateral grant assistance in the world (2015: 14). Of about $134.8b total world ODA, the U.S. provides roughly 14 percent (2015: 2). And, despite being spread around 60 overseas missions in 160 countries, a small amount of funds can and has bought a lot of needs satisfaction, public support, visibility, and trained personnel that can move on to both public and private sector employment and have wider effects on governmental effectiveness.[7] Put in perspective, DA provided by other donors such as DFID is much smaller in amounts and for shorter projects; regional aid donors such as IDB provide sectoral funding for even smaller, intermittently staffed projects that last for very short periods of time, often less than one year. The multiplier effect of such efforts would have to be even smaller than those of USAID. Of course, USAID has been criticized for failure to "scale up" many of its projects. This is largely a problem of host country regime receptivity and support. There has to be a host state partner for all ODA which, among other manifestations, provides counterpart contributions in the form of cash or in-kind support. That demonstrates the host country regime stake in the program or project (at least for the regime governing at the time the grant or loan agreement was signed).

As suggested, DA projects provide TA and training to technical professionals mostly in the executive branches and specific line or spending ministries of host countries. DA has little direct effect on either voters or legislators/policymakers. There have been quite successful USAID projects to strengthen parliamentary budget office analytic capability (e.g. Romania), and to train media personnel in public budgeting and finance in order to enhance their writing on public finance and financial policy (e.g. Bulgaria). But overall, the expected driver of governmental effectiveness is the combined expertise, example, and influence of the enlarged executive cluster. But voters suffer from the effects of poverty and ill-education on their eventual turnout and polling choices. They are often illiterate, that is, easily persuaded by demagogic rhetoric on policy matters as tax and trade. Demagogues in most regions are successfully able to peddle myths focused on beliefs and communal identities via social media that facilitate the suspension of judgments and elimination of doubts. Empirical responses on technical policy matters increasingly fail to translate in such contexts. Nevertheless, DA election projects can benefit officials, voters, and civil society institutions such as the media in improving elections, thereby legitimating governments that are elected. Voter education DA programs are often feared by regimes as threats to their incumbency. For that reason, they often "regulate" to the point of banning such projects in particular countries (e.g. Ukraine and Russia).

Despite the view that elections are often the trigger for democratic development from such analysts as Pastor (2004), electoral institutions, including professional election administration and independent oversight of the balloting and counting processes, should be considered as necessary but not sufficient for the development of political democracies. The weakness of host country electoral institutions even after DA projects is a problem of limited ministry buy-in and for the tendency, where there has been buy-in for officials to change, diminishing support for previous aid-assisted reform efforts. Where DA provides grants for capital works such as schools and hospitals, effectiveness is also limited by refusal or indifference of host country regimes to pay for regular operations and maintenance (O&M) to keep the assets functioning. The political trade-off for regimes is that funding for operations and maintenance often cuts into budgets composed mostly of salaries, benefits (i.e. supporters) and debt service commitments (important in order to obtain more loans for infrastructure asset projects!).

What can DA do about stimulating growth? Growth is often constrained by structural supply-side factors that are persistent rather than cyclical. DA cannot be expected to change deeply ingrained laws or policies; operational DA can only create a knowledge base and some support for those changes over time—it cannot change "structures". DA may be expected to generate economic growth from its projects when this depends on strong states that (a) can control macroeconomic policy and (b) which have the political will to make the necessary structural supply side changes, for example, elimination of laws restricting hiring and firing of personnel. Strategic level results depend on the willingness of governments to solicit and adopt lessons over time from DA advisors. Ukrainian policymaker intransigence illustrates that this often does not happen. Two decades of DA lessons were largely ignored by the central government, mostly in the western part, and adopted only by selected cities. In some cases, minor changes to standard official forms were considered "structural" and required new laws; the GFMIS for instance was and is only a management tool or system yet still requires parliamentary and/or presidential approval for design, bidding and installation in most countries, for example, Jordan and Honduras. In other countries such as Bulgaria, reform of PPB budgeting systems varies by city. DA work with receptive mayors produced dramatic and almost instant results; other cities fail to reform their systems despite TA and capacity-building by the same teams from the same DA project and evidence from neighboring cities that service funds could be saved and results improved. In Nicaragua, frequent change of counterpart personnel at MOF finally led to the derailment of efforts to develop and install a PPBS-type system as a product of the World Bank "Budget Strengthening and Internal Audit" project there in the late 1990s.

But DA, as indicated, has improved PFM systems to facilitate better choices for managing public budgets to ensure fiscal discipline. In this effort, driven by conditional loans to improve fiscal databases and provide substantial training of MOF, treasury, and tax officials, DA has been very successful in all regions. PFM assistance, however, has had minimal effects on the allocational efficiency (AE) of both wealthy and poor countries. Failures to do so have provided openings for traditional populists and ultranationalists in fringe parties and groups that have threatened centrist parties and policy agendas. Further, programmatic intentions to improve AE often run afoul of partisan needs to please local voting constituencies, which may be composed of rival ethnicities, religions, and groups that control sectoral ministries responsible for allocating program funds by budgetary functions that cover geographic areas. DA projects have facilitated electoral democracy and stronger civil societies but the scaling-up effect on governmental effectiveness, translated into quality of life, has often been the missing link in an expected causal chain.

For, as is known, the economic growth on which both political and economic development depend is a function of increased aggregate demand. Without the monetary means to consume and invest, recessions and depressions occur which destroy lives and open the door for political demagogues of all stripes. If consumption is weak, and investment is low, only government remains as the stabilizing force, hence the spate of largely successful fiscal stimulus programs in many countries in response to the global financial crisis of 2008–2010. DA can only provide advice on how to design stimulus policies that may lead to higher demand. It cannot create a consumer class that will actually raise its consumption enough to make a difference to macroeconomic stability. For example, despite being a BRIC country, the average income of about 90 percent of Indians is only that of either the most destitute SSA countries or neighboring Pakistan and Bangladesh. Only 10 percent of the country is about the level of either OECD or Central and Eastern European countries—roughly the middle and upper classes. Ninety-seven percent of all Indians have never been on a plane and 93 percent of all Indians still work in the informal sector in small enterprises (*The Economist*, 2018b: 16). Structural, legal and regulatory reforms are required to improve the educational system and to remove obstacles to firms trying to scale up. Only such efforts in the short term can lead to the development of a middle class in the medium term that could energize growth and development. Such policies depend on the political will of regimes, which has not been there for the sustained periods needed.

Further, even with DA support, a country's public policies can only affect wage levels indirectly (e.g. mandated sectoral and local minimum wage levels), neither can they require industries to invest unless they are SOEs driven by state banking system loans (e.g. China). Nor can greater public spending for stimulus programs and sectoral assistance necessarily mean that the spending is properly targeted for maximum value for money (AE and TE). These are local choices about which overseas aid, other than the conditional program loans of IMF and World Bank, cannot directly control. DA can improve investment climate and bureaucratic professionalism through new PFM systems and methods. Such systems facilitate online approvals for customs and trade transactions that can reduce opportunities for corruption and cut commercial and public sector transaction costs. Country political structures such as federations can magnify the effects of DA by spreading funds to sub-national levels as well as the central government. As noted for India, they can enhance positive sub-national competition for investment by improving institutional systems, such as permit clearances, instead of engaging in the usual negative competition to provide subsidies and favors to firms to spur local investment. The cash surpluses from greater fiscal discipline, applauded by international donors and credit agencies, can then be allocated to appropriate levels and sectors to reach more people in need through a federation, rather than one central government or an authoritarian regime that, by its very structure, facilitates the reward of insiders.

Notes

1 Suppose the nudge doesn't work, momentum stops and "virtuous circles" (Levy, 2014: 50), as were found in Taiwan, go into reverse? Suppose "institutional incrementalism" (2014: 176) doesn't produce results for democracy and development? The effort to produce a "small wins" can become big losses if not monitored carefully and followed with course corrections in response to negative performance information. Russia, for example, was nudged toward democracy by U.S. aid programs after the transition in the 1990s that produced only minimal results and a decidedly illiberal regime that rules today as neo-Stalinist. Reconstruction of Russia to be an open economy was of secondary importance. The entrenched Russian regime of today is driven by populist nationalism and supported by state security forces and irregulars. "Liberals" seeking an open political system work incrementally to win local council elections (symbolic rather than substantive victories, given their lack of authority) by focusing on small-bore issues such as broken apartment elevators and potholes.

So far, they have gained majorities in 17 of Moscow's 125 districts and split 13 more evenly. The Putin regime fears that a "ring of hostile municipalities" around Moscow could turn into "centers of protest". But opposition support is mainly from the middle classes while pro-Putin districts derive from the grittier working class which is much larger (BBW 2017d: 47). Levy suggests that where virtuous circles go into reverse "no simple reform can substitute for in-depth, country-specific knowledge and informed judgment" (2014: 50). In such places as Russia the trick for locals is to use survival skills to get the circles going in the first place as real opposition to a regime that is unafraid of using deadly force to remain in power.

2 The classic historical fiction novel on the activities of this brutal tyrant and serial populist nationalist is *La Fiesta del Chivo* (Feast of the Goat) by Mario Vargas Llosa.

3 Economics should provide toolboxes for analysis of institutional, organizational, and policy problems. But economics is usually not enough for insights into the complexity of problems or trying to solve them without creating even more serious ones. Such scholars as Riggs (1964), Perrow (1974), Weick (1979), Crozier (1964), and Zimbardo and Ebbe (1970) have provided road-maps of what to look for where institutional roles fail to match organizational job descriptions and insights into why they often do not match for cultural, psychological, sociological, and anthropological reasons. But the guides are complex and application to specific contexts requires the keen insight, country experience, and informed judgment which depend on the observer. Given time and mandate constraints, however, the aid policy prescriptions are less focused on applied research on the behavioral determinants of institutions than on channeling and controlling the results from existing roles and systems. Strengthening internal control and audit systems is for these reasons a simpler more effective means of achieving governmental efficiencies and program effectiveness.

4 Chemonics International, for example, is still known in the industry as the "fertilizer company".

5 This classic book focused on policy hubris and program failures mainly in U.S. agricultural modernization efforts around the globe in developing countries.

6 See Vicki Golich and Terry Forrest Young (1993), "Debt-for-Nature Swaps: Win-Win Solution or Environmental Imperialism in Bolivia?", Institute for the Study of Diplomacy, Pew Case Study Center #187.

7 Many of the applied projects my unit developed, which were then funded by LGI/OSI for up to a year, were small with the largest being $100,000 (most were less than half that). Fees and "multipliers" were disallowed which kept projects (and bidders) small. But these ground-level policy and administration projects were enthusiastically implemented and produced books, papers, workshops, and articles that had substantial spread effects in the host countries in which the NGOs, universities and charities worked. Funded projects covered such topics as: training effectiveness, health care efficiency, educational reforms, budget and tax systems installation and use, and participatory budgeting for capital projects (Armenia). The honor and pride in implementing an OSI project was an important factor for success. See, for example, Grupo Propuesta Ciudadana (2006); Staronova (2007); Guess (2007).

9 Targeting Aid to Threats Against Governmental Effectiveness

Three of the four noted threats in Figure 0.1 directly affect state effectiveness. They can undermine states, hollow-out institutions with servile, unprofessional cronies, damage budgetary stability and destroy services and programs throughout many countries. Can ODA make a difference to stemming the ethnic and populist nationalist forces? We have noted that it can and has made an important difference to macroeconomic stability in many regions among rich and poor countries alike through installation and use of PFM systems and analytic tools to measure and control economic aggregates.

Nativist Threats and Attempted Remedies

But targeting ethnic and populist nationalist forces is different from working with the specific experiences of state modernization in that the nationalist problem is harder to define. There are not clear actionable components with levers attached and signs pointing out which way to pull them for maximum effect. Poor country sects, tribes and ethnicities are assets for leaders and demagogues to exploit for power. As complex as they are, they are a given in each setting, a part of the cultural context which investors and traders must understand to do business. Citizens and service users of the minority or disfavored current sect must either accept their fate or try to increase their power through the ballot box and electoral systems or mobilize pressures for greater shares of the budget. The latter invites repression in many poorer countries. Wealthy countries use sects, tribes, and ethnicities in the same way, to favor dominant or perceptibly threatened religions, races and groups by attempting to target and exclude minorities as either the wrong ethnicity (even if they have been indigenous for decades or centuries) or as unwanted immigrants (threatening jobs, incomes, and dominant group hegemony). Problem definition is hard and cause–effect relationships are tenuous and hard to attribute to policy action. In this fluid methodological context, demagogues are able to use social media and exaggerated claims as "facts" which resonate well with their often angry and left-behind bases.

An improved economy, better health care, or education for whole countries or particular regions can only make a difference, if at all, in the longer term.

Improved voting rules and electoral systems, if sustained and supported by regimes, can build firewalls to withstand nationalist threats by strengthening democratic development over time. Ethnic and sectarian government can become representative of all groups. By the 1950s, Costa Rica, for example, was the first Latin American country to include the Socialist Party in elections for parliamentary seats. While most other regional countries fought unnecessary wars with Communist and Socialist opposition groups for decades, Costa Rica has had inclusive governance and moderate regimes elected with partisan contestability ever since. Installation of single-member voting districts to pinpoint accountability and plurality vote elections with run-offs between the top two vote-getters can also widen the representational base and moderate elected regimes. Direct presidential elections can prevent the problem of differentials in popular vote and parliamentary representation. But such reforms take time and require regime support. Regime support in many cases naïvely presumes that leaders will suddenly become reasonable, generous, and threaten their own power bases. There is also the additional reality that, even in developing country democracies, unelected leaders are often indicted for corruption and imprisoned by their former opponents. That provides an additional disincentive for regimes to support electoral contestability.

Nevertheless, using available tools and methods it is possible to improve USAID DA programming to try and make host country states more effective and democratic. First, country counterpart funds can be accounted for more transparently. They are often in extra-budgetary fund (EBF) accounts where it is often difficult to trace amounts entered or contributed to ODA. Counterpart funds should be clearly linked to inflows of donor aid (including aid provided in kind) and managed under specific procedures, taking into account the requirements of the donors concerned (Allen *et al.*, 2013: 399). To this end, ODA targeted for budgetary and fiscal strengthening should require that these activities be organized as on-budget funds. They would then be part of the budget process and the final approved budget but earmarked for the special purpose of aid counterpart funds (2013: 400).

Second, more efforts need to be made to find a state institutional partner that can drive the reform process. DA depends on functioning states in target sectors; aid programs are often designed with their initial assistance and support. There have to be local partners and government officials, in MOFs or sectoral ministries that are supportive throughout project implementation. As seen in countries such as Haiti, without functioning states, NGOs can be partners but often have few links to actual government officials that can make and execute policies. Haiti has been called the "Republic of NGO" for this reason—it receives substantial ODA but little of it has improved state capacity.[1] In short order, then, DA is expected to create functioning and effective states when politics intrudes and counterpart officials in weak states are regularly removed or leave. This destabilizes both the state and the aid programs. In a tragic paradox, DA to improve state effectiveness depends on a minimum level of stability and effectiveness that are a precondition to improve them. Operational DA projects are expected to create big things like democracy and economic growth that depend on effective states when there are too many links in these causal chains that DA cannot control. Despite the reality of unstable or failed states with which to work, the public aid debate is captured by the abstract conceptual jargon of the international aid community—civil society, sustainability, institutional and state modernization, and "development" itself—which often lead to exaggerated expectations. Should a representative and legitimate state partner not be found, the aid funds should not be disbursed. Regime buy-in is essential and disbursement otherwise leads to waste, fraud, and abuses of power.

Third, state modernization methodologies can be applied, evaluated, and compared for results more precisely. State modernization programs and projects were common in the late 1990s and early 2000s from World Bank, DFID, USAID, and UNDP. The goal was to target central government ministries to achieve cost-reductions and modernize systems. The means to this would be a methodology guide the review and classification of functions in order to clarify them and eliminate unnecessary redundancies. Functions, such as policy, regulatory support, and service delivery would be clarified, rationalized to examine if they fit with roles and structures. The results could then be used at the ministry level to determine whether functions should be lifted, decentralized, deconcentrated, or privatized (UNDP, 2001: 55). The methodology was applied to the Ministries of Agriculture and Justice in Latvia, for example, in vertical reviews to link functional performance more tightly to their objectives. So, existing functions such as state investment planning and enterprise management would be eliminated after review and replaced with a regulatory function of market activity (UNDP, 2001: 11).

But the review processes that were intended to make breakthroughs in public administration reform often were sub-optimal and led to the self-fulfilling prophecy of non-applicability (2001: iv). Experience with the functional review of the Bulgarian Ministry of Social Protection in 1999, financed by DFID, produced enthusiastic participation by ministry officials over months of review sessions. Policy papers were developed and discussed; functions were combined and eliminated on paper; even new structures to house the new functional arrangements were proposed. But under the Civil Law-like Soviet legal and regulatory system in force, nothing could be changed, structurally or functionally, in any ministry without Council of Ministers approval. Not even minor forms could be modified without such central approvals. Predictably, the Bulgarian state was a constraint to state modernization and improvement. Similarly, ten Ukrainian ministries were included in functional reviews (1998–2001) which produced analyses, papers, and recommendations. But the regime-state failed to monitor either the functional review process or to produce effective procedures to monitor implementation of results (2001: 50). That left ministries "free" to try and implement agreed-upon measures on their own. But of course that required Council of Ministers approval, which never happened. Give that the Ukrainian state is largely corrupt, bloated, and ineffective, the state reform methodology had little effect other than solidarity-building for civil servants.

Moreover, the method is complex, labor-intensive and ultimately quite subjective. The likely consequences of this or that removal or addition of function to a ministry would be debatable and lead to more reviews and process. Such reorganization exercises are similar to those found in universities where faculties and staff debate about efficiency, results, and the likely implications for change on their turf, ego, and power relations. Universities as well as state bureaucracies view efficiencies to be at the expense of effectiveness, especially if decisions are made by staff officials that have little technical experience with line activities, for example, in urban transport or health. These are two core roles oddly not mentioned in the method, for instance. Additionally, if the goal is to decide whether roles should be eliminated, decentralized, deconcentrated, or privatized, the standard fiscal federalist review of intergovernmental roles and responsibilities often results in recommendations for changes consistent with how much subsidiarity (decentralization) or efficiency (correspondence between benefit area and public sector service provider) is required. Functional review-type methods are still improvements over the old mean–ends aid evaluation debates where the ends or objectives were given and the means or techniques were viewed as questionable. That led to tinkering with lower order concepts and machinery, such as personnel (Packenham, 1973: 116). The functional review method seeks to get behind the purposes of roles and functions and to rationalize them for better policy and service results. But that in itself is an amorphous process seemingly leading to paralysis by analysis.

Another method to reform states used by several donors is civil service reform. Such donors as the World Bank and Asian Development Bank have employed these methods to reform pay and employment systems. The problem targeted was twofold: determination of who was getting paid and how much civil servants should be paid. The first problem tackled the ghost worker problem of salaries collected by someone on the payroll that either is not there or to other persons (Stevens, 1994a: 115). Personnel or establishment rosters are notoriously incomplete for varieties of reasons, ranging from deliberate omissions to incompetence. If rosters are not linked to governmental accounting ledgers by codes and then to the treasury payments systems, payments can be made regardless of status and whether or not budgeted funds exist. One of the state reform systems discussed is the GFMIS which in real time links accounting and treasury transactions and balances and withholds payments if the linkages are not verified beforehand. That solved most of the problem of fiscal leakage and indiscipline related to public sector salaries. The second problem pertains to incentives. Poorer country civil service salary differences between highest and lowest grades are minimal. That means most make about average salaries which reduces any incentives for better performance and promotions. The "compression" ratio is high in such systems. In practice, many civil servants in poorer countries have several jobs and show up to use official offices based on their own private schedules. So official civil service disincentives have little effect on performance. Additionally, pay and grading exercises, recruitment and promotion are typically compromised by sect, ethnicity, race, and partisan affiliation of the ministry.

Thus, the ODA tasks have been to determine who should get paid, why they should be paid (i.e. what real qualifications they have and even whether they should have been recruited), and then establish how to design systems that will incentivize the civil service to work harder for more rank and salary. That meant at minimum the decompression of ranks, increasing the salary range from highest to lowest levels. As Stevens noted for Tanzanian reforms, the trade-off often becomes between restoring pay levels and retrenchment (1994: 73). Very often the state is both bloated with staff and is unproductive or ineffective. The need is to reduce unnecessary staff (by elimination of both "ghosts" and unnecessary or redundant workers) and increase pay (via decompression which raises the total salary bill in many cases) for needed work performed. Donors have been more successful redesigning civil service systems than retrenching staff. The prospects of being down-sized in economies with few other employment options often leads to violence against both the regime that proposed such "civil service reforms" and the donors that advised them. The problem remains severe in poorer countries but the practical steps for remedy are unclear in state contexts under threat from ethnic and populist nationalism trying to bring regimes down. Gregory (1994: 34) for instance, found all the major problems in Somalia: over-sized work force, low pay, lack of clear definition of functions and responsibilities (an opening for "functional review" methods), and a complete lack of incentives, motivation, or efficiency. Donors firmly believe that implementation of reforms for these problems will be beneficial despite any measurement errors (Gregory, 1994: 60).

But few regimes have been willing to gamble that benefits to them would be greater than short-term costs to their longevity and well-being. For example, the IMF recently froze the second tranche of a loan to Tunisia because it was moving too slowly on fiscal reform. The fiscal deficit had climbed to 6 percent in 2017 and thus the regime imposed a 1 percent increase in the VAT to try and bring it down to 4.9 percent. But this brought thousands to the streets in protest against economic hardships from the IMF austerity policy for Tunisia. Fiscal deficits are a narrow measure of fiscal rectitude, an easy technical accounting target that can be met by standard policy changes of spending cuts and/or revenue increases. The target should be the regime and government which employs 20 percent of all workers in the public sector at a cost of 14 percent of GDP (*The Economist*, 2018c: 44). But layoffs or redundancies would bring even more angry protest because the private sector could absorb them. This is the dilemma of political regimes that would like to satisfy social needs without making the necessary structural reforms that could allow greater private sector growth. In many cases, the IMF's programs look cruel when other conditions on structural reform could bring even more regime instability and social protest.

For regimes interested in reform, simplifying state activities into core transactions is another method of increasing effectiveness in the short term. Transaction analysis is a simpler way to determine how well administrative systems are functioning, to identify the needed changes, and then to plan a sequence of steps to reduce the number of decisions and approvals required for each transaction. The method focuses on which participants are involved in producing a decision product, for example, license, office furniture acquisition, particular safety inspection, or maintenance job. The internal audit unit (not external consultants) would then target the transaction and perform analyses on constraints to timely and effective actions and how they might be eliminated. The transaction analysis method was successfully used in Kosovo, for example, in a PFM fiduciary risk assessment to review core transactions in procurement of capital equipment and personnel resources—recruitment, hiring, firing, promotion (DAI, 2013: 6). This is similar to the earlier call to face the complexity of joint institutional action during forward planning and to include implementation steps and potential constraints in initial planning for programs, services, and capital projects. Pressman and Wildavsky (1984: 141) long ago noted that the frequent complaints of federal officials about government fragmentation that impedes program results is similar to that of aid officials lamenting unstable regimes in poor countries. By identifying clearance points during policy formulation that would stop or delay implementation, better results could be obtained. In the context of an intergovernmentally financed and managed economic development program for Oakland, that meant, for instance, focusing on approving applications, committing funds, and negotiating initial agreements (1984: 145–146). The results of this approach to join formulation and execution led to eliminating the separation of project design and construction. Responsibility and authority were now placed in the hands of one institution, a single budgeted position, and a single official.

The intent of the functional review and transactional analysis methods is to improve systems and cost effectiveness at ministry levels and to encourage scaling them up to the entire government. That would move results from the sector or pilot program level to mainstream: improving overall state effectiveness. The scaling issue is similar to that of whether to pursue a pilot project first to try and obtain a visible small win or to roll out the full mainline program first? Government reformers in Pakistan in 1999–2000 decided that pilot fiscal decentralization projects, limited to several districts in one province, would be risky in that the approach could lead to failure (ruining chances for a revision and restart later) or that political capital existing then would not be available for a future effort—successful or not. So they rolled out an entire program supported by a small ADB project with later funds added on by DFID. While relatively successful in a technical sense, the program was soon engulfed in small-bore personality and institutional turf battles which were later engulfed by regime change and state failure itself, neither of which the small project could prevent. The hope is that successful sectoral projects such as the ADB fiscal decentralization effort, will be picked up, transferred to other jurisdictions, to other tiers of government, and adapted to meet their special circumstances.

Such "scaling up" happened in the Canadian federation, which devolved the local economic development authority from the federal government in Ottawa to the Tsawwassen First Nation or indigenous people. By removing them from dependence on fiscal transfers and eliminating their tax-exempt status, in return they gained full fiscal and political autonomy. They now pay sales, income, and property taxes in exchange for regulatory and political autonomy. By creating investor certainty to make and enforce contracts, the new status has led to an economic boom (BBW, 2017a: 32). The First Nation is now a model of how a local development model can be scaled up for the benefit of the federation, while serving as an example of how to resolve such local secessionist conflicts in other countries, such as Spain with Catalonia. The policy analysis for design was based on standard fiscal federalist theory which provided grist for a beneficial trade-off that resulted in more beneficiary correspondence for the Province and more subsidiarity or authority and responsibility for the First Nation.

Another national policy area in need of successful smaller-scale examples has been social assistance. National program design efforts have proceeded from the notion that low subsidiarity was needed to cover large benefit areas (nations, provinces) for economies of scale to achieve high correspondence. But a more innovative question was how to provide social assistance benefits that could also improve recipient behaviors in education and health? As one answer, a new type of social assistance program was created by combining local needs and national delivery efficiencies in the poorer countries of Latin America. The new programs combined cash transfers with in-kind support, making the receipt of cash assistance conditional on meeting certain health and/ or education requirements. CCT programs have typically incorporated targeting schemes to identify the appropriate recipients. The conditional support provides funds in exchange for the recipient's agreement to purchase certain items or to carry out specific investments in activities such as education, health, and/or food. As such, while the government does not necessarily provide the goods in-kind, they represent a hybrid of income transfer and in-kind assistance programs. Focusing on nutrition, education, and health, the CCT program goal is to alleviate long-term extreme poverty rather than just providing shorter-term relief.

CCT programs were developed recently, primarily in Latin America, and later transferred to Mozambique and Turkey. After Mexico initiated its program in 1997, several countries in Latin America—Brazil, Colombia, Honduras, Jamaica, and Nicaragua—also adopted similar CCT programs. A similar program design is now used in New York City as well. The primary difference between these programs and the other types of social safety net programs is that while cash transfers are used, like income transfer programs, the cash is expected to be used for specific purposes. In exchange for mandatory use of public services, such as health care and education, the recipient is expected to purchase the cash goods in the regular market. For example, Colombia provides school subsidies and Honduras awards education vouchers to poor households to increase the education of children living in poverty. Supplemental grants are also provided in many program countries to improve the health and health education of their poorer citizens (Guess and Husted, 2017: 147). Thus, as CCTs indicate, design flexibility for successful programs can encourage rapid scaling up, within countries and by transfer abroad.

Finally, components of state reform programs can be scaled down as well as up. For example, the first integrated financial management system in Latin America (IFMS) was the administration and control system component (called *SAFCO* or *Sistema de Administracion Financiera y Control*) of the Bolivian Public Financial Management Operation initiated in 1987 by the World Bank (IDA). The system consisted of budgeting, internal control, cash management, and audit sub-system modules linking the MOF with 15 central ministries and other decentralized entities. As is common, the tax administration sub-system was initiated separately and not linked to the IFMS.

Nevertheless, the 1987 SAFCO project (which is one of three components in the Bolivian Public Financial Management Operation) was the first full IFMS in Latin America and served as the model for other projects, such as SIGFA in Nicaragua, and many current operational systems that were once implementation projects (Dener *et al.*, 2011).

While this project had a volatile history of successes and failures, its deeper significance lay in the generation of consciousness for the value of financial management improvements to both accountability and public sector performance. It also generated demand for additional improvements in other regional countries. It served as the foundation for USAID's work in the area that became the Regional Financial Management Information Systems Program I (RFMIP I) in 1989. Out of these experiences grew a solid technical commitment to the IFMS (or GFMIS) as a powerful means to improve accountability and resource allocation in Latin America.

Decentralization of the IFMS to municipal governments or scaling down has been a more recent occurrence. The RFMIP II only began to focus on this objective in its 1ast year: 1997–1998. Other donors have operated from the premise that for lack of local capacity reasons central IFMSs must precede the installation of local IFMSs. As one respondent noted, the evolutionary sequence for IFMSs has been in practice: (1) MOF or spending ministries, (2) autonomous agencies, (3) state enterprises, and (4) state and local governments. Since few IFMSs are fully functional at the central government level, only those countries with lengthy experience in IFMSs have taken the next steps. For this reason, only Bolivia has devolved its SAFCO down to the subnational/local levels. Conversely, in other cases, such as Ecuador, IFMS successes at the local level (in the capital city of Quito) flowed upwards and became the basis of national systemic level improvements to control spending and its allocation. Thus, the successful local IFMS was scaled up to the national level (Guess and Jutkowitz, 1999).

The key to success for a scaling up or down then, is that multiple tiers of either unitary or federation states work together and that private and public stakeholders are included in planning and setting objectives. For example, Prime Minister Modi of India has supported a massive campaign to clean up India and recycle rubbish into compost and electricity. Indian cities generate more garbage than any others in the world and their supplies are growing along with wealth, consumption, and urbanization. Only 28 percent of collected garbage is treated and processed while the rest ends up on often hazardous dump sites that damage both health and the environment. The central government now subsidizes compost plants and he has mandated the purchase by electricity generators of power from the seven existing waste to energy plants. Fifty-six more are under construction. In the city of Mysuru (population 1million), trash collection is funded by property taxes and fees and households must separate wet from dry waste (Pradhan, 2018: 34). Thus, the combination of intergovernmental cooperation, aligned incentives, common objectives for solid waste management, and supportive local officials and stakeholders has made local projects scalable to the national level. The model of waste-to-energy is simple and could be adapted for use in poorer countries with weaker states. But lack of state support and fewer incentives, together with weaker CIP processes to plan and finance capital projects, would make implementation and thus scaling more difficult. Though India has used no overseas aid for their city solid waste management efforts, DA can and has been used in other contexts to support CIP strengthening and to deepen learning of analytic and appraisal techniques for designing and measuring the impact of environmental energy projects. The Indian example suggests that DA-supported efforts to scale up can work elsewhere in the energy–environmental sectors.

As for how any of these complex efforts, many of which are successful in strengthening the components of the state that increase effectiveness, can reduce or prevent regime-threatening ethnic or populist ultranationalists, this again depends on how effectively regional and local citizens are linked to regimes and governance. DA can support efforts to tighten these linkages through projects that strengthen public accountability systems. And that is in part an election systems and administrative design and enforcement problem for the longer term. The regime response problem is made more difficult by structural constraints of ethnicity and sectarian-dominated ministries and states that deliver distorted programs and projects that magnify allocational inequities, generating even more ultra-nationalism in the name of the "people" and the "nation".

Targeting Aid to Regional Problems

Table 9.1 provides a summary review of recent U.S. ODA allocations to programs and projects. Much of this was discussed above. The U.S. aid classification is similar to other donors, both bilateral and multilateral, which reveal allocations to sectors and countries. The U.S. government provides about 14 percent of total global ODA amounts (Tarnoff, 2015: 2). The allocational differences of U.S. DA are less between rich/poor countries than its emphasis as a tool of foreign policy. It is targeted mostly to low-income countries (44 percent), low- and middle-income countries (41 percent), upper-middle-income (15 percent) and high-income countries (0.06 percent) (2015: 16). Like the British DFID program, DA also focuses directly on democracy-building and governance improvements (13 percent), for example, elections, media, unions, civil society organizations, and political parties. Other ODA donors focus on these objectives only indirectly, through such programs as PFM strengthening (e.g. Swiss Aid).

All USG "International Affairs" spending from multiple agencies and accounts (core and shared) are collected in budget function #150. This does not include all Defense Department Security Assistance (SA) funding which is in account #050 ("National Defense") and often becomes a shared expense between the State and Defense Departments to be spent, for instance, in conflict and post-conflict country contexts.[2] SA supports DA and other forms of #150 spending in complex crisis states such as

Table 9.1 U.S. Overseas Development Assistance Patterns

Region	Major Country Recipients (Tarnoff, 2015: 16)	State Threats	% Aid (FY 2013) (Tarnoff, 2015: 18–19)	% Sector (Tarnoff, 2015: 20)	Type of Aid Allocations(Grants 22%; Cooperative Agreements 46%)
SSA	Kenya, Nigeria, Uganda, Tanzania, South Africa, Sudan, South Sudan, Congo, Ethiopia, Mali	EN	39.2%	Health 36% (42% to SSA)	DA, HUM, CCF, HEALTH
MENA	Jordan, West Bank/Gaza, Syria, Egypt, Lebanon	EN	23.5%	Humanitarian 19% (to SSA Ebola; Haiti earthquake; Sahel drought)	DA, ESF, SA (DOD), CCF,HUM
Afghanistan/PAK	About 20% of all USAID funding	EN	19.2%	D&G 13% (66% to Jordan, Afghanistan, Egypt, Iraq, Pakistan and South Sudan)	ESF, SA (DOD)
ASIA/PAC	Philippines, Indonesia, Vietnam	EN/PN	8.0%	Economic Growth 11% (67% to: Egypt, Afghanistan, West Bank/Gaza, South Sudan)	DA
LA	Haiti, Colombia, Mexico, Ecuador	TP	7.4%	Agriculture 6% (54% to: Afghanistan, Bangladesh, Haiti, Colombia, Ghana, Mali, Ethiopia, Pakistan, Tanzania, Uganda)	DA
EUR/EURASIA	Ukraine	PN/TP	2.7%	Education 4% (basic and post-secondary workforce development: Afghanistan, Ethiopia, Lebanon, Liberia, Pakistan)	ESF, CCF
ALL		TP		Environment 3% (Land rights management and deforestation: Colombia, Ecuador, Indonesia, Mexico, Philippines, Sudan, Ukraine, Vietnam)	DA

in the SSA and MENA. The SA component is also often part of shared funding for ESF (in #150) targeted to strategically important countries, usually where major conflicts are ongoing and threats to the state are serious. The #150 account amounted to only 1.4 percent of the total USG FY 13 budget, of which 38 percent was spent by USAID and 32 percent for "other foreign aid" (Tarnoff, 2015: 14). USAID is funded from multiple accounts and its appropriation is in the annual State Department Foreign Operations legislation (2015: 10). The functional categories used by USAID core programs are: (1) Economic Support Funds for strategic countries like Iraq and Jordan; (2) Development Assistance (DA or ODA); (3) Humanitarian Disaster aid; (4) Military Security (from the DOD budget); (5) Global Health; (6) Complex Crisis Fund: an un-allocated pot of funds for unanticipated crises such as the Ukrainian conflict with Russia and required plantings for resettled Sri Lankans and Tamils; and (7) Food for Peace or the P.L.480 Title II program where USAID provides agricultural commodities for emergency and non-emergency needs (2015: 12).

These functional expenditures are largely targeted by USAID to the two regions (SSA and MENA) with the greatest ethno-nationalist threats to effective governance and state stability. Very little ODA has been targeted to regions with traditional populist (TP) problems or PN issues. Regions such as Latin America that have evolved from the raw populist nationalism of the past to more traditional populist concerns must respond to these problems largely alone (without much ODA) and through its robust local politics and relatively strong institutions. Overall, whether USAID programs or projects are effective or not, the overall organization is quite cost efficient. Administrative expenses (overheads) were only 0.085 percent of FY 16 (2015: 11).

Is the regional and country allocation by USAID in Table 9.1 optimal? Probably not … But it is probably sufficient for the mix of complex policy and security problems that the major countries in each region face. A case could be made that poor countries need all of the above functional allocations in greater amounts and in marginally varied proportions. What is missed by one donor is likely provided by other donors such as UNDP, AusAid, Swiss Aid, the Asian Development Bank or DFID. Thus, by program, perhaps the simplest aid to allocate is ESF, DA and Health to countries working to improve quality of life and governmental effectiveness. ESF, DA and Health Sector aid realistically need more time to achieve results and funds to maintain them. The hardest aid to allocate is DA and SA aid to the fragile and failed states, that is, those needing rebuilding from wars where the same ethnic-sectarian groups that caused the conflicts now vie for power and threaten any new solutions from regimes or aid donors. If funds from the Complex Crisis Fund, International Disaster Assistance, and Humanitarian Aid are hard to allocate, they are even harder to use effectively since the situations on the ground change daily and locally trained personnel are usually not available or trained to performance-inspiring levels. Even more problems lie at the project implementation stage, which will be discussed in Chapter 10 below.

The aid from USAID is targeted to meet the challenges noted: macro-economic and fiscal instability (Economic Support); ethno-nationalism (EN) (virtually all types of U.S. aid); populist nationalism (PN) problems (receive DA, Economic Growth, and Complex Crisis aid); traditional populist problems (TP) (receive almost no ODA from any donor, except election management and civil society strengthening). For, as noted in Chapter 3, TP consists of the perennial issues whipped up by local political leaders, those of insufficient jobs, divisive land issues, inadequate (often rural) incomes, and needed public works. Land tenure security and management issues have been important in Latin America and involve not only natural resource conservation and usage but also financial security and stability since, without a title, loans will not be forthcoming from local banks. This local traditionally populist issue has become a national issue in Ukraine, where long-standing restrictions on sales and purchase of farmland prevent sectoral investment, growth, incomes, and jobs in a country already suffering from the devastating effects of civil war with Russia and its eastern zones.[3] Local populist officials have spread the myth that an open land market will lead to further poverty and destitution, which resonates in the largely Stalinist–collectivist culture. That mindset has been largely immune from the effects of DA aid which largely transformed neighboring Romania and Poland. Most Ukrainian farmers must lease their landholdings to firms rather than increase their own productivity and incomes from better yields of sunflowers, corn, sugar beets, wheat, and soybeans (Gomez and Choursina, 2018: 30. The tendency to leave traditional populist issues out of state threats is reflected in (Table 9.1) the allocation of only some U.S. aid to the European region (2.7 percent) and a small part of the 3 percent spent on environmental programs in all regions.

The geographic rationale for the aid breakdown was contained in earlier discussions of regime and governance threats. And recall that the USAID budget for ODA and ISA is not the entire U.S. Government aid commitment, which includes DOD funding for strategic, military, and geopolitical objectives.[4] To summarize the regional threats briefly, the Latin American/Central American region has had fewer problems of separatism and ethnicity-based nationalism. Historically, as noted by da Cunha (1944) minority Indians in countries such as Brazil were dealt with summarily and often brutally in scorched-earth military campaigns to "pacify" them in order to build states that covered national territory. This was of course an early instance of "pacification" in order to "save" the clients program rationale, seen later in conflicts such as in Vietnam and El Salvador. Otherwise, recent Latin American nationalism has been largely constructive to strengthen states and relationships within and between regions of nations which, helpfully, speak common languages, mostly Spanish or Portuguese. Some states such as Brazil, Mexico, and Argentina, have developed as federations facilitating the scaling up and abroad of institutional and programmatic innovations such as CCTs and BRT (bus rapid transit) urban transport for low-cost high performance means of moving large numbers of people in densely packed urban corridors, for example, Mexico City and Quito.

Common nationalism has been an advantage for a shared project of democracy, which offers multiple models to transfer and adapt between countries and abroad. Ironically, former colonial powers such as Spain and Portugal often receive aid from their former colonies. This shared cultural nationalism has worked in countries such as: Uruguay, Costa Rica, and Venezuela (which offers a cautionary example of what can go wrong via distortions in a democratic electoral system perversely designed to destroy a wealthy, developed country). As in France, national unity has long been a political project in such countries as Mexico and Brazil. Another regional advantage that has kept states strong, and popular nationalist movements weak, has been the influence of regional international agencies such as: OAS, PAHO, World Bank, IDB, and USAID which was founded with a southern hemisphere focus. Saturation by these agencies with educational fellowships, state training, workforce development projects, farming and agro-industrial projects, health care systems support and anti-poverty efforts has been a distinct advantage. No other region has had this kind of coverage from multiple aid agencies, and has left few openings for identity politics, any declines in the moderate middle classes, or the rise of fringe parties in most countries. Those that remain are distinctly exceptional (e.g. Venezuela) and have had peculiar geopolitical circumstances (e.g. Cuba) to explain why. ODA has added to this favorable mix of circumstances; both democracy and government effectiveness have gained.

Externally driven threats to domestic Latin American states still exist in the form of narco-criminal and related gang violence in Mexico, Colombia, and Central America. Efforts to take advantage of federalist structures and to strengthen local law enforcement agencies have been hampered by the continuing restriction on training from USAID, stemming from the infamous Uruguay program to wipe out Tupamaro opponents to the government in the 1960s.[5] Haiti has been a more intriguing example. It is an enigmatic, tough, and exceptional case of a persistently weak and corrupt state that has left its people in poverty and ill-educated misery, despite years of U.S. DA projects and NGO work (Downs, 1988). Whatever micro or sectoral reforms take place at the project levels there, unfortunately almost none of them have been scaled up to strengthen the state and to ensure effective governance. The country has been noted for its reliance on NGOs to deliver basic education and health services which have had few spread effects that build up state capacity.[6] As noted in Endnote 1 of this chapter, the successful BRH-AU project to build precisely such state capacity in public financial management and policy analysis was ended by a devastating earthquake in 2010.

Naturally, this many aid attempts to improve matters in Haiti with so much money over so long a period of time has produced a robust explanatory industry. Theories of failure range from: (1) racist (the other side of the island is the DR which is mostly white and prosperous, if corrupt); (2) the political culture (the persistent belief and practice of Voodoo even by MOF and BRH professionals with PhDs from Oxford and Harvard) works against rational progress. For, the beliefs place a supernatural, fatalistic and deterministic variable between policy cause and attributable and measurable effect. That has produced unpredictable, bizarre, and damaging results; Harrison (1985) calls these beliefs and practices an example of a "damaged culture" that has impeded the development and quality of life for almost a century there; and (3) divine judgment: religious fanatics such as Pat Robertson have even blamed Haitians for 2010 earthquake as divine retribution for profligate living! A more sensible explanation might just be incredibly bad luck—in 2010 just weeks before the earthquake, Haiti was noted by many for its development progress which according to most had never reached that stage of advancement. All these explanations have surface plausibility but divine judgment. But even the last one adds to the fatality part of the political culture and prevents positive action. And the effects of a damaged local culture quickly wear off with emigration—as is known. Haitians in Miami have thrived for many decades to the envy of many poorer and often black Americans living in the same parts of town.

By contrast, the Sub-Saharan Africa region is not as fortunate as Latin America. Many countries have suffered from repeated episodes of ethnic and populist nationalist leaders and movements that destabilize states and inhibit their reconstruction. The trajectory of resource-rich Zimbabwe is almost prototypical of poor countries in SSA except that it may have suffered less violence and bloodshed than its neighbors. For all his bad press before and after his recent abdication, Robert Mugabe gained power as a local hero leading opposition to the white racist regime of Ian Smith. In 1965, Smith had declared independence from London rather than bend to British demands to enfranchise the then Rhodesian population. Mugabe finally forced Smith out in 1979 and won election as the first leader for his Zanu-PF party, after which he remained in power for 37 years. To maintain and aggrandize power, he began a series of black racist or nationalist policies including land and industry confiscation from white farmers and industrialists which he termed "indigenization". His regime also forced the resettlement of white farmers on other plots (Campbell, 2018: 48). This began Zimbabwe's descent into an economic abyss as efficient farms became unproductive subsistence plots.

Thus, Mugabe's nationalist power policies were based on standard "race and land" slogans and programs which resonated with the black ethnic and racial majority. To further his ethno-nationalist credentials, his army massacred 20,000 members of the Ndebele ethnic minority in the 1980s (2018: 51). To deal with the rapid descent into widespread poverty, he created new money and printed more of it in order to spend more funds from the treasury to benefit his needy but obedient followers. His "zollars", for instance, were electronic dollars called "bond notes" that officially had parity and could buy one U.S. dollar. But the fictional currency had no value to pay for imports nor did it work as a means of exchange in domestic commercial transactions (2018: 49). By destroying property rights, land tenure security, and rule of law, Mugabe had instituted "rule *by* law" which does not inspire either domestic or international investment confidence and merely stimulates more corruption. Following his 2017 abdication, the task has been to build on functioning institutions such as the auditor-general and court system and to rehabilitate a relatively solid infrastructure that has fallen into serious disrepair. Unlike most SSA countries, Zimbabwe once had a sound road, railway, and power grid network that spanned rural and urban areas. The prototypical pattern to political power in SSA then was the rise of the populist nationalist hero of an opposition rebellion against a colonially supported regime; ethno-nationalism to maintain and expand his power and credibility among the loyal base; and followed by irrational economic and financial policies that lead to macroeconomic instability. This familiar multi-stage trajectory has nothing to do with reforming or strengthening the state to deliver needed services, programs, and infrastructure.

To restart the economy and take advantage of its soil that once produced the breadbasket of the continent, Emmerson Mnangagwa will have to induce the Chinese and World Bank that it has become creditworthy enough to pay back any new loans for reconstruction.[7] That will require an effective state that can forge proper fiscal, monetary, currency, land tenure, commercial transaction, and social safety net policies. Proper design of them is relatively straightforward from international best practices. But implementing any of them would require a new regime that can force institutional compliance. And financing them will require convincing creditors that, even at probable concessionary lending rates, the newly constituted state and regime no longer plans to defy the laws of financial physics (2018: 48) with bizarre policies that have no credibility and are proven failures wherever tried, e.g. Venezuela. The U.S. can help by providing funds for economic growth (to develop financial and economic policies); DA (for national and sectoral socioeconomic programs); and environmental (for land management) assistance from its #150 account.

MENA country states suffer from autocratic and theocratic regime policies that suppress any political opposition. That removes the accountability and regime legitimacy link and adds to poverty, poor services and lack of basic human rights. Most MENA countries suffer from almost permanent sectarian religious, factional as well as populist nationalist movements that continue to threaten and weaken further already illegitimate and weak states. Several MENA countries have received U.S. aid regularly for almost half a century; many MENA states including those receiving U.S. democracy and governance or "D&G" aid have degenerated into lengthy civil wars. Most are still considered necessary "strategic partners" by the U.S. despite their lack of real progress on democracy or the creation of effective governance. This is an ongoing geopolitical dilemma where preferred disengagement by the U.S. is considered a higher risk than the costs of continued engagement. Nevertheless, there have been aid-attributable successes. Countries such as Syria, Jordan, Egypt, Lebanon, and West Bank/Gaza remain top recipients of U.S. aid through the multiple programs of education, democracy and governance, and economic growth (Tarnoff, 2015: 19–20). Substantial SA is also provided by USAID as well as defense allocations by DOD in countries such as Syria and Iraq. The most stable and effective regimes in the MENA region are Jordan, Tunisia, Lebanon, and Morocco which have received large amounts of ODA funding. Aid assistance at the micro-sectoral level has also produced important (if hard fought against high odds) successes, such as the GFMIS for the Government of Jordan (Campbell and Guess, 2012) and the finally functioning BRT system in Amman.

To review the main threats to state effectiveness and what overseas aid from all ODA and SA sources can do about them then, we identified the two major threats of (1) poor-country ethno-nationalism and (2) wealthier country populist nationalism, both of which are led by demagogues with intense followers. Both threats were discussed in earlier chapters.

Poor Country Ethno-Nationalism

We have reviewed several country cases such as Liberia, Ethiopia, Nigeria, as well as Zimbabwe in the SSA region. An extreme case of this problem, as noted previously, is in the MENA region where Yemen has suffered years of civil war, tribalism, jihadist violence, poverty, and now a proxy war between the Shia militia Houthis, backed by Iran, and a Sunni militia led by Saudi Arabia and backed by mainly the U.S, several Sunni Arab states, and local militias. The Yemeni conflict has left 21 million of 28 million people in need of humanitarian aid. A proposal for a federal state and a parliamentary split or partition between the north and south, turned into another power dispute and case of personal betrayals between the two leaders (the former Sunni president Ali Abdullah Saleh, ousted by a 2012 coup and recently murdered in 2017) and his former Vice-President

Abd Rabbo Hadi. The ongoing conflict will have to be resolved by outside mediators and any efforts to strengthen state institutions (again) and to develop a new governing structure will require local demand from a source viewed as legitimate before any outside aid can supply funding, technical assistance, and training.

In such unstable contexts of ethno-nationalist and religious nationalist sectarian war, ODA or SA improvements cannot be gratuitously supplied. Such contexts will require humanitarian, security, and complex crisis aid foci until the fighting stops and legitimate leaders and stakeholders appear with an interest in growth and development of the country or territory. Rational though federation solutions may be, they remain mere textbook models until locals see the benefits of this structure and a strong need for governmental effectiveness to provide services and programs to whole nations rather than simply to sectarian, tribal, or ethnic kin. Otherwise, non-state actors will continue to fill the vacuum.[8] Such ethnic and religious sectarian groups have regularly killed aid personnel and harassed broader sectoral aid efforts in health in Pakistan for years. In such contexts, the threats apply to both sectoral/quasi-federation or national aid efforts. Neither can work, as indicated, until the fighting stops and the sides begin talking about trade-offs.

Wealthier Country Populist Nationalism

Populist nationalists are not qualitatively different from ethnic nationalists in that both use group membership status dog-whistling as a means to gain, maintain, and expand power. Members of such groups led by cultural often racist zealots and demagogues can be found in all forms of government: unitary authoritarian or democratic and federation. They mostly arise in wealthy countries and such leaders often combine both group/sectarian ethnic and populist national causes effectively to achieve the same ends. Populist nationalists claiming a national following typically focus on opponents in sectarian conflicts, like the British–Northern Irish conflict that ended in the Good Friday Agreement of 1998. That conflict ended finally when mediators and reformed leaders agreed on a path to reconciliation through maintenance of constructive ambiguity and avoidance of forced binary choices.

To reiterate, the design and implementation of aid, either intergovernmentally or internationally, to defuse or weaken such destructive movements and to generate regional income and employment opportunities, is not easy. The ongoing conflict in Catalonia is a recent example of populist nationalism destroying both the regional economy and one of the most structurally decentralized governments without attaining any real independence or gains in "freedom" for adherents of greater autonomy/independence (Cercas, 2017). The number of successfully implemented and transferred schemes and projects to accomplish allocational efficiencies that have reduced ultranationalist threats is not great. Better results have been attained at the sectoral or micro-federation levels if they can be scaled up to the national levels (which often they are not).

Notes

1 An exception to this was the 2009–2010 project between the Central Bank (BRH) and American University's School of Public Affairs to provide in-country public financial management and economic policy analysis courses leading to MPAs for the 20 students initially selected. The $400,000 project was paid for by the Government of Haiti. Students were in service from other ministries such as MOF and Health and would return to their positions after graduation adding to state capacity. The second group of 40 students had been selected for 2010–2011 by BRH when the earthquake hit, destroying the BRH classroom building and killing several program staff and participating students.

2 The distinction between DA and ESF, which includes "international security assistance" (account #152) or SA and the Foreign Military Sales Program" is somewhat arbitrary in that the design of U.S. aid frees poor countries from spending on targeted items and allows them to "fungibly" use the funds for their own purposes (Kaplan, 1967: 283). The FMSP finances U.S. military equipment via loan guarantees or credits, for example, fighter jets for Saudi Arabia. This used to be the largest item in the U.S. foreign aid program (Guess, 1987: 19). Despite the shared nature of the DA and SA programs particularly in SSA and MENA, nevertheless, the DOD defense budget function #050 and the #150 accounts remain separate. But the budget numbers by functions, that include all agency spending, for them are valid, reliable, mostly transparent, and can be disaggregated for more detailed analysis.

3 The recent Lithuanian/French/Polish/Russian/English film "Frost" by Sharunas Bartas vividly recounts the tale of a young couple driving a humanitarian aid van from the urban stability of Vilnius into the maelstrom of the Donbas region where they encounter lives torn apart by the war and are finally engulfed in the conflict themselves (Bartas, 2017).

4 Facts commonly cited facts about U.S. DA efforts by USAID include that at $31.2b in FY 2012, economic foreign aid was only 0.9 percent of the U.S. budget and 1.4 percent if military aid is included. Including all aid, the top five country recipients were Afghanistan, Israel, Iraq, Egypt, and Pakistan, demonstrating that economic aid is tightly linked to U.S. security and foreign policy object-ives. The top five USAID countries are different, and do not include Israel, because they are a smaller set of countries fully aided by the U.S. Government (Tarnoff, 2015: 16). In addition to the ODA from the U.S., an additional $900m annually is allocated for policy-level conditionality activities through the Millennium Challenge Corporation (MCC). This has been called the GOP alternative to USAID and allocates funds on the basis of country achievement of gains in big-ticket policies such as good governance, reduced corruption, and better macroeconomic performance. MCC spends money for such activities as school construction, improved business systems, and registration systems. MCC provides merit rather than needs-based aid. In some cases, MCC policy-level

objectives are achieved through the support of operational systems such as health, education, and anti-corruption, for example, internal audit and procurement systems. Other areas, such as macroeconomic improvements, which are advised by multiple donors such as IMF with their own conditionality, are harder to attribute to MCC spending. Moreover, there are doubts about such conditional aid as the catalyst for "virtuous policies" (Hirschman, 1971: 205). Often, Hirschman argues, aid-hungry governments accept conditional aid at variance with their own policy or program preferences and then backslide later or sabotage any measurable results attained later (1971: 206). Nevertheless, there can be achievements at the operational level if the aid is both conditional and run through country systems (decentralized) without unnecessary reporting burdens. For example, USAID DA covers, as noted PFM improvements and fiduciary risk assessment systems at the operations level. PFM improvements improve efficiency but do not necessarily lead to better macro policies. At minimum, fiscal databases and information sources are improved and made more transparent. As in other policy areas, the PFM goal is long-term aggregation of skills leading to more analytics, better data, and more circumspect decisions based on comparative research of what happens elsewhere. But the reality is that security and policy-level rationales are always a better political sell than the often invisible drudgery of improving operational systems. In sum, longer-term strategic-level aid usually has less direct effect than shorter-term operational aid that builds needed systems for the future.

5 The still classic film on this episode involving police chief Dan Mitrione's torture escapades that led to his kidnapping and murder there is *State of Siege* by Costa-Gavras (1972).

6 An excellent case study by Charles Downs on how DA can be disbursed most optimally in a country without a state partner is: (#117) "Negotiating Development Assistance: USAID and the Choice between Public and Private Implementation in Haiti" (#117) (Pew Case Study/Institute for Study of Diplomacy, Georgetown University, 1988).

7 It will also have to convince IMF that any new policy of fiscal austerity or budget consolidation would work against its growth and development. Past IMF program loans came with austerity advice and conditions which, after years of local non-compliance, has ended any new loan possibilities without major structural and policy changes. Because of major arrears on past IMF–World Bank financing, Zimbabwe was effectively cut off from international loans by its bad credit ratings. For the popular local view of the IMF, listen to the 2014 Nigerian hit song called "IMF" by Seun Kuti. www.youtube.com/watch?v=8fGcf3GODKE&spfreload=10; Many IMF conditional loan negotiations are used by both partners as a planned distraction from regime efforts to reform. But in the case of Mugabe there was no effort to reform. In practice, IMF often defers or waives most of the harshest conditions in private after much public fanfare during negotiations and after mission departures.

8 Some non-state actors such as ISIS were made up of former members of state militias that defected or went rogue. The personal suffering from this constant institutional instability where few can be trusted was brought home powerfully in the 2016 film by Licinio Azevedo *"Train of Salt and Sugar"* or *"Comboio de Sal e Acucar"*, a film from Portugal/Mozambique/France/South Africa. The rail journey from Nampula to Malawi by people risking their lives to exchange

a few bags of salt for sugar is used as a metaphor for the tenuousness of life during the brutal civil war in 1989 Mozambique. During the journey, the state militia who are protecting the passengers occasionally turn against them and conflicts frequently break out among the militia whose loyalty to any regime or state is tenuous. Along the way, guerrillas destroy tracks and attack the train, killing many passengers. During these attacks, the militia must put aside its internal power games and hatreds to repair the track to prevent everyone from perishing. The point is that civilians are accountable to the army and the army is accountable to no one in countries with failed states.

10 Specific Problems with Design and Implementation of Aid

Introduction

To be effective, in supporting the creation of effective host country governments, overseas aid must meet two criteria leading to sound design and implementation matching objectives. First, it must be optimally allocated by sector and function within countries. Programs and projects should be focused and scaled to specific outcomes; and the aid projects must be staffed and managed effectively consistent with national and sectoral objectives. Again, based on the above sectoral and regional aid allocation analysis, the thesis here is that the bulk of U.S. DA and SA is allocated to appropriate sectors and functions. Instead, the major problems lie in the second area of project implementation. Since many aid performance problems involve personnel issues, relations with local contractors, and unexpected events that occur during implementation, they are hard to correct with legislation, other than to decentralize more authority and responsibility to the project management level. For, as noted by Levy (2014: 38), there is no necessary inevitability that governance improvements will follow growth. Incentives are required by domestic officials and aid project designs to induce competitive institutions with checks and balances and separated powers. A 2003 audit of 669 of 4500 Brazilian municipalities to uncover frauds in procurement, such as fake receipts, over-invoicing, and phantom firms were posted on the internet. The results of the transparent audits induced voters to support those mayors who had the best results for re-election (2014: 159). The difficulty of inducing such reforms in transparency and participation to improve governance is revealed by the fact that even in this strong federation democracy, critics opposed the audits.

ODA operates largely on the premise that governments can be induced to reform by civil society action. Direct leverage on regimes and states by donors is minimal, leaving the intermediary institutional layer as the main target of influence. Support for CSOs by aid has been an important vehicle for its allocation and use in all regions, for example, the noted ICHD participatory capital budgeting efforts with multiple Armenian small towns (ICHD, 2006). Most such bottom-up initiatives are sectoral-level programs that attempt to create quasi-federalist features in target countries. For example, the Pakistan RCT (randomized controlled trial) effort to determine school treatment with parent information, time spent, book availability and test scores relations; El Salvadorian community-level educational fiscal monitoring committees; Ugandan educational public expenditure tracking; the Kenyan RCT to determine "contract teacher" effectiveness; and the Indian RCT to determine learning achievement (Levy, 2014: 166–167) The premise of such aid projects is that more of them can create more pressure to reform whole governments. However, not all of them have been scaled up and the perennial question has been how can that objective be incentivized?

1. Design

Three criteria should be met for proper aid design: first, the design process should be: decentralized enough to allow focus on the problem(s); second, technically sound for the context; and third, be able to anticipate major implementation obstacles and include alternative project responses. The design process should lead to projects that are responsive to the real needs and demands of all the major stakeholders.

Decentralized Design Process

Much of the ODA design process for larger donors, such as USAID and the World Bank, has been decentralized over the past several decades. More allocation and design decisions are made at the local mission level or by regionally decentralized units (e.g. the World Bank) without requiring lengthy approvals from HQ for new projects or changes during implementation. For example, USAID mission directors, if delegated the authority by their Assistant Administrator, can approve activities up to $100 million, but anything at or above $25 million still needs to be put before the Contract Review Board (CRB) at USAID HQ in Washington, D.C. before being put out for procurement. Many USAID mission directors, especially in large host countries, have this authority (Rozner, 2018). The U.S. aid programming process is described and contained in annual publications called "Country Development Cooperation Strategies" (CDCS), the most recent of which for Ethiopia is for 2011–2018. Without recounting the details, this typical country CDCS provides the rationale for programs, planned outlays and net resource inputs by sector and project, including performance measures for the mission's 120 projects costing $12.8m/year (USAID, 2017a: 70–73). Each CDCS is comprehensive and lists other country donor outlays (e.g. Irish Aid and DFID) for major projects (2017: 77). It describes USAID's inter-donor cooperation that includes a "productive safety net program" (2017: 14) that requires building on World Bank plans with the Government of Ethiopia (GOE) in that sector. For its objective of "accountable governance and peace", the CDCS lists working with CSOs and hosting dialogues between CSOs and the GOE as the major means. In the area of strengthening governmental effectiveness, it notes specific work on USAID-GOE procurement reform. The stated overall goal of country aid is to move Ethiopia to middle income status through work on the economy and society. The CDCS is thorough, well researched, and based on identified country problems. But there is no overall country evaluation of aid results for Ethiopia—by for example, UNDP or any other donor or aid research institution. CDCSs are a plan of USAID DA programs and projects with performance indicators and some activities. USAID missions, like that in Addis Ababa, are the main funding provider and overseer of all projects, including longer-term efforts.

In general, projects have often had major impacts on governmental effectiveness only to be reversed later by changes in regime and country oversight personnel. USAID or any other ODA donor is quite powerless to prevent such interruptions. For example, an important key to success of the 12-year $34m Ethiopian USAID project (1996–2008), called the Decentralization Support Activity Project (DSA), was the cultural context of discipline and a new regime that, after 17 years of civil war, needed legitimacy and a free hand in design/implementation of proposed financial reforms. That meant the new regime carefully scrutinized who was to be allowed into the local "reform tent". The regime viewed the management of public money as the heart of sovereignty and was suspicious of foreigner prescriptions and imported techniques. It made sure that any resources taken from aid agencies contributed to doing the right things correctly (i.e. effectiveness). Contextual and regime support conditions were right in that reform was urgent and the DSA team was trusted. The context was also a weak state that urgently needed to establish control and legitimacy. The means to this end was a rationalization program intended to establish central control of the public finances and increase the capacity of regional officials to implement development projects. In textbook fashion, the state would be strengthened in order to diffuse and devolve authority while maintaining control of local fiscal and political events. Uniquely, this regime took ownership of the DSA project by ensuring that it would be built into the Ethiopian cultural features of discipline and conservatism while keeping at bay the Bretton Woods institutions and their near obsessions with macroeconomic control (i.e. budget cutbacks) in exchange for reform support. Added to the complexity of the project and regime's task was that in the interests of enhancing its legitimacy through state modernization, the regime was implementing a political decentralization program at the same time as DSA public finance and fiscal decentralization reform (Peterson, 2015: 8–10).

The DSA project team was intimately aware of the local political culture and the need to harness values and practices in order to build trust in the new PFM systems and methods. As to the basic question of whether senior officials would actually support the fiscal reform, the project team discovered that while part of the political culture superficially seemed to be an impediment (i.e. too conservative), the prevailing uncertainty allowed the operational dimension of that culture (i.e. discipline) to embrace change. All it took for success was to harness local leadership with these enabling features of the culture. Though a daunting challenge, the team selected the right regional leadership which energized ground operations and sustained the project.

The DSA project work plan proceeded logically from basics of budgetary classification and coverage to the introduction of cost centers using simplified analytic information. Here began a series of intrusions from other aid donors, notably IMF in this case, which worked against the DSA project timeline in that the IMF wanted sophisticated program-performance budgeting systems installed in the shorter-term (2015: 210, 219–220). Even under the most advanced country conditions, the perennial problem of program performance budgeting systems is that they require sophisticated management skills (which are often a proxy for higher pay) if they are to work at all. The interference problem surfaced early on with a task force report written by an overseas auditor who wanted advanced budget reforms in Ethiopia despite the fact that the traditional object of expenditure budget could not even account for or control off-budget funds, for example, social rehabilitation funds. Instead, DSA was focusing on transaction controls through cost centers and an improved but simple chart of accounts and budget classification as well as basic policy reforms such as a new macroeconomic planning framework and fiscal transfer formula. As indicated, the common sense project logic was that public and performance management could be the focus only after fiscal administrative capacity was established. The IMF repeatedly attempted to derail the roll-out of traditional budget reforms by demanding that the GOE regime change the DSA focus in order to facilitate advanced program budgeting systems in Ethiopia (2015: 81, 90–91). In contrast with IMF arrogance, the World Bank recognized the constraint and respected the needs and capacities of local officials. It supported continued strengthening of the traditional line–item budget by the DSA team. These kinds of intrusions by competing and self-styled dominant donors occur in many countries and damage the effectiveness of aid to strengthen states.[1]

Another major frustration with aid project design and implementation is to achieve success and have it come unglued later by changes in personnel and top-level regime support. Following the end of DSA, the government opted not to sustain the PFM reforms and instead to follow the advice of the Bretton Woods group and go for "perpetual reform", including accrual accounting and budgeting, and program-performance budgeting. By 2011, the public finances suffered serious problems due to budgetary indiscipline and loss of financial control as functioning systems fell into disuse. For example, 58 percent of the finance offices no longer bothered to reconcile cash balances from bank statements with balances shown on the ledger cards; internal auditor roles were compromised by interference from finance departments despite purposely separating them as a check and balance (or essential internal control design feature); and accounting backlogs returned and account closures were no longer performed (2015: 121–122). The original drivers of reform: favorable Context, government Ownership, clear and limited reform Purposes, and sensible Strategy (COPS) all were overwhelmed by donor squabbling and intrusions. The contextual advantages evaporated quickly. The overall failure of financial reporting and attendant control led to more corruption, since the "check-out counters had been removed from the store!".

Organization is the way government is structured to perform its core functions (2015: 26). A new organizational and institutional problem arose in sustaining the DSA reforms. That was the merger of finance and planning organizations into a new MOFED that was both incapable and unwilling to assume responsibility for the core function of PFA/PFM. MOFED later rejected the creation of a PFM steering committee that might have sustained the reforms (2015: 94, 229). Without such basic top-level support, the public finances deteriorated. Again, aid projects, however well-designed and staffed, cannot alone deal with such instabilities. Since aid is rationally planned by donor but irrational in that all donors are rarely taken into account by host country regimes or individual donors themselves (except often in a competitive sense), little can be done by project funders to remedy the intrusion problem except protest. At the country level, donors often compete to have country officials sign loan or grant documents that enhance donor staff performance metrics. They often have little concern for duplication or waste and at best presume they can "coordinate" matters later during implementation. Much aid then works at cross-purposes at the country level despite being sensibly planned by individual donors for target countries. The Ethiopian CDCS did note other donor efforts and offered coordinating devices. But the host regime, conversely, is often interested in generating the most aid, some of which might be used to substitute for locally budgeted funds. The regime can also claim credit for amassing aid, if debt service burdens do not become unsustainable. And project counterpart funds can always be found "in kind" that do not really sap local resources. In the case of Ethiopia, USAID earned the GOE's initial trust for DSA by providing exceptional support and oversight staff and flexibly trying not to set the agenda for PFM reform (2015: 42).

At the strategic allocation level, project and program funds are often criticized for spending on long-term abstractions, such as democracy and human rights. The criticism is twofold. First, the aid diffuses Western universal values that stoke up ultra-nationalism, both narrower ethnic and wider populist. Second, it wastes funds that could otherwise be directed at operational and sectoral programs that can improve state effectiveness. For, state weakness is the virus that stokes and energizes nationalist threats to both stabilization and reform.

First, Western values of universal human rights, democracy and rule of law are viewed by nativists and nationalists as not universal at all. Ethnic and populist nationalists claim that nations are sovereign and different and shaped by their own history, culture, and race (*The Economist*, 2017m1: 54). Other nations (France at the time) could not impose their version of liberty and equality on others (on Germany at the time, for instance, which claimed its own special knowledge of what such values meant for its locals). Political conflict over the meaning of such "universal" values could often then be between friend and enemy—not national citizens seeking compromises. The inherent factionalism and sectarianism whipped up by nationalist thinking around the meaning for locals of "universal" values is evident. The tragic paradox is revealed in the tale of Vladimir the peasant who was offered whatever he wished by God if his neighbor would get twice as much. He chose to lose one eye so that his neighbor would be blinded. Despite the culturally specific Slavic pessimism of this tale,[2] it demonstrates the tendency of nationalists to make choices that harm themselves, often out of injured pride, at the expense of the entire nation, for example, Poland falling out with Germany, its biggest trading partner and source of investment. The sensible answer to economic insecurity is programs and projects for schools, roads, civic improvements, more funds from the central government, as well as the authority to spend them. Instead, nationalists prefer triumphal arches and monuments (2017m1: 57).

Those who would repel Western universalism (e.g. the popular Vladimir Putin in Russia; Viktor Orban and his Fidesz Party in Hungary; and Jaroslaw Kaczynski and his Law and Justice Party in Poland) argue that they have simply different values that favor ethnicity, race, and historic ties to blood and the soil. They have viewed Western lectures on human rights and democracy as arrogant, naïve and often hypocritical, given recent happenings on race and populist nationalism in the "universalist" countries, such as the U.S. Destructive nationalists are often populist politicians who follow a standard script: exploit economic and physical insecurities by claiming special connections to the "people"; recount tales of corrupt elites, crooked immigrants, misleading media and sinister conspiracies (2017m1: 57). The Philippine authoritarian leader, Roberto Duterte, for instance, employs a "keyboard army" to purvey his half-truths in order to feed his base and strengthen his power and popularity. His message: only a strong, ethnic culture and powerful government can keep you safe (2017m1: 57). To dictators and authoritarian regimes, diffusion of Western values of checks and balances, separation of powers, rule of law, and federation governance are indeed contrary to local values. But the values are contrary, not to those of most people, but mainly to autocrats and nativists. Western values constitute threats to their rule and promise transformation of such systems to link the actual needs of people with responsive and effective governments. Thus, the values are not actually in conflict; the conflict is and has always been between democracy and autocratic dictatorships. In short, if U.S. DA did not grate on "local" regime values in authoritarian countries, it could be criticized as poorly targeted. CSOs in authoritarian countries such as Russia and Central Asia have long been targeted along with donor support from the U.S., Britain, and the Open Society Institute.

Second, after nearly thirty years of mainly U.S.-led efforts to build democracies and effective governance abroad, many of the same host country regimes and governments around the world have become increasingly autocratic, illiberal, and authoritarian, for example, Turkey, Poland, Hungary, and Thailand. While aid workers and scholars recognize that best results have often been obtained small-bore at the sectoral and micro levels (albeit with larger projects), much U.S. (and British) aid policy efforts have instead been at the transformational or strategic level. The aid has been allocated to build democratic institutions and practices where underlying support for effective governance has usually not existed. The overall approach has been called: "outreach to populations or social engineering" (Jeffrey, 2017: 28) and often relies on NGOs and strengthened civil society organizations. Their public participation campaigns have been designed to stimulate greater freedom of expression and public choice. These large-bore or "transformational" missions with corresponding projects and programs have been intended to remake country political cultures (2017: 31) driven by progressive or liberal values and practices. Important gains have been achieved as noted in micro or technical areas of democratic sub-systems, such as election systems, and revenue mobilization. For example, U.S. DA successes in streamlining tax and customs administration in such countries as Georgia and the Philippines have resulted in: greater revenue generation to finance local budget needs; increased public willingness to pay taxes from perceived stakes in the system; and creation of the taxpaying cultures necessary to strengthen accountability for services and responsiveness by governments to local needs. Such aid successes have been scaled-up and provide needed strength to governing states. These small wins have generated momentum for the creation of "virtuous cycles" of reform (Levy, 2014) that in the aggregate, strengthen governmental systems and improve local and regional services delivery. Despite these successes, allocation of aid funds to finance similar revenue mobilization programs and projects by all donors was only 0.07 percent of total ODA (USAID, 2017a: 2). In short, the operational systems-level successes have not been supported by necessary aid allocations and have instead often focused at the strategic country level. Beyond such institution-building successes at the sub-systems and micro levels, unfortunately the overall strategic thrust of U.S. DA has largely produced superficial and formalistic gains that have been quickly reversed by authoritarian and populist leaders around the world. Moreover, deeper values of Western democracy often perversely design out or ignore home-grown injustices in the political culture, for example, caste and the class discrimination practices in South Asian countries such as India, Sri Lanka, and Nepal.

In fact, there were earlier historical precedents for successful transformational U.S. aid efforts such as in Japan, Germany, and the Marshall Plan after WWII. Since these programs led to successful results, why not perform the same trick elsewhere? U.S. doctrines about promoting constitutional democracies overseas began in Latin America with the concept of political development, which buttressed policies and programs through applications from about 1945 to the present. One important problem that led to even more stress on strategic transformational efforts of the past decades has been the mistaken emphasis on means and techniques, rather than ends. Large-bore, complex, and messy problems, such as how to create democracy and good governance, were transformed into objectives which were then taken for granted. This has been an example of how an analytic tool, such as cost effectiveness analysis, has been distorted and poorly applied. Cost effectiveness analysis is used where primary ends and benefits are given (e.g. lives saved from a railroad crossing gate or homes served by weekly trash collected) and the task is to figure out the least monetary cost of attainment. Non-monetary costs, such as institutional rules and cultural practices as well as the value of a human life, can be ignored for calculation of the lowest cost/unit of benefit (Michel, 2001: 79–80). But ends such as democracy are abstract and almost, by definition, full of non-monetary costs and benefits. Despite these measurement and methodological problems, when aid disbursal did not produce these ends, the common inference was not that the larger transformational objectives were out of line but that something was wrong with the techniques. That led to constant tinkering with aid machinery, personnel, and lower-order concepts (Packenham, 1973: 116). It also led to new fashions and approaches (such as tighter monitoring and evaluation of expected results) rather than challenges to the basic assumptions or goals (1973: 117). As will be noted, the over-emphasis on performance measurement, monitoring and evaluation has become the new "Digital Taylorism" (*The Economist*, 2015c, 36) that has resulted in aid goal displacement. Such self-defeating patterns have persisted and explain much of the ineffectiveness of development assistance to strengthen governments and improve their performance.

The charge is that instead of targeting the aid to defined problems and needs, it is often programmed to serve long-term democratic goals that reflect more U.S. or British vanity than local needs. A recent example of aid to the primary Philippine agricultural sector is telling. The constraints of land tenure insecurity and failure to move from primary growing and export to secondary processing and manufacture in that country have been known by experts for over 50 years. Successful World Bank projects to develop small farmer forestry production for supply of pulp mills there date back to the 1970s. Yet, the examples were not transferred to other sectors, nor scaled up to the central government. All this occurred while the U.S. spent and still spends funds on the distractions of democracy rather than at the proper micro-sectoral level to stimulate growth and development.

The response to these arguments is that despite all the fanfare of nation-building by the Bush and Obama administrations, aid for democracy and governance was actually very small: only around 13 percent of FY 2013 USAID aid allocations (Tarnoff, 2015: 19). SA and DOD allocations for armed conflicts added more funds but they were based on strategic military policy considerations and not allocation of DA. While U.S. foreign policy drives aid policy (Guess, 1987: 6) to a large extent, in this case it cannot be argued that the larger policy goals significantly distorted USAID allocations. Additionally, if state effectiveness is the aid goal to prevent destructive nationalism from overwhelming societal institutions and order, which eventually demand military solutions, soft aid in the form of D&G can help stabilize them and legitimize regimes. Aid to strengthen election administration, the independent media, an independent judiciary, rule of law (to move away from rule by law) and CSOs or NGOs that provide intermediary layers between states and the people, is necessary. Only the British and U.S. aid programs have had this focus. The aid has not directly produced democracies in the examples given because host regimes have to be willing to support the generally positive results of the aid projects. They often have not, and in many cases have opposed the very institutions that could have strengthened their states.

In addition, the specifics of such apparent aid failures as the Philippines are often more nuanced. Failure to make traction on land tenure and secondary processing, for example, reflect local elite preferences and special interests that constrain policy solutions. Strengthening civil society activism to secure land tenure and to provide credit to move from primary to secondary processing are worthy objectives but require the support of the banking system and a regime that wants to empower many small landholders. Strong civil society institutions are necessary to put issues on the agenda, build support for them, and force them to be taken up by regimes. Indirectly, democracy aid can benefit state effectiveness. So far, direct aid has made little difference to regime preferences. It is the preferences and not the aid that have prevented growth and development.

Second, in addition to problem-driven planning and responsiveness to major stakeholders, aid design should provide technically sound evidence that the context for the aid project is and will be favorable. In an extreme sense, one would like a stable context with strong institutions for projects to be implemented. But since those are the objectives rather than conditions, most aid projects would fail the test of likely success in what would be high risk contexts. While conditions vary for aid success, a typically favorable context would include top-level regime support that ensures project appropriate regulations, financing, and authorization of needed project decisions (Guess, 2005a: 179). Such conditions rarely exist at the beginning or prevail at the end, as demonstrated above by Peterson (2015) in the Ethiopian PFM reform project. Nevertheless, many conditions can be identified during aid design and planning, and assessed as to their severity as a constraint to success. For example, the contextual risks for aid support for current efforts in Pakistan to privatize the state airline PIA should be clear. The countervailing institutional forces will be unions, and the historic political and patronage links between PIA and the regime. Such donors as ADB conduct contextual analyses of the short- and medium-term costs and risks before project approval. For example, before approving an extension and expansion of the Pakistan fiscal decentralization project in 2000, ADB wanted to know the potential risks of nuclear war from the current conflict with India! It was noted that warhead exchanges could diminish both project results as well as local government tax bases, all of which had to be weighed in the proposed project's cost/benefit calculus! For most projects, however, the contextual review is intended to see if at least some favorable conditions exist and whether predictably unfavorable ones might be changed during the project from additional official and public support if it goes well. Otherwise, aid planners are well aware that regime and project support is tenuous and cannot be counted on for the duration of this or any other similar project.

The operational problem is that some design problems related to context may not be resolvable by sounder technical analysis of costs/benefits, by requiring more/better technical assistance and training, through stronger conditions, or even by structural reform of aid institutions (because of unintended consequences). The reason is that to be successful in a government reform project in often corrupt and unstable contexts means that trained individuals must take on security risks themselves. For security they will be depending on national police and security institutions which typically will have less interest in their welfare while working to uncover corruption than in maintaining their institutional and personal loyalties and patronage links to the regime. For example, internal audit agencies in wealthy countries are functionally designed to produce evidence of conflicts of interest and to reveal embarrassing transactions and networks. In poor countries, the audit agencies typically lack independence and become part of the conflict of interest problem themselves. This is a serious problem in developing and transitional countries where throwing out dirty laundry can mean death and family threats (Nelson, 1983). Similarly, aid focused on financial sector reforms often targets the banking sectors. This often means the application of forensic accounting and auditing skills to inspect invoices and check premises to ensure that banks are not financing with fraudulent loans and international money laundering (e.g. Afghanistan with its thriving opium trade). Commercial bank loans are granted in such countries with scanty financial records making it difficult to gauge creditworthiness or to foreclose on defaulters. The difficulty of tracing paper trails at the source of loans naturally leads to personalized lending which often appears to be, and actually is, corrupt and incestuous. The Afghanistan International Bank (AIB), for example, must demonstrate compliance with international transparency rules to maintain its clearing relationships with foreign banks such as Standard Charter and Commerzbank (*The Economist*, 2017d1: 70). Aid to improve accounting and reporting skills in order to perform these necessary tasks and to meet the management requirements runs up against the powerful disincentives and dangers of using these new skills in both the state and private banking sectors. In short, accounting and auditing staff gain the skills but are often afraid to use them.

This is unfortunate in that building an accounting and auditing culture, via PFM aid and World Bank scholarships to gain international qualifications, is an example of how the provision of narrower technical skills, in this case to "count beans", can be scaled up to strengthen both states and private sectors. For example, efforts in war-torn Afghanistan to build an accounting culture through the provision of common professional norms can lead to wider benefits. They could lead to a greater entry of needed foreign investment from investors that have greater confidence in formal records and the transparency of public fiscal and private financial data (*The Economist*, 2018d: 67). That would lead to the reduction of the large informal sector and greater access to loans from banks, which now constrains growth. Greater trust can ultimately result in a country where corruption is now a normal way of doing public and private sector business. But the security constraint on the use of new accounting and auditing skills must be tackled first.

Third, in addition to contextual obstacles such as regime support, institutional obstacles to implementation should at least be considered or anticipated in the aid risk framework. Most donors have some form of pre-commitment risk assessment for programs and projects. The ADB process was noted previously. The ideal process would anticipate implementation obstacles and opportunities and deal with them beforehand. Standard evaluations that examine project experiences for lessons would not be of much use for complex, multiple-objective, intergovernmentally funded and shared management projects such as the Oakland

EDA economic development effort. The Herbert Simon notion of evaluation as the "implementation of programmed decisions" (Pressman and Wildavsky, 1984: 177) would not produce many useful dos and don'ts. Aid projects do not take place in static worlds of programmed decisions: "good" and "bad" take on multiple meanings during implementation (Pressman and Wildavsky, 1984: 178). The process of implementation itself alters the policy or project, making it hard to draw decision-relevant lessons. That is, implementation evolves over time. Lessons learned from any "similar" project experiences then would not be similar enough and probably inapplicable. That is why the superficially useful "what works and what doesn't" approach to aid projects seen in the media and some guru books is not very useful for actual management or policy lessons.

In the Oakland EDA case as in many aid projects, a stated objective was to induce jobs and raise incomes of depressed regions or cities by providing infrastructure that would stimulate new investments and generate economic growth (1984: 154). But the theory may have been flawed in that such local economic development or LED projects often transfer employment from one part of a community to another; the hard-core unemployed are unaffected because they lack skills and experience. Thus, the "development" project becomes multi-objective, more complex and harder to evaluate other than to view it as a very large combined public works and social services effort, such as the TVA project in the Appalachian region of the U.S. In any case, implementation of aid projects like that in Oakland face the "multiplicity of decisions" and "complexity of join action" problems that require "decision points" and "clearances" all along the way and reduce chances of project success (1984: 102–107). Pre-agreement among decision participants for unexpected events presumes knowledge of which institutions will appear, which new decision-makers in those institutions might want additional clearances, what denial of clearance would mean to implementation and so on. That would be impossible to do during the design or planning phase for all but the simplest of projects, that is, one objective and one institutional overseer, such as a rural tertiary road.

Unanticipated consequences and uncertainty surround complex aid projects in both wealthy and poor countries. Both sets of countries are faced with institutional poverty in the sense of the lack of positive redundancy, and decisional uncertainty, as explained by Caiden and Wildavsky (1974). In this context, the second best solution is to provide field management with the needed flexibility to change course during implementation without lengthy delays. Even that solution has to be qualified for field surprises, as indicated in the Appendix case of Pakistan. In general, project management needs maximum authority and flexibility to modify budgets, change personnel and change course subject to, for example, rapid USAID approval (or denial and explanation) by the Chief Technical

Officer (CTO). Built in at the design stage, that would result in better results during implementation.

Even with greater line or field discretion and authority, design errors for complex projects still surface in specific cases. The argument here is that they are dramatic, with splashy broad-brushed portraits of waste and incompetence, but practically of less importance for overall ODA efforts, by USAID or other donors as well. For example, in implementing the Macedonian local government strengthening project in the mid to late 1990s, the Chief of Party was prohibited, as all of us were, by the Mission Director from talking with anyone from the central government without USAID clearance. The rationale was that the project should not be talking to the central government if it is supporting local government development. The local USAID decision was hardly a sound recipe for how to strengthen intergovernmental fiscal and management mechanisms in Macedonia. That order led to the absurdity that the COP could not talk to his landlord who was also Minister of Trade, about heating and repairs without going through USAID! Many other well-designed project implementation work plans have micro-managed by USAID or contractor HQ personnel to the point of interfering with the delivery of results. That is less "goal displacement" than simply instances of annoying and irrelevant interference with necessary project work.

Other projects have been designed on the theory that the locals "don't know how" when it turned out that donors didn't know either. For example, USAID funded two agricultural research stations in Guatemala without ensuring communication lines between them. Nor was there effective communication between USAID and the MAG. Paddock and Paddock (1973) documented such "aid follies" early on. Many have done so since.[3] The Paddocks attributed many of them to constant changes in, and elimination of, personnel, meaning that discontinuous experts often initiated programs followed by others who constantly "reinvented the wheel" (1973: 10). As juicy as such tales are, descriptions of aid follies are often written by people who lack street credibility. They have been sacked from projects multiple times; they are on do-not-hire lists of donors; and they had personal grudges from being always "right" and "not listened to" by the blockheads above them. By contrast, the Paddock's materials were derived from multiple sources in the field, such as bush pilots, and could be verified in USAID reports. Another Guatemalan project described was a rice drying and storage project that was intended to contribute to the ongoing anti-guerrilla campaign (a U.S. foreign policy objective at the time). Consultants came and went, equipment arrived too late or too early for supervised installation; and builders didn't follow specifications that were often in English. Despite its obvious unworkability, USAID claimed it as a success in deterring Communist guerrillas! (1973: 20). On land reform, they found that USAID had no more foresight than the IADB and followed the stale policies of putting more funds into electricity generation and industrialization than in the agricultural sector (1973: 264). Since we still haven't even solved the problems of subsistence farming and poverty in Appalachia, their point was that we shouldn't be inflexibly telling the Third World how to solve theirs (1973: 303).

Thus, the aid design problem is often one of: arrogant experts that assume no local knowledge and presume their own (1973: 62–65); in-house donor jargon that even other donors, for example IADB, cannot follow in joint meetings or reports; and the use of federal budgetary and accounting terms which makes mutual understanding harder, for example, "re-obligations", "obligation year budget", "program loans", "sector loans" and so on (Guess, 1987: 58). Such instances of poor planning and panicked implementation responses to pick up the pieces continue. To compound the problem, USAID is still often inflexible about listening to contrary opinions from its staff or outsiders, and often closed-minded in telling hired experts initially what they should find after their review missions end! As we have seen, host country governments such as Ukraine often ignore aid advice and others such as Pakistan argue that they know how to fix their problems and simply need the money. Most of these kinds of predictable intrusions should be anticipated in advance and the question is, under the circumstances, what is the best way to negotiate the best project work plan during implementation?

Corruption and Aid Context

In addition to potential design follies from arrogance, bureaucratic micro-management and inflexibility, aid projects in most countries must confront corrupt ways of doing business in varying depths and intensities for both private and public transactions. Again, this is part of the context for which USAID must assess risk to project success. Corruption is defined by the CPI as the misuse of public power for private benefit. The CPI measures the perception of corruption by multiple institutions and people conducting daily transactions in each country. Corruption in the countries used as cases in this book (Table 2.2) is unsurprisingly distributed. Wealthy countries with large private sectors have higher ratings (e.g. U.K. and Spain) than poor countries of SSA, Latin America, FSU/CEE, or Asia (e.g. Nigeria, Brazil, Egypt, Hungary, or Indonesia and China) with smaller private sectors having much lower ratings. In countries with larger private sectors, one might expect greater instances of public corruption in the form of violating state regulations to move the funds and get the job done. In such contexts, state bureaucratic over-control clogs systems, and prevents services, programs, and projects from being completed. In order to satisfy local needs, local public officials often have to develop ways around regulations. They may take a fee but the purpose is not private gain but moving the money and completing their tasks. This was Mr. Johnson's dilemma (Cary, 1939): developing creative systems to get a road project in Northern Nigeria completed but at the cost of violating almost every modern public financial management norm of good British practice at the time.[4] But his actions could also be described as good, creative management that got the job done. In such contexts, private suppliers to aid projects may want bribes to facilitate their efforts to use their networks and contracts to get public projects completed. That makes sense if you want the project completed. The danger is that a confident local leader with apparent authority, together with local "mirroring" behavior that tolerates bending financial rules for empathetic reasons of "social reciprocity", will keep at it, leading to perpetuation and expansion of petty corrupt practices, whatever their utility (*The Economist*, 2016b). Values and practices of the local political culture then directly facilitate "corrupt" practices in such contexts. Nevertheless, contractors and even aid agencies may look the other way for such charges euphemistically called "administrative expenses". They may want to complete projects and get paid; but post-audits usually turn up their legal and regulatory misdeeds and they are sacked and/or jailed.

Conversely, in countries with larger public sectors (% GDP) and smaller private sectors, official corruption would likely describe the national way of doing business, e.g. Russia or Nigeria. These are states where "cultures of corruption" closely describe how business is conducted. Aid project design has to recognize the constraint and either not disburse appropriated funds that fail to meet internal control standards (controls that reflect accounting and treasury practices) or obligate and let them be spent with falsified papers that, after audit, would implicate all parties in a technically corrupt practice. Early U.S. military assistance to Iraq faced this problem: a large appropriation that could not be spent because of suspect financial controls.

Moreover, aid design and planning must face the contextual constraint that corrupt practices may be required to do most things necessary for project successes. There are many remedial suggestions but these often apply to the future, not the next fiscal year! For instance, a workable strategy for identifying and reducing corruption at the local level in developing and transitional countries could be to support institutions that focus on smaller but high-impact (mainly sub-national) instances of corruption from the strategic level rather than on larger, systemic problems at the operational level (Guess, 2005). The core of the approach would be to focus on fiscal transactions related to municipal services delivery, for example, infrastructure, transit, water, sewerage, education, and sanitation. The suggested mechanisms are accounting/reporting and oversight via improved internal audit and control systems. While efforts to treat "ethically impaired" officials and contractors via training and counseling are important, the focus should be on strengthening institutional efforts to attack well-known opportunities for misappropriation and diversion of funds that are often related to extortion and kickback payments for contracts. Many have found it useful to distinguish fraud from theft, systemic from periodic corruption, and big vs. small corruption. These distinctions are academically interesting but often boil down to a range of opportunities for public diversion of funds that ultimately should be eliminated. Such transactions occur in developed and developing countries with differences in regularity attributable largely to the efficacy of local control institutions and to the professional capabilities of their staff.

The impact of corruption on the public is variable not constant. Much of the high public impact corruption occurs in municipal service finance (Guess, 2005). Quantitative service delivery surveys indicate that people sense that poor services and corruption are linked and support remedial action. Low public impact corruption consists of transactions either too large (strategic in amount as well as analytical level) or too alien (perceived as victimless) from community cultural systems altogether. Surveys indicate weariness and helplessness in the face of stories about these kinds of misdeeds. Responses reveal a kind of fatalism and passiveness among the public. Allocating enforcement resources to low impact corruption may then produce few returns in the quest to institutionalize anti-corruption norms. The contrary cases of Armenia, Malaysia, Guatemala, and Romania (which all focus at the strategic level to deal with low impact corruption), suggest that focusing on high impact cases through management-level reforms seems to be more effective. The Romanian DNA national anti-corruption agency was discussed previously. Following this approach, modern systems of internal controls and audit systems target high-impact fiscal transactions, incrementally building support for wider investigations into the abuses of power which divert funds from activities and services that benefit common people.

Again, from the aid design perspective, the need is to estimate the severity of local corrupt systems on the transactions that will affect the project, that is, the decision and clearance points noted previously. How serious are these potential problems for the implementation of the aid program or project? If this can be done to the satisfaction of USAID, for example, they must ensure that post-transaction audit and control systems are in place. The implementation system should centralize and enforce financial control norms and decentralize authority to transact business and manage results to the project level. Through this kind of "New Public Management" method, used for decades in advanced Commonwealth countries such as Australia and New Zealand, the interaction of oversight and audit institutions to hold managers accountable for financial and physical results in an incremental flow of sequential transactions, is likely to produce the best value for money.

2. Implementation, Reporting, and Oversight

The second criterion for effective aid programs and projects logically is that they be implemented properly. If aid can facilitate state effectiveness in countries where regimes and states are threatened by ethnic and populist nationalism, then most of the aid problems need to be sorted out at the project level. Donors such as USAID deliver pots of cash to countries for programs and projects. The funds may be insufficient or not allocated to the most needed regions, countries, and local partners. But the funds are there. Despite the many tracts written about donor structural problems, and reading between the lines of aid evaluations that conclude either projects were successful or beset by the perennial "coordination" problem, it is during implementation that most constraints occur to aid effectiveness. Institutional incentive remedies to straighten out rules and processes that encourage perverse actions must be identified and applied at this stage. Some are caused by context: local corruption, overseer and partner instability, multiple cultures, and parallel institutions such as those Mr. Johnson faced (and relished) in Nigeria. But most are from micro-management problems: intrusions by home office contractor firms; intrusions by donor country office staff; goal displacement derived from excessive or irrelevant reporting requirements; and/or project personnel problems. Devolution of authority to the project level in order to flexibly deal with personnel, budgeting and work plan issues can improve matters dramatically.

The charge that U.S. aid is targeted to the wrong level was noted above. The emphasis has seemingly been on strategic goals involving societal transformation rather than more tangible operational objectives in sectors and locales. But strategic objectives are usually translated into sectoral objectives that require strengthening civil society institutions or governmental organizations; and operational projects often require civil society institutions to achieve their objectives. D&G aid is only 13 percent of annual spending by USAID. Nevertheless, the charge sounds plausible. For, the mistaken policy premise was that, since aid could transform economies and produce effective governance in one spot, it could do it elsewhere. That was the conclusion reached from experiences with aid for effective central and local governance in Eastern Europe post-1989. This may have been premature given the turn of events in core Visegrad country regimes toward political illiberalism in recent years, for example, Poland, Czech Republic, and Hungary. The aid conclusion was that the trick worked a few times before so it could be repeated elsewhere. But the "trick" was poorly specified.

In early post-transition Balkan and Eastern European governance aid projects, the focus was initially correct and successful then later revised based on criteria irrelevant to results on the ground for building effective governments. In Albania from the mid to late 1990s, the U.S. program was called "public administration" and projects focused on strengthening local government services and systems. Since subnational units were deconcentrated parts of the central government, this required working closely with the relevant functional ministry which was Interior under the communist system. The results were successful for not only the five local governments that could now plan and execute services, including in some cases the capacity to contract service delivery, but also for inter-governmental relations in that the now ministry knew that local finances were insufficient and recognized the disincentives caused by the existing system of central fiscal transfers. The approach of working with both levels of government, concentrating on central and local systems and techniques to improve discrete activities, for example, financing sanitation services and paving roads, worked well, and additionally built up support for local mayors. The project resulted in several unplanned items not in original scopes of work (SOWs) or later work plans but which contributed to effective government, such as the ability to allocate local grants to local organizations for small public works as water filters to control garbage flowing into lakes, designing a new transfer formula for the Ministry of Interior, and developing a technical paper series of best practices on core topics such as pricing public services, developing local revenue bases, planning capital projects, and contracting-out services. The project implementation approach was incremental, trial and error, and in many cases, learning by doing. That required flexibility from the USAID mission and the contractor. Both were forthcoming for the duration of these projects. Reporting burdens by the COP and project team were reasonable and often handled informally by meetings between the USAID mission director and the team.

By contrast, a similar SOW for Bulgaria several years later was hamstrung by process and reporting requirements imposed by the USAID mission on orders from the HQ in Washington. These were derived from new congressional democracy-building and performance requirements. The thrust was that since such projects would be contributing to democracy-building and larger strategic objectives, all activities should be quantified, measured, and reported regularly. On the familiar management theory that "what gets measured gets done", USAID developed "democracy indicators" for its projects, composed of dozens of indicators for each activity that were to be reported by field personnel. The emphasis was properly on results and performance. But the continuing problem with such "new scientific management" and "digital Taylor"-type approaches (*Economist*, 2015c: 36) are the personnel and management costs of the increasing demand for performance indicators, by USAID in this case, but by most governmental agencies providing services, for example, excessive educational reporting of test results in order to obtain fiscal transfers. The emphasis on achieving measured results often ended up incentivizing behavior unrelated to the actual objective of delivering DA to increase effectiveness of local officials or educating students. The resultant reporting burden and distortion of activities becomes "goal displacement". The new practice was an example of "digital Taylorism" (*The Economist*, 2015c: 36) in honor of the early 1900s' "scientific management" theorist Frederick Taylor, who developed and encouraged the concept of workflow analysis to increase efficiencies i.e. the mathematical streamlining of industrial workplaces. This foundational and useful modern management theory, in part the basis of the Functional Review state modernization methodology discussed previously, was now being applied almost mindlessly and without judgment or insight by leaders and managers less interested in the problems created by goal displacement than on gaming results to obtain better ratings and more funds.

Specifically, the problems of this more controlled, micro-managed and heavily scripted approach are threefold: (1) field personnel often didn't know how to install systems in the new environments in the short term. Effective installation of personnel or budgeting systems required time to convince local officials; (2) the approach also put projects in central and local government silos that were not supposed to interact. Since pre-existing systems were a function of laws and personnel that were often from the central government, this became a major communications constraint that prevented building trust; and (3) the causal linkages between better budget processes, wider tax bases, more professional personnel, and improved health care efficiency, for example, and democracy were, and are, debatable. Attributing democratic results from a collection of technical activities from one project over a mere several years was highly abstract at best, and flawed to the point of creating operational constraints where none existed before. The predictable results were that either (a) the activities were "gamed" to match the indicators and results expected, or (b) they were simply reported as spectacular successes that, of course, would lead to surprises later when the systems unwound. The project required extra layers of costly and time-consuming monitors and evaluators to whom field personnel would report, followed by many hours of extra meetings and reviews to analyze results before forwarding them up the chain of command. What could have been mostly replicated from the cultural and institutional contexts of Albania to other Balkan countries such as Bulgaria to create small-bore systemic successes was prevented by the intrusive bureaucratic requirements of aid delivery in the name of creating the whole-systems reform of democracy-building.

The question is, what is the way forward for aid allocation? What should be done via DA feasibly to improve governance, in what contexts, and how? First, the "winning hearts and minds", "values-driven, outreach to populations social engineering", "transformational" (Jeffrey, 2017: 31) missions and projects have not succeeded and cannot succeed in achieving these strategic level ends and structural changes. The goal of such efforts is nothing short of transforming whole political cultures and the perverse incentive for aid workers is that Congress actually wants to hear this is being done in reports. This is true whether the context is a failed, fragile, or centralized state. Additionally, adding democratic targeted metrics to otherwise useful sectoral projects unrelated to democracy-building is a useless distraction. Second, in these contexts changing political cultures and institutions require incentives and incremental efforts at the micro-sectoral level. Examples are food aid, disaster assistance, emergency health sector aid, educational reform (e.g. Afghanistan) and technical programs to strengthen revenue, public expenditure planning, and execution systems as well as central banks (e.g. Iraq) (2017: 26). This kind of targeted aid can and has worked to create micro-successes in difficult contexts such as Syria, Ukraine, and Yemen (2017: 32) and easier ones such as Albania, Macedonia, and Bulgaria. Third, the objective should be the creation of country federations or sectoral quasi-federal systems as the most citizen accountable, policy responsive, and sustainable type of governance. This requires working to strengthen central governments enough to devolve authority and responsibility for particular administrative and financial functions and policy sectors. The objective should be effective governmental performance rather than broad-scale democracy. Since federations are rare and hard to achieve, efforts to build on quasi-federal systems should be made incrementally. The latter can be, and have been, created by redefinition and reassignment of intergovernmental roles and responsibilities to devolve authority for particular functions.

Goal Displacement from Reporting/Supervision Requirements

We have noted that small systems improvements at micro-sectoral levels can counter some of the threats from ethnic nationalists to state integrity and effectiveness. This operational focus can provide core services without the necessity of reforming whole states beforehand. An example was the necessity of getting social safety nets to Albanians caught by the transition of the early 1990s. The socialist state had ceased to function and social assistance and benefits were needed to avoid famine and further social unrest. The World Bank designed an emergency social assistance program of individual and local government transfers that provided space for more in-depth state reform efforts of fiscal, monetary, and other sectoral areas to begin. The Bank also supported successful efforts in 1992–1993 for macroeconomic stabilization and recovery in the agricultural and construction sectors (Sewell and Wallich, 1995: 255). For later threats from populist nationalists, efforts to decentralize government finances, revise fiscal transfer formulae, and broaden management and political authority defused hatreds fanned by group leaders with unrealistic demands for more jobs and higher incomes. Thus, micro-sectoral aid DA projects rather than broad social engineering programs can build states from the ground up, through the piecemeal systems, methods, and skills required to conduct analyses and operate them. Such projects can create incentives to improve country service and program delivery by building capacity that is in demand. The supply of aid products are actually demanded by local officials and personnel. We noted that aid devolution can assist in the task to convert aid into an asset in demand, that will be used. For officials, charged with carrying out reforms, improving service performance and productivity, or implementing capital projects under budget and on time, need incentives. Besides the obvious financial incentives that can be built into construction and service delivery contracts for better performance, and greater authority and discretion to actually manage for results, an additionally important incentive is to remove unnecessary reporting burdens.

Much of government effectiveness relies on professional personnel. For that reason human resources constitute large components of state budgets. Such officials need to know that their work is valued and that they are reporting on it to reveal progress, pinpoint problems, and signal the need for remedial action by superiors. Often, reports require large quantities of superfluous data that are not understood, read, or acted upon by superiors. The reports waste time and are simply make-work in most cases. The reform of Milwaukee City budget systems from traditional object of expenditure "input" spending and reporting to a system of "outcomes" budgeting that would link resource inputs to actual outcomes, for example, deaths and injuries from fires or infant mortality rates, began with the elimination of reporting burdens as an incentive for action. The line-item reports buttressed line-item controls on budget execution by the city council (legislature) that clogged service delivery and prevented management from taking necessary actions. As the then director of the city budget department told me, for the success of complex reforms "don't talk to the accountants and get rid of reporting burdens". It worked there; it can work anywhere.

Aid reporting burdens are often justified by serving accountability goals. Reporting reams of spending data may provide grist for variance analyses. They could lead either to efforts to reduce budget execution instability, often revealed in large planned–actual differences by year or year-on-year, or they could lead to further efforts to reduce discretion to transfer and reprogram funds in order to reduce the variances and be more plan-consistent. The latter effort to micro-manage and script results in advance fails to allow for the usual unplanned interventions, such as less revenue available than planned or major unplanned expenditures. The entire reporting effort becomes narrowly focused on pre-control of management behavior rather than encouraging management to achieve programmatic results with more discretion. Modern systems focus on post-transaction expenditure reporting that allows decisions to go forward and auditors to examine results in detail later without impeding budget execution and service delivery. Real performance gains are made by changing incentives that affect managers, in our case aid project-level personnel.

Beyond the standard problem of reporting spending, which is made easier by GFMIS real-time minimum clearance systems that are in use now in even the poorest country, is the additional burden of reporting physical or service results performance. In the name of broader, deeper accountability, systems have been added that require performance "metrics", "benchmarks" all of which aspire to "replace judgment with standardized measurement" (Muller, 2015: 18). These new "scientific management"-type requirements permeate governments in the U.S. and OECD countries now in both domestic and international activities. They have added a new layer of make-work that has the same defects of narrow spending data reporting: the reports are unread, often not understood, and rarely discussed or acted upon. The situation is somewhat paradoxical in that the effort to move from useless reporting on inputs to output/outcomes reporting that analyzes the link with inputs and leads to better cost effectiveness requires the new type of reporting. Thus, the incentive to perform the latter must be based on the removal of unnecessary input reports that no one reads. That essential quid pro quo is often missing in the rush to reform. The benefit of such exchanges for DA would be less need and expense for clerical data entry accountants and more funds then for program staff that do the analyses and actual delivery of programs and projects. The aid would become more effective by making a greater impact on host country state effectiveness.

In short, "metric madness" (Muller, 2015: 23) has led to false accountability systems that result in the not uncommon problem of "goal displacement". That is, the metric replaces the end that these means ought to serve (2015: 27). Given the stakes of keeping jobs, getting raises or adding more staff, people will focus on satisfying a single measure and goal at the expense of other more important organizational goals that are not measured. Officials forced to spend time on reporting metrics are often pushed to game performance measurement systems, especially in the important fields, such as education where testing madness has become the problem, and law enforcement where more arrests somehow become greater productivity to overseers.[5] Since goals and metrics are often imposed by others who do not actually understand the work required (2015: 28), it is important that metrics be developed and used by technical line officials, at the operational level, who actually know about task complexity and do the work. It is also important that metrics be used for internal analysis by practitioners rather than external evaluation by publics who typically fail to understand their limits (2015: 31).

The development and use of metrics is especially a problem in DA evaluations. The challenge for aid is to encourage judgment, initiative, and motivation through proper oversight without stifling autonomy (2015: 31). This means ensuring that line practitioners develop the metrics and that they are developed by other similar practitioners. In this way, reporting burdens can be reduced and streamlined to improve real results without generating "false accountability" numbers for consumption by unknowing publics. Estimates of the reporting burdens vary by agency and purpose and are not aggregated in one reliable figure. One empirical study of management control systems for 99 defense contracts found the "quality, detail, timeliness and cost of information did not have a positive effect on project control" (Overman and Lorraine, 1994: 195). Despite these findings, "most managers still believed that collecting and reporting information led to project control". Data is reported because it must be reported and it preserves the illusion of control, that is, it has symbolic value (Guess and Farnham, 2000: 129). All this wastes time and scarce resources that could be used for better program delivery.

Those who have worked for aid agencies know that much profitable time is spent on recording what should already be known or implied in the ongoing work. Many feel that the burden is to overcome the presumption of distrust between staff and line officials in aid agencies or HQ and field. As such, no amount of reporting would reverse that presumption. The Swiss Aid agency (SDC) may have the least burdensome reporting requirements. Their projects are smaller and stress sectoral and micro-level results for intended beneficiaries. Program directors assume that pre-screened qualifications and professional integrity of project executors should be enough for accountability purposes. Other programs, such as the Soros Foundation's Open Society Institute, operate smaller projects conducted by NGOs, charities, and universities. These, as well as British Aid (DFID), also rely primarily on professional qualifications expressed in their proposals and past performance records rather than pushing field staff to report during project execution. Aid reporting for DFID projects, for example, is often handled in working lunches with the country ambassador. The Fulbright Program is another example of light reporting requirements. The assumption has been that academics and graduate students are working and studying in countries for professional reasons, that they want research data and publications, and that shirking behavior only harms the grantee. Given the high professional output of grantees over the life of the program, this assumption is valid.

Conversely, larger donors seem to have less trust in grantees and project executors and are obsessed with the apparent need to please larger publics and parliamentary or legislative sources of funds such as Congress. For a time, USAID pitched the U.S. food aid program as a major boon to the U.S. agricultural sector through its purchase of P.L. 480 crops from farmers in almost every U.S. state to be sent overseas. The intent was to broaden the base of lobbying for aid during annual budget appropriation hearings. The problem is that farmers are less interested in the rest of what DA does in target countries, and mandated reporting for other publics that is generally indifferent makes little difference to the aid program's acceptability by voters. In fact, many voters think the U.S. aid budget is as much as 25 to 30 percent of annual spending and any contrary facts are "fake news", to use the popular term. Other donors such as the Asian Development Bank have the heaviest reporting burdens and provide the least discretion to field personnel. What is planned and approved must become the actual project and results in this line of thinking. Our months of field work in Kyrgyzstan under an ADB contract for "Social Services in Development in Osh and Jalal-abad", for instance, was spent mostly inside spinning elaborate narratives for interim and annual reports to ADB HQ in Manila. Project staff was prohibited from making the smallest adjustments to budgets or personnel without HQ approval. Such approvals, if ultimately successful, often took weeks and months, by which time the changes were often unneeded.

The most burdensome, given the potential for excellent results on many projects, are those requirements of USAID. Over the years, trust has declined between HQ and field staff. Some of this may be justified by occasional rogue consultants that turn up and wreak havoc. Others may just be incompetent or inexperienced and somehow made it onto the final project team. The case in the Appendix provides colorful examples of such types and they are not uncommon. Controls must be exercised and supervisors need data and information from someplace on which to act with proper authority. For that reason, project-level metrics and supervision, without major intrusions by contractor home offices or USAID HQ, are essential. Their roles should be to support project staff where justified and to act swiftly to make personnel and work plan changes if required. They should also support project team efforts to gain the trust of host country ministries and the political regime. Often that does not happen. Peterson (2015) noted how USAID did support their efforts for such purposes in Ethiopia. Instead, to cover these implementation uncertainties, USAID now requires burdensome reporting to provide the illusion of accountability. USAID supervisors (as well as contractor home office overseers) are often unable to judge the quality or relevance of field technical work. In Romania, for example, our teams made certain that supervisors received top grades for the least complex work of local government budget reform and that the difficult tasks known to us to be practically impossible to achieve in the short-term were left out of evaluations altogether. Like others, we simply gamed the systems to get rid of these people so we could work with our counterparts in local governments, which were the budget and public works officials.

The USAID reporting burden is so onerous that aid contractors decades ago installed units with extra staff to monitor and report data first to them then to USAID for double accountability. Once the perverse incentives are established at the center, they diffuse downward into program and project management, contaminating their work with guilt and/or duty-driven needs to generate data for the required metrics. For example, the DAI Technical Assistance Management Information System (TAMIS) was established in the 1990s as a sophisticated M&E system for project reporting that would also demonstrate to USAID its commitment to excellence and accountability. Other large contractors developed their own similar reporting systems to win approval and hopefully new contracts based on such costly and redundant commitments. They have merely duplicated the problem of excessive reporting burdens that drive up project and contract costs and waste scarce aid budget funds.

USAID DA may not provide enough funds or for long enough periods, but those made available are not used effectively, in our view, because of regulatory constraints from mission level on down and internal personnel problems. Implementation is quite centralized with perverse incentives for false accountability and against allowing local responsibility. This places much of the burden for effective aid to create effective states on the actual aid worker. It is believed here that the most important determinant of effective DA is the field work of experts in continuous relations with local counterparts, that is, "on and off the job training". DA works best to develop relationships of trust between neighbors that create healthy interdependencies. Human associations have always existed prior to the state and they cannot simply be reordered by rearranging state institutions through fear or material incentives (Grygiel, 2018: 91). Effective states depend upon these networks and social regulatory rhythms. Aid, properly designed, can strengthen these associations which can improve state effectiveness. Delivery of better DA projects to improve local services and programs often leads to growth and development. But necessary personal and institutional networks, systems, and relations are hard to build and take time. DA is more than the Victorian, "Mrs. Jelleybee" of Dickens' *Bleak House*-type solicitude for the spiritual and material welfare of others, that is, the international do-goodism associated often with NGOs, charities, and foundations. DA seeks to build larger institutions from multiple encounters with aid field workers fostering trust through such daily relationships for the life of the project as part of accomplishing TOR tasks. The success of DA depends on the field worker and team learning from recipients while also giving lessons to them.

Effective DA project field work can be illustrated by the behavior of Admiral Peary who in the 1890s spent extended time with Eskimos to learn from them such vital facts (then rejected by most "experts") for polar exploration as: that their dogs could be trained for travel; their clothes could be adapted to the environment; their igloos worked better than most tents; that these primitive people had something to teach, and that civilized men did not have a monopoly on knowledge (Huntford, 1999: 29). It is the Peace Corps-type approach to development where extended time is spent in the field exchanging lessons and building relationships. In contrast with this bottom-up, egalitarian learning, almost anthropological approach to technical work, the expeditionary project of

Captain Scott represented the British class stereotype: class-riven culture, rigid hierarchy over functional efficiency, blind obedience, and aloof, top-down command (1999: 112). The Scott mentality and approach frequently represents the strategic policy-level aid project or program that fails to build on-the-ground relationships on which institutions must be based. The operational approach at its best means that several years of aid project working with locals are going to be required to develop field-level relationships between aid workers, among the members of associations, and between the associations and the states after the aid project work has ended. This requires socialization and interaction with functional counterparts and their families. The top-down command and control, or short-term "parachuting" in consultant approaches, are contrary to this normative ideal of operational field work.

While most aid field workers are versed in the relational approach, strategic policy officials, concentrating on reporting, evaluating, and supervising field teams from afar typically are not. Successful examples include the USAID: West Bank Gaza water scarcity project; the West Bank Gaza PFM project, working with corresponding Israeli sectors; and the creation of Albanian and Macedonian local government finance associations or GFOAs by large numbers of their cities in the late 1990s. To work, such technical/functionally based topics had to encourage open debate in order to create opportunities for trust. DA projects have done this repeatedly at the functional, operational level in multiple sectors. The Swiss aid agency (SDC) targets broad goals such as growth-promoting projects to strengthen trade and investment in market economies. Historically, they have focused on democracy-building, civil society projects and, more specifically, on small-scale agricultural programs at the operations level, such as production of cheese by the rural poor in countries like Ecuador. More recently, they have moved into another critical operational area: public financial management (PFM). They emphasize development of databases for macroeconomic policy reform, and planning–financing systems for infrastructure projects. For instance, the "Strengthening PFM in Colombia" project was a five-year effort worth $7.37m of which SDC covered $5.8m with local counterpart contributions amounting to $1.5m. In short, the SDC model of an independent DA agency properly focuses on operations-level projects with great success.

Notes

1 As a former member of the budget division of IMF's Fiscal Affairs Department charged with TA and training to improve budget information and allocation systems, I can say that IMF has never actually seen a successful program budget implemented anywhere.

2 The dark Slavic humor is revealed constantly in local jokes that somehow always end with a punchline where everyone dies or suffers from disease. Working in Tartu, Estonia on a USAID local government project for DAI,

I greeted my ethnic Russian Estonian assistant with: "Well Maria it looks like it's going to be a nice day." She—"Yes, but don't worry, it will get worse later!" Russians are famously noted for their dark Slavic jokes, such as:

> A dozen workers from the Urals were visiting Stalin in his office. After they left, Stalin was missing his pipe. He told his aid Poskrebyshev to see that all the workers were questioned. A few minutes later, Stalin found the pipe in his desk and told Poskrebyshev to release all the workers. "But Comrade Stalin, they have all confessed."
>
> Joke from *Stalin's Barber* by Paul M. Levitt
> (New York: Taylor Trade Publishing, 2012).

3 See for example: Graham Hancock (1996) *The Lords of Poverty: The Power, Prestige and Corruption of the Multibillion Dollar Aid Industry* (New York: Mandarin Press). Can't imagine him getting more aid jobs after this blistering indictment of the incompetence and lack of integrity in the aid business! See also, Patrick C. Heilman (2017) *USAID in Bolivia: Partner or Patron?* (New York: FirstForum Press); Dambisa Moyo and Niall Ferguson (2009) *Dead Aid: Why Aid is Not Working and How There is a Better Way For Africa* (New York: Farrar, Strauss and Giroux); and William Easterly (2006) The *White Man's Burden: Why the West's Efforts to Aid the Rest Have Done Much Ill and Little Good* (New York: Oxford University Press). The others are all measured critiques that argue for better program and project design and better coordination during implementation, and which propose structural changes in aid donors.

4 In the 1939 novel, the action takes place at a Colonial station near Kano in the Muslim part of Nigeria. Johnson is a wily local (real name Bauli) who works for Rudbeck the political officer or ADO who likes road-building. The district officer (DO) Blore deals with tax collection and is also a judge—he suspects Johnson of no good; Bulteel is an old hand who likes roads and wants to see the 100-mile Dorua road project go north to Fada to link with Kano. The context consists of trying to work the project through in multiple cultures governed by parallel institutions: colonial British institutions, parallel native institutions (the courts), and local Muslim culture and institutions that feature their own treasury system. Rather than the complexity of a joint action problem (Pressman and Wildavsky, 1984), this is a problem of single decisions taken in the context of joint cultures and shared institutional authority! The local Muslims actually oppose the road and the *zungos* or temporary work camps that could become permanent and threaten their native authority. Johnson was a dreamer and believed in his own words as soon as he invented them. That was the origin of his financial dexterity. Tring is the UK regional auditor who is suspicious of Johnson, and wants to know if his road payments were from the British or native treasury, and why the road project was running into cash flow shortages. Johnson moved funds freely around between accounts, capital and current, personnel and non-personnel, and even fiscal years to pay workers from imaginary cash accounts. This violated the British budgetary rules and the standard chart of accounts for journal and ledger entries. He simply made up account titles and paid from them. Lack of clear accounting rules for

account definitions were a contributory factor, a product of implementing a project in the context of multiple cultures and institutions. For example, Johnson entered the purchase of a cow as an expense for personnel milk supplies but instead of a payable or incurred liability he entered it in the exports file because he expected it to become a hide. Why not? one might ask. At the end of Johnson's short career as project financial accountant and manager, Bulteel argues that British financial control regulations were too rigid and, if followed, there would have been no Dorua road or even a British Empire! Rudbeck was also reprimanded in Bulteel's report, not for fraud/embezzlement which is what Tring wanted but rather for "unorthodox accounting" and "overspending votes".

5 An important origin of this activity is the *New Public Management* reforms beginning in the 1980s and aimed at strengthening the results orientation of the public sector. The emphasis was to shift the focus of control from inputs to outputs in order to achieve accountability for performance targets. Pioneers were the UK, New Zealand, Australia, Sweden, and U.S. state and local governments. This was a growth industry starting in the 1980s in developing countries as donors sent consultants and teams to make institutions more accountable. Results have been uneven with most responses incremental and piecemeal. The major problems were: time consumed in developing and measuring results; failure to link fixed variable costs to service volume relationships; failure to include any incentives for those making changes to routines and repertoires; institutional inertia from teachers, railway, and other unions; and fear of political backlash from producing evidence of weak performance. For our purposes, the more important failure is the time and resources consumed in implementing results measurement systems that actually displace program results. See Brian Levy, *Working With the Grain: Integrating Governance and Growth in Development Strategies* (New York: Oxford University Press, 2014); and *Public Sector Reform: What Works and Why?* (Washington, DC: World Bank, 2008).

11 Summary and Conclusions

This book described three common features of the international governance problem: (1) centralized but weak states incapable of providing effective programs, services and infrastructure; (2) rigid structures lacking internal flexibility between levels of government and branches of government. The centralized and inflexible governance structures have minimal separation of powers or checks and balances; and (3) weak central governments which have been unable to mediate legal, fiscal, policy, and management tensions that arise from normal operations of a complex state. Unable to anticipate or manage tensions, states have often taken refuge behind more rigid and authoritarian policies and operational controls over management. The controls extend to political opposition to its poor policies and management that maintain poverty and prevent growth. They have often been forced into such policy responses by the pressures of ethnic and populist nationalist groups and their leaders which, in most cases, reinforce bad decisions, such as circling the wagons by ruling groups in Zimbabwe and rejecting international pressures for open societies and markets, for example, Brexit.

We then argued that institutionalized federation can most effectively respond to these problems and strengthen democracies through three features. First, strong central governments counter-balanced by independent sub-national government levels are essential. Vertical intergovernmental relations are worked out through periodic reassignments of fiscal and political authority. These may devolve authority or centralize it depending on the policy function and need for efficiency and responsiveness. Instead, the literature and technical advisors often argue for straight decentralization as a simplistic remedy for governance problems. This unintentionally often leads to community-based corruption and the authoritarian control of cities and regions. Second, effective checks and balances for policy corrections are required. This is the notion of countervailing power or "supplying opposite and rival interests" for "self-defense" (James Madison, Paper #51) against institutional and special interests, to preserve a fairer pluralist bargaining democracy, which was an important feature of his contributions on the proposed new U.S. system in the *Federalist Papers* (Hamilton *et al.*, 1961: 322); and third, separation of the political division of labor is required to prevent power grabs by one branch or leaders representing that branch.

But serious constraints exist to transferring, building, or adapting these features abroad. Despite the common sense rhetorical and empirical support for the above three propositions, major practical problems exist in transferring and adapting the decentralized democratic federation model from countries with stable, U.S.-style contexts overseas. Adoption is limited by at least three constraints. First, the powerful opposition of authoritarian regimes and alternative-value secular and religious (e.g. Islamic) systems offer illiberal models of growth and development that produce gains for only the short term. This political culture or contrary value problem limits the ability of any good governance or democracy-building programs to achieve more than operational gains in particular sectors. Values are political convictions, such as secular and liberal or extreme religious zealotry. Within each value cluster, detailed nuances can be identified and linked with political behaviors. Second, host country interest groups oppose reforms and have well-oiled and corrupt links to regimes. The values of such groups and sects dominate the political culture and often prevent the adoption of decentralized federalist systems and solutions. Their concentrated special interest influence is evident in: botched privatizations, crony state bank lending, crony public contracts, and the persistence of tax havens. Thus, federation remains a useful goal and can only be approximated by microsectoral projects and programs to decentralize governmental finances and political authority to local governments. Such efforts can create quasi-federalist structures as interim solutions.

Third, democracy-building programs themselves are flawed on at least two fronts. First, programs expect institutions from developed democracies such as elections, civil society organizations, and public sector management systems to work in host locales without major interference from local cultural and historical values and practices. An important goal instead for effective governance should be normative centralization and operational decentralization of fiscal, management, and political systems. Central governments should be strengthened to deliver effective programs, projects and services; discretion and financing should be devolved to subnational levels and particular sectors to increase responsiveness and accountability to local populations which builds support and legitimacy for central governments in the process. Democracy-building programs often target one governance level or another without linking the two comprehensively. For effective state-building, DA works best at the microsectoral level, rather than at an unrealistic whole-systems level where the sudden transformation of local political cultures and institutions is expected to suddenly create democracies (Jeffrey, 2017: 28).

Second, false accountability structures (Muller, 2015) are imposed on aid programs in the form of strategic-level rules that require intense operations-level reporting and encourage goal displacement at the program level.[1] Tarnoff (2015: 40) fails to mention this as a problem in his analysis of "Too Much Accountability?" Aid workers fit their activities to abstract goals and objectives, attributing their actions to impossible results. Though collectively, the activities add up to such happy outcomes as growth, prosperity, peace, and democracy, country policymakers are often surprised later when it turns out to have been a donor-created Potemkin village. That they have "gamed" the system would be an understatement. Often driven by the need to show success and keep the funds flowing, donor rigidity and lack of consistency during implementation limit the effectiveness of already-limited impact "good governance" programs. The result is that donors often do not utilize their immense technical expertise properly to strengthen governance in general and federalism in particular. They frequently seem to lack practical knowledge of how to deal with growing fragile and failed state problems and are unable to respond effectively when they occur. Of course, development aid organizations are but one actor in the geopolitical policy matrix. Additionally, they often lack influence within bilateral country policy-making institutions. Britain may be the exception here. While meeting the annual UN aid target of 0.7 percent GDP, it spends more from its budget on aid than diplomacy (1.2 percent of every £1000 for DFID vs. 0.2 percent for the Foreign Office). But its aid policy design and implementation still takes place within an unfavorable institutional context where six other departments handle international policy. Nevertheless, we argued that these three constraints amount to soluble, actionable administrative and policy problems.

In short, despite aid project follies:

1. Donor aid programs are about as effective as could be expected for the small funding amounts and short time periods allotted to them. Structural changes of aid programs to make them more independent might help. But overall, given the range of donor programs, countries receive about what they can reasonably absorb and use. They always need more of it. But they could manage the competing donor programs in their countries better, to maximize results in multiple sectors. The incentives for regimes to take the funds and for donors to spend the grant funds or have the loan papers signed are too great.
2. Ultimately, trade and investment should replace DA in all but the poorest countries in conflict and post-conflict contexts. As we have noted previously, this will not likely happen, given aid fatigue in OECD countries and growing trade protectionism. More private investment depends on the creation of strong states that can provide transparent and predictable legal and regulatory frameworks. It is

a paradox that trade and investment require effective states which can only be created by reformist regime with external nudges from aid. New methods of combining the capital markets with NGOs to deliver core municipal services effectively have been developed. Social Impact Bonds (SIBs) developed in the U.K. for example, have been used to finance and deliver services that previously had been thought to be the exclusive domain of the public sector (Guess and Husted, 2017: 108–109). The bonds are sold to finance NGOs to deliver service result targets based on predetermined industry norms by each service. Thus, they combine the smart use of performance metrics with aligned financial incentives to get the jobs done. Such innovations as SIBs can spur petrified states and corrupt civil service and contracting systems to improve.

3. DA cannot prevent eruptions of traditional, ethnic, or populist-driven nationalism. Growing nationalism is fueled by culture and identity issues that material goods and incomes cannot usually diminish. Success of nationalist movements depends in part on demagogic leadership that distorts facts which are amplified by social media. They also are driven by what seems to be a permanent expectations/reality gap. DA cannot prevent these occurrences from weakening states. SA can help stabilize the security problems, and Civil Affairs units of the military can design governance structures and service delivery systems as they have in many countries since WWII. The second-best solutions lie in micro-sectoral aid projects scaled up to national states and domestic efforts to reduce allocational ineffi-ciencies by redesigning fiscal transfer formulae to incentivize sub-national state-building as a multi-tiered buffer against threats to central governments. Such domestic responses could defuse and perhaps have prevented the Catalonia secessionist crisis and others like it.

4. Nor, as we have seen, can DA directly and quickly create political democracies. Aid stabilized the Taiwanese economy but it developed its own systems for creating governmental legitimacy and account-ability consistent with its political culture. Aid also had nothing to do with Costa Rican democracy which was a product of its own political history. The U.S. cannot export democratic norms such as tolerance, compromise, contestability, and accountability. It can transfer models of sub-systems that work in the U.S. to facilitate the operation of its federation, such as participatory budgeting, election administra-tion and supervision systems, judicial institutions, commercial laws systems, and analytic methods to improve service delivery efficiency and effectiveness. It cannot ensure that any of these are scaled up to national governments.

5. More DA funds are clearly needed to prevent further state failures to stabilize governments. This can be done through expanding the

amounts spent in the existing portfolio of functions, sectors and countries. Specifically, more innovative efforts need to be made directly in state modernization. Projects to strengthen and develop participatory training of trainer systems, local government borrowing capacity, domestic revenue mobilization or DRM, PFM improvements such as medium-term expenditure frameworks (MTEFs), more NGOs to work as SIB executors, and greater management capacity for particular services such as urban transport and health have had dramatic effects in countries such as Romania and Bulgaria. Institutional incentives need to be designed to increase demands for such improvements. The supply of skills and capacity through aid training programs will not by themselves generate demands for their use. Most important is that successes be scaled up. And some of these efforts have indeed been scaled up: many of the personnel who worked on USAID local government projects later entered high positions in their central governments and have become reformers in multiple areas, for example, social protection policies in Bulgaria. These direct state-building efforts at sub-national levels have been successful in many regions and should be expanded in size and length and increased in number.

6. USAID DA programs target major socioeconomic problems in its host countries and missions. The funds are allocated to programs and apportioned by projects in each sectoral area as indicated in CDCS documents prepared by permanent USAID missions. CDCSs are replete with local knowledge and insights based on multiple stakeholder interaction. One can almost say they were the wrong stakeholders in retrospect. But determined efforts are made to gauge local needs and opinions in each country before aid allocations and execution of projects. The strength of state partner commitment is always judgmental and based in large part on the value of taking reasonable risks in-country to get the aid delivered. The context is risky. Aid is a risky business. The machinery must take this into account and make the aid work under unstable conditions. The fact remains that strong, effective governments will be required to implement and sustain these projects. Much work fails after projects end for lack of O&M from state budgets and lack of interest now that USAID personnel have gone and high pay rates have ended. Nevertheless, as indicated, the focus of DA should remain on state building: personnel training and recruitment systems; budget and IFMSs; elimination of in-country perverse incentives working against use of skills and systems gained through aid projects; stronger and independent internal control/ audit institutions; stronger sub-national governments; improved fiscal transfer formulae and more cost-effective taxation, fee or charge systems to finance state budgets.

7. Major reforms to the State Department or USAID are not going to happen. Secretaries will come and go with orders to modify the number of management positions, eliminate titles and functions, consolidate activities, decentralize operations, centralize oversight for operations, and so on. As in university reorganization efforts that absorb time and resources in mostly raucous and inconclusive meetings, the actual effects are hard to gauge or attribute to the reorganizations. There are simply too many unintended consequences in large public bureaucracy reorganizations to be worthwhile. British Aid DFID and Swiss Aid SDC are more effective because their projects are smaller and shorter in duration. Reduced scale allows greater focus on staff and results. Oversight of aid projects is much less top-down and handled in monthly meetings that include not only the aid agency representatives but often the country ambassador who takes a personal stake in the ODA results. This contrasts with the metric madness and top-down, distant, mechanical command structures that often oversee large donor projects from USAID and the World Bank. More important than structures that organize and deliver core functions are the quality of personnel and leadership who occupy positions and how they interact informally to get decisions made and implemented.

8. Thus, the major contribution to aid project ineffectiveness is the level of personnel and management problems arising at the project level during implementation. Problems of inappropriate project design have been noted as part of continuing aid follies that affect all donors. Corruption and weak state partners are a permanent contextual condition of most aid projects. They are givens and must be dealt with by deft and experienced aid workers and officials in the field. To perform such difficult management tasks, such professionals clearly need all the budgetary, personnel, and management authority possible, subject only to post-audit review of transactions and decisions as is normal in many Commonwealth country public management systems. Aid should be as much as possible tailored to local counterparts and beneficiaries by field personnel to the extent possible, that is, CTOs, USAID Mission Directors, and project COPs. This may be easier said than done in larger missions with multiple complex projects and few top personnel interested in granting wide discretion to project people under them. USAID directors and CTOs that have followed locally sensitive, labor-intensive tailored approaches often run into trouble with superiors that rigidly follow guidelines, as *Mr. Johnson*'s supervisors found out. As revealed in a few anecdotes and the antics of personnel in the Appendix, there are major problems at the country and project personnel staffing and management levels. Improvements here can make the most difference to improving aid results and to producing actual host country governmental effectiveness.

All this means that USAID must take a harder look at proposed project personnel. To do that, requires more evaluation personnel at the design and approval stages and information on individual past performance. Such requirements have been in place for decades, and past performance has always been part of the bidder project evaluation score and process. But too often USAID misses evident weaknesses in the proposed personnel; or selects the least-bad in order to prevent the project from stalling, which would potentially mean unobligated project funds left over and embarrassing questions to be answered.

At the country level, donors vie to unload grants and loans for particular purposes, e.g. several donors may have civil service reform projects in one country, and need the regime's approval. This destructive competition wastes funds that could be usefully combined in an ideal world or at least tailored by the regime to avoid overlap. Regimes may also go for projects that offer the least intrusive conditions demanding local reforms, for example, Chinese infrastructure loans, but which at commercial rates can threaten country debt sustainability and hence its financial condition. As indicated, USAID CDCSs note other major donor projects in-country and suggest the need to "coordinate" (the universal elixir) with them. That rarely happens in the competitive world although project staffs often socialize in-country to everyone's benefit.[2] Country reports need to detail the effect of all aid, joint and several, on sectoral developments.

As stated, the real aid is delivered in the field by line workers and project staff. Managing these operations well will have the most impact on aid goals, both strategic and operational. To reiterate, it is critical to maximize COP discretion to manage his or her project budgets and staff. In the process of implementation, it is also critical to cut down on reporting burdens and oversight by distant generalists who waste substantial amounts of valuable time.

Notes

1 The biblical characterization of this perennial phenomenon is: "straining at a gnat while swallowing a camel!"
2 In Nepal, for example, our World Bank team leader forbade us from talking with the IMF mission despite the similarity in SOWs dealing with public expenditure management issues. I knew one of them and found out he played tennis. So members of both missions played tennis and we ended up sharing vital information despite the naïve prohibition of the Bank's team leader.

Appendix: Managing Development Projects in High Risk Environments

The Case of Pakistan

George M. Guess and Dennis DeSantis

Background: USAID in Pakistan

For more than 60 years, the United States and Pakistan have worked together to forge a relationship that benefits the people of both countries. This cooperation has produced transformative ideas and institutions that are still considered landmark accomplishments for Pakistan. In 1947, the United States was one of the first countries to recognize an independent Pakistan and to extend considerable assistance for the establishment of key institutions. With U.S. support, Pakistan was able to undertake many notable development projects, such as the Institute for Business Administration, Jinnah Postgraduate Medical Center, the Indus Basin Project, Faisalabad Agricultural Institute, and a variety of other efforts that laid the path for Pakistan's Green Revolution. In the 1960s and 1970s, the United States was a major donor for the construction of the Mangla and Tarbela dams which, at the time of their completion, accounted for 70 percent of the country's power output. In the 1980s and early 1990s, the United States helped build the Guddu Power Station in Sindh and the Lahore University for Management Sciences, which is now considered to be one of the nation's top business schools.

More recently, U.S. civilian assistance to Pakistan has delivered real results on issues of greatest importance to all Pakistanis: energy, economic growth, stability, education, and health. In addition, when natural or manmade disasters threaten Pakistan, the United States has been quick to respond. Over the past decade (2006–2016), the United States, through USAID, has given Pakistan nearly $7.7 billion of funding. Pakistan remains one of America's largest recipients of foreign assistance, a sign of long-term partnership and commitment. USAID's 2016 programs in Pakistan focused on five key areas: energy, economic growth, resilience, education, and health. All USAID efforts in these five sectors incorporate the cross-cutting themes of gender equality and good governance.

DA has been a major tool of U.S. foreign policy. According to Markey,[1] this became clear in the 1990s when the U.S. dropped aid altogether and imposed sanctions on Pakistan. During the Cold War, Washington intended Pakistan to serve as part of its defensive bulwark against the Soviets' southward expansion into the Persian Gulf, first by drawing it into a treaty alliance and later by using it as a conduit for sending money and weapons to the Afghan *mujahedeen*. All the while, Pakistan's leaders—usually dominated by the military—pocketed resources for the fight against their principle adversary: India. In the 1990s, Washington's policy concerns shifted to nuclear non-proliferation, but neither threats, nor costly sanctions dissuaded Pakistan from testing, *weaponizing*, and even sharing its illicit technologies with other states like North Korea and Iran. In the late 1990s, the first author of this case worked on designing a fiscal decentralization project in Pakistan for the Asian Development Bank (ADB). Under the required heading of project failure risks he listed nuclear war with India which became a real threat a short time later, requiring his evacuation from the country!

Introduction and Overview

Practical Concepts in Development (PCD) is a fictional for-profit, Washington, DC-based international development consulting company specializing in private sector development, evaluation and health.[2] PCD was 15 years old in 2010, and employed nearly 100 people, and had worked in 65 countries implementing both long- and short-term development projects for multiple international donors. In Pakistan, this consisted of 25 local professionals and technical Pakistani staff as well as numerous other support staff for a total project figure of around 100 people. PCD would thus be considered a mid-sized aid development firm. Large U.S. firms execute about $150 to $200m in projects yearly and employ 400–700 people. They have been collectively known as "beltway bandits" because of their proximity to the funding source (USAID) from their DC and the Virginia and Maryland suburb offices. Over the past five years, the firm has enjoyed steady and sustainable growth, reaching $40 million in annual revenue, with profitability above the industry average. PCD's reputation and status in the development community has been growing, and the firm feels that it is on the cusp of breaking into the top tier of development firms. The culture of the firm is entrepreneurial, growth-oriented, and technical. The management style has been evolving from a centralized owner/manager approach to a collaborative, decentralized approach to broaden management skills and opportunities. PCD's main client is USAID, which provided 85 percent of its contracting revenue. The remainder is from a variety of sources including the World Bank, State Department, and the U.S. Trade Development Agency, among others. In 2010, the firm won a USAID competitive bid for $25 million over five years, to implement the evaluation of the $500 million USAID Private Sector Development portfolio in Pakistan. U.S. DA to Pakistan focuses on issues of greatest importance to all Pakistanis: energy, economic growth, stability, education, and health. Consistent with the emphasis on growth, the private sector development portfolio is implemented by 14 different contractors, and PCD will design and conduct a monitoring and evaluation project to efficiently identify and track a set of standard project and development indicators. The project, based in Islamabad, has five long-term expatriate staff members, 25 local Pakistani staff, and a large number of short-term expatriate and Pakistani consultants.

PCD won the contract in part because of its superior past performance on similar projects. For instance, in Afghanistan it had successfully evaluated several projects for USAID. In Pakistan, the terms of reference required the contractor to develop performance indicators and a system for monitoring USAID's portfolio across all projects, which included: micro-credit, banking and financial sector development, and commercial enterprise financing and development. Monitoring and evaluation of project impact would proceed according to its approved management plan in Pakistan by collaborating with the 14 contractors implementing USAID's projects in these multiple sub-sectors of the private sector development program. Evaluation would be based on the results of measures derived from indicators agreed between PCD and implementing contractors. They measured progress and results through such indicators as: on-time performance of project objectives; personnel turnover; actual spending vs. projected spending; reduction of unemployment; and sub-sector growth, operating margins and profitability. Project implementation performance indicators were clearly important to both USAID and to PCD. A methodological difficulty that came up immediately was how to measure results across diverse sectors and activities, such as: enterprise development, finance, private sector projects, and environmental projects. How could their impact (i.e. outcomes), such as jobs created, businesses started and increased revenues be measured and attributed to diverse projects in different locations and sub-sectors?

PCD, as noted above, is a for-profit international aid firm. Since USAID began delegation of DA implementation to contractors decades ago, the largest bidders in the development business have been for-profit, e.g. Chemonics International and Development Alternatives, Inc. (DAI). Non-profits, such as World Learning or International City and County Management Association (ICMA), find it easier to bid as sub-contractors for teams led by for-profits. To perform the prime contractor or team leader role requires a much larger scale and the ability to manage large, complex USAID projects according to USAID's detailed accounting and reporting rules. "Profit" meant the firm bid on contracts for clients such as USAID and would charge an agreed-upon, fully audited "multiplier" that was roughly twice its operating costs. It would then add on another small percentage to that figure for profit. Such profits would be distributed to shareholders in firm stock, often firm employees and others that could purchase it as a private firm. PCD was not a "public" firm or listed on stock markets. By contrast, a "non-profit" firm, such as International City-County Management Association (ICMA) was mission driven and less bureaucratic than a private firm. NGOs also made profits ("retained earnings" consisting of revenues over expenses) but they were treated as "reserves". In practice, other than for treatment of "income" by the U.S. tax code, this may be a distinction without a practical difference since both must report project progress to clients in the same way. The reporting burdens are the same.

Like most bidders, PCD bid on mainly USAID contracts with particular terms of reference or TORs to implement them through field projects around the world. It is also possible to submit unsolicited proposals to USAID with novel approaches to particular development problems in specific countries. These are often not funded, the projects are financially much smaller, and it would be difficult for a firm to remain in business and meet the payroll based on a portfolio which hoped for wins on unsolicited proposals. At its HQ, PCD had a staff of around 100 consisting of proposal-writers, contracts specialists, procurement specialists, subject and regional area experts, and project support staff. At any time, it would be bidding on several USAID projects in order to smooth out its revenues and ensure that cash management problems did not occur from sudden gaps in revenue flows in the face of fixed expense obligations. That meant that PCD personnel had to perform reconnaissance on upcoming bids, travel to target countries, locate local firms and personnel, meet with donor clients, and return to prepare the proposals by the due date. This was high pressure work and required the use of teams of diverse personnel focused on winning the project for the firm. PCD would grow, depending on how many wins it could obtain, thus maximizing its revenues and ensuring positive cash flows during the fiscal year. In this way, PCD could hire more personnel and increase its capacity to bid on more projects with the hope of obtaining even more wins.

Upon award, the project became the "jewel in the crown" for PCD, becoming the largest overseas implementation project with a high profile in an important country, with potentially a large amount of follow-on work both in Pakistan and throughout USAID. Monitoring and evaluation was also a practice that PCD had been trying to "grow" into by winning more project bids. Monitoring and evaluation (M&E) of aid programs and projects was, and still is, a popular technical practice area for international development work, and especially that financed by USAID. Other donors such as DFID and World Bank also financed evaluation work but that was much harder work to "win" for a medium-sized U.S. firm with most of its experience and funding from USAID. Nevertheless, PCD now had an opportunity to showcase its management and technical expertise and ability to work in high risk environments. In addition, once PCD successfully performed on a large contract in Pakistan, given geopolitical policy realities, the likelihood of winning more work in evaluation and other practice areas would be increased.

As luck would have it, a few months into project implementation, problems began to emerge from three sources:

a. ***Personnel and Staffing Issues*:**

Andrew, a first-time Chief of Party (COP), was specifically requested by the USAID Project Officer, Kathy during the proposal development stage. The operative oral phrase often used by USAID is they would "look favorably" on PCD's bid in such a case. While technically not allowed under USAID contracting, this is a not infrequent back-channel request. Kathy was in her first assignment with USAID and in charge of the historically high budgeted Private Sector Development portfolio. Kathy's position was the Chief Technical Officer (CTO) or person in the mission to whom USAID project implementers would normally report on technical/physical progress. The perverse incentives operating at this stage were fairly clear. PCD wanted to win the contract. Senior PCD staff likely knew of the conflict of interest if told by those preparing the proposal, putting the team together, and negotiating the contract with USAID which meant both personnel and budget issues. But they also hoped it would all work out during successful implementation. To have protested at this stage on ethical, conflict of interest grounds would have been naïve and self-defeating. It might have scored points with moralists negotiating the final contract at USAID but might have raised broad questions about PCD's competence for future work.

It soon became apparent that:

1. Kathy, while familiar with the Pakistan environment, had a weak grasp of USAID contracting regulations and protocols, and was inexperienced in development practice. In other words, she was an area specialist but not into the time-consuming complexities of USAID reporting requirements, some of which are onerous and can even lead to the goal-displacement of important project work in the field by bureaucratic process requirements. USAID places a premium on performance by experienced field hands on its projects. By contrast, Kathy was very young and inexperienced to land such a large and important role in a key country on her first posting.

2. On the basis of their personal friendship, Andrew became more responsive to Kathy's management rather that PCD's home office, which often led to arguments bordering on insubordination with the Washington senior manager. Effectively, he was reporting to her and viewed her as his superior rather than the home office PCD. This is the dual reporting problem faced by public sector managers who have to serve multiple masters.

3. Andrew entered into a personal relationship with Sarah, who was one of the long-term expatriates, and they moved in together. Sarah then became his live-in partner and subordinate on the project. Such relationships are not uncommon in the tight camaraderie of development teams working in the tight quarters of development projects. Some chiefs of party (COPs) even claim their more successful projects have higher numbers of close interpersonal relationships, which reflects greater camaraderie and leads to better project results.

4. Pakistani staff complaints that Andrew was abusive to Pakistani staff and that he lacked sufficient management and technical experience were increasing. Project feedback channels are formal and informal. COPs may have a set time for weekly complaints; often serious ones come from back-channel sources that want to remain anonymous. A good COP will listen to both, investigate them, and make personnel changes accordingly.

5. Andrew's progress in getting the 14 contractors to agree to a standard set of measurable indicators was slow. These contractors lacked confidence in Kathy's approach to reaching agreement through Andrew on a final set of performance measures that would apply to them. Since knowledge of how to evaluate presumably won PCD the contract and USAID evaluated his qualifications positively, one has to assume he must have known that uniform indicators for the contractors would be an essential first step for the project to go forward. The contrary incentives here should be obvious: contractors seeking indicators that would make them look good; COP needing performance indicators that would also produce valid and reliable data fast.

b. *Environmental and Security Issues*:

1) Street bombings and kidnappings were increasing, as were roadblocks and the presence of Pakistani military to guard against possible terrorists strikes. Curfews were imposed by the government. Security problems were more nascent in the mid-2000s. They are much more serious now in 2016.

2) Unplanned security costs increased more than 100 percent over budget to comply with office, vehicle, and staff housing security standards implemented by USAID. This is clearly a large increase from the planned and approved budget. But to have budgeted 100 percent more for security on the chance that security would deteriorate further could have lost PCD the contract on cost. Guards, hard structures, hard vehicles, and security equipment were needed. In this case, USAID did not want to cover these additional security needs and costs by increasing the budget or redirecting

funds from the technical component. The original budget did not include actual "hardware" equipment costs and trained personnel. It focused on the "software" of security procedures for project personnel with curfews and flashlights, which were much cheaper. With the changed context, PCD engaged USAID in a discussion of several security cost issues without reaching final decisions. PCD wanted to know who would hire the security personnel and who would train them? Who would own the guns and the ammunition and then what would be done with them after the project ended? Who would pay for kidnapping and personal liability insurance? The insurance oversight is odd since, as of the early 1990s, firms had insurance for such events. These problems are known in advance and their resolution is tricky, requiring flexibility from both contractor and donor. For example, the firm for which the first author worked (DAI) carried kidnap insurance for him to work in Pakistan. When asked how much, the president told him that it was a secret as they could torture out the figure—a sensible response.

These discussions and negotiations are more common now as most USAID target countries increasingly have security risks for aid personnel. Estimated additional costs of security were now around $500,000/year. PCD would make about 7 percent profit on the $25m contract or about $1.75m which breaks down to $350,000/year on the 5-year project. Thus, PCD coverage of all extra security costs would wipe out all of its project profits and produce a 5-year loss of $750,000. There would be little incentive for it to continue under these constrained circumstances. The cost coverage issue depended on USAID's treatment of "foreseeability" or whether the costs were "unanticipated" and "unforeseen". Decisions on this issue by the USAID IG (the Inspector General) or the professional development association lobby group would take about six months. In the meantime, USAID wanted its TOR implemented at the original budget and the clock was running to achieve milestones in the PCD management plan for its project. The question for PCD at this point would be whether to walk away from the contract to preserve its company profitability and risk future USAID work or continue as good professionals and fight it out later with USAID?

3) Electrical blackouts surged in the summer, required more generators and renovations, in response to increasing security risks.

4) Expatriate staff, led by Andrew, resisted restraints on staff movement during off-hours, and tighter security standards. Sarah was reported by ISI (the Pakistani Inter-Service Intelligence military agency) to be going out at night, taking taxis and generally

"going native"; she was becoming a "loose cannon" to PCD and to the project. Kathy went even more "native" than Sarah, dressing immodestly for Pakistan and going out to late-night parties. Both of them attracted the attention of the ISI. While civilian and military governments alternate, nearly all civilian political leaders play along with a regime-dominant army to form a permanent establishment that protects its narrow interests at the expense of the vast majority of the population.[3] The ISI is part of this army establishment and still concerns itself with the Kashmiri issue as well as monitoring foreign personnel working in Pakistan. During the first author's ADB project work in Pakistan in the early 2000s, it became evident that their driver couldn't drive. He ran over at least one bicyclist and roared through red lights regularly. Recognizing that we would all be killed at some point, he approached the project assistant (or RHM (right hand man) as we called him). The RHM met with the security chief in Bhutto's Palace (our project's central office) and came back with the explanation that the driver was a "spook". I told him that was fine but to tell his chief to find a spook who could drive. We had a new spook who could drive the next day. Negotiation can work wonders even at this low level of operations.

5) It became impossible to travel to parts of the country to visit sites, and increasingly difficult to travel to contractor meetings.

6) USAID was under lockdown, requiring two days' notification to enter the facility under very strict security procedures. USAID staff could not leave the facility. This is not unusual. Even under "normal" conditions in Pakistan, one could not enter the USAID compound without authorization beforehand. In the first author's case, it wasn't a problem since the project was funded by ADB and we only went to the USAID facility to eat cheap hamburgers. For the PCD project, it was a problem since the CTO was there. The way around this fortress problem was to meet the CTO informally in a restaurant and report over lunch. That USAID officials couldn't leave the building was less of a problem given their intense paperwork routines. One USAID official in Honduras told me once they rarely travelled outside and got most of their country information from the Peace Corps.

c. *Political issues*:

1) A Special Ambassador was appointed for Afghanistan and Pakistan, ranking above the U.S. Ambassador to Pakistan, adding another layer to the official bureaucracy.

2) The Special Ambassador, a known micro-manager, took de facto control of the USAID Program, severely limiting the control and

input of the Country Director. All checks written over $1000 had to be approved by him! The Country USAID Director remained accessible to U.S. contractors. But he had no discretionary budget control which limited the flexibility of all USAID projects to achieve their objectives. This micro-control of financial transactions centralized the flow of U.S. DA in Pakistan even further than noted above.

3) The Special Ambassador wanted to contract directly with Pakistani consulting firms, eliminating the implementation and oversight of many U.S. contractors, putting the PCD project at risk. That is, he wanted USAID to directly plan and deliver DA, which was the original intent of foreign aid in 1961. But the growth of program scale and task complexity resulted in the gradual delegation of the implementation of DA contracts to private contractors and NGOs. To eliminate PCD in this case, as well as for other USAID projects in Pakistan, meant in practical terms finding "certified" local firms, rebidding all contracts, and training cadres of new people—a process that would take years. The notion that local personnel could do the project better than U.S. contractors and that LOE (level of effort) should be allocated to them is a perennial issue. Since it was known that local firms could never meet bid requirements and legal compliance issues, such as functioning internal controls on spending, the fear was inducing more corruption and opacity into both contracting and project management control. This led to the fear that his call for new bids would be simply a "front" for bids prepared by "silent" U.S. partners. Some also feared that U.S. foreign aid would lose its political clout in Congress as a supporter of U.S. firms (e.g. "buy America" procurement provisions and other examples of "tied aid") and employment if the bid policy were changed. Others argued that if locals knew how to perform these tasks, they would already have done so and that international assistance from any donor is therefore not needed. For comparative purposes, regional donors such as the Asian Development Bank working in Pakistan have smaller, shorter projects and do use a greater percentage of local LOE to implement its projects.

4) The Special Ambassador shielded himself from direct contact with U.S. contractors.

d. *Management Issues*:

a. Given the loss of control over personnel and angry feedback from staff, it became apparent that PCD would have to replace the

COP. This was not an uncommon situation: COPs are replaced all the time on USAID projects usually with the rationale of moving ahead in a different direction with a different leader. The question was, how should PCD proceed? Andrew as COP had authority over the check-book and the lives of 100 people. Angry COPs can sabotage projects, and have done so before. Andrew was already "dissing" PCD among Pakistani officials and local staff. He was clearly out of control.

b. Recognizing project problems early on, PCD tried a number of mitigating techniques. It sent Home Office advisors out to the project office in Pakistan. It invited Andrew back to Washington for consultation. PCD held several phone conferences with Andrew in the field. All were ultimately unsuccessful.

c. Thus, having decided to sack Andrew, a visiting team was organized which included the CEO of PCD. But it informed Andrew that he was sacked prior to informing Kathy and USAID. Though this was a serious violation of protocol, the rationale was to prevent Kathy from informing Andrew that he was about to be sacked. The team then set up a meeting with Andrew at which USAID and Kathy were present. In this latter meeting, PCD notified Andrew and USAID simultaneously that he was being fired. Later, Kathy was notified separately by USAID that she was fired as well.

The project raises interesting questions of how all these problems might have been avoided in the first place. What should PCD have learned? What might USAID learn about procedures to implement projects in dangerous or "current-conflict" situations?

Questions

1. *Policy*: What strategic actions should have been taken to salvage the situation by: USAID HQ, USAID Pakistan, and PCD? How could future projects with similar objectives be better structured?

2. *Management*: Classroom participants should be assigned and simulate or play the assigned roles of: Andrew, Kathy, Sarah, USAID and the USAID angel of death team around the issue of Andrew's termination and what should follow. What should USAID require of departing project COPs? How can USAID be assured that the COP actually leaves the country after being relieved of command?

   • How did that lack of rule clarity, and the failure to anticipate this, limit the ability of Andrew to actually manage the project? Which rules should have been clarified or replaced? How did this rule ambiguity lead to the larger management issues that finally derailed the project?

- What management options existed for Andrew on the issues of: security and personnel? What would you have done given his circumstances and why?

3. *Project Planning*: How would you improve the TOR for this and similar projects? What language should be included to clarify liability and security rights and obligations for all parties to the contract?
   - Often planning and implementation issues are settled but not resolved and they resurface on other development projects in other contexts, leading to more problems. Is there any evidence that USAID produces "precedent" from its projects and reworks its rules accordingly?

4. *Content*: Despite successful bids, all USAID projects require approval of a work plan by the CTO in-country before work begins. Contractors must deploy personnel almost immediately and have around 30 days to produce an approved work plan. Some projects even founder at this stage and USAID terminates the agreement with the formerly successful contractor. What should the work plan in this case have provided before USAID approval?
   - It is often argued by contractors that the project work is ill-structured in that, given country contextual surprises, it usually makes no sense to implement as it stands. Contractors can make these points during formal comment periods before bidding after seeing the TOR. They can also make the points after the successful bid but during final negotiations with the CTO and USAID personnel while preparing the project work plan. Was there any evidence that this was done here? What issues should have been raised?

5. *Diplomacy and Negotiation*: Diplomacy is needed to resolve issues and reduce conflict through realistic, arms-length negotiations. There must be a clear framework with explicit rules to guide issue resolution. For instance, which the first author assigns his graduate classes cases which, focus on the design of IMF structural adjustment programs for Zambia and South Korea respectively. IMF provides clear rules with program design driven by the explicit, transparent and often debatable assumptions of its macroeconomic models. Local MOF officials often disagree with IMF demand but most issues are resolved given the relatively tight fiscal framework and the need for valid and reliable fiscal data in support. Local officials are left with choice of means to attain IMF program objectives if they want more loans and continued access to international credit markets. By contrast, for USAID project implementation, rules and criteria to guide management are often vague or non-existent. Field guidance is provided by USAID/PCD for financial transactions and financial and physical progress only. Issues must then be settled ad-hoc through formal and informal meetings. Issue resolution is also constrained by the need for aid contracting firms to maintain profitability and the

USAID need to maintain credibility and political capital with the U.S. Congress.

It is clear from the badly understood and weak communications on this project at the outset with the TOR, at the personnel appointment stage, during implementation with the staff, and for the final replacement of the COP, that the diplomatic element was missing from this project. Diplomacy can be high or low: it may be required during a Cuban missile crisis with high stakes involving top officials or more commonly at the other end of the scale resolving lower-level field conflicts on projects that involve personnel and higher-level country officials + the home office. This is the triangulation problem commonly faced by aid people from companies and NGOs executing development projects overseas.

- How might conflict resolution mechanisms have been improved for this project? How could PCD have had better field intelligence on the project and anticipated what was happening? Aid personnel often complain about supervision and evaluation of their work by inexperienced generalists often interested in power and personal games. Would provision of personnel by both USAID and PCD of personnel with greater technical expertise and experience have improved communications here?
- Overseas aid or DA should be a diplomatic tool. Lasting personal relationships are forged over the course of long projects. Locals learn about the U.S. development business and often fit perfectly while others become cynical of the entire business. Locals also gain insights into the functioning and operation of a USG institution working overseas. They witness the relations between home office project personnel, the COP and themselves. What conclusions can you draw on these themes from this project? How might USAID improve its delivery of aid as a diplomatic tool?
- How could USAID design its programs for evaluations and private sector development to reduce ambiguity and potential conflict? Could the evaluation process be formalized to produce faster and more accurate agreement on program objectives, means and results? Could the private sector development program include grants to small businesses and local NGOs to design criteria and eligibility requirements and suggest evaluation measures? What other suggestions could you make to reduce conflict and ambiguity between the key project partners (i.e. USAID, PCD home office, PCD field staff, PCD local project staff, local private firms and local NGOs) in this case implementing these programs?

Notes

1 Daniel Markey, (2016) "Subcontinental Drift", *The American Interest*, Vol. XII, No. 1, pp. 88–90.
2 The people, companies, events detailed here are fictionalized for teaching purposes, but are based on the authors' many years working in international development.
3 Volume VII, Markey, *op.cit.*, p. 89.

References

Abend, Lisa (2017) "The End of *Convivencia*", *Bloomberg Business Week*, October 30, pp. 13–14.

Adolino, Jessica and Charles H. Blake (2011) *Comparing Public Policies: Issues and Choices in Industrialized Countries* (Washington, DC: CQ/Sage Press).

Allan, William A. (2013) "Managing Foreign Aid Through Country Systems", in Richard Allen, Richard Hemming, and Barry H. Potter (eds), *The International Handbook of Public Financial Management* (New York: Palgrave Macmillan), pp. 540–553.

Allen, Richard, Richard Hemming, and Barry H. Potter (2013) "Managing Extra-budgetary Funds", in Richard Allen, Richard Hemming, and Barry H. Potter (eds), *The International Handbook of Public Financial Management* (New York: Palgrave Macmillan), pp. 396–411.

Almond, Gabriel (1960) "Introduction: A Functional Approach to Comparative Politics", in Gabriel A. Almond and James S. Coleman (eds), *The Politics of Developing Areas* (Princeton, NJ: Princeton University Press), pp. 3–58.

Amanat, Abbas (2017) *Iran: A Modern History* (New Haven, CT: Yale University Press) (Review in *The Economist*, 2017, November 18, p. 72).

Aud, Shannon (2017) "Decentralization and Primary Health-Care Systems in Sub-Saharan Africa", Capstone Paper, Schar School of Policy and Government, (Fairfax, VA: George Mason University).

Azevedo, Licinio (2016) "Train of Salt and Sugar" or "Comboio de Sal e Acucar". (Locarno: 69th Festival Internacional del Film). Available at www.pardo.ch or (accessed 2016).

Azour, Jihad (2017) "A Time for Action", *Finance and Development*, Vol. 54, No. 4 (December), pp. 4–9.

Bardhan, Pranam (2017) "Characteristics of Populism", letter in *The Economist*, October 19, p. 12.

Bartas, Sharunas (2017) *Frost* (Locarno: 70th Festival Film del Locarno), August 2–12.

Bedell, Janet E. (2018) "Romanian Folk Dances: Bela Bartok", *Overture*, January/February, pp. 23–24 (Baltimore Symphony Orchestra).

Bernstein, Lenny and Dennis Brady (2016) "In Flint, Failures at Every Level", *The Washington Post*, January 24, p. A1.

Bershidsky, Leonid (2018) "This Stat Says Iran is Ripe for Change", *Bloomberg Business Week*, January 8, pp. 11–12.

Bird, Richard, Robert D. Ebel, and Christine I. Wallich (eds) (1995) *Decentralization of the Socialist State* (Washington, DC: World Bank).

Bird, Richard M., Christine I. Wallich and Gabor Peteri (1995) "Financing Local Government in Hungary", in Richard M. Bird, Robert D. Ebel, and Christine Wallich (eds), *Decentralization of the Socialist State* (Washington, DC: World Bank), pp. 69–119.

Bloomberg Business Week (BBW) (2018) "Agenda: What They're Worried About", January 22, p. 43.

———. (2017) "The Price of Australia's Complacency", October, 9, p. 33.

———. (2017a) "A First Nation For the 21st Century", October 9, pp. 30–32.

———. (2017b) "Amazon Gets a Good Deal in Ohio. Maybe Too Good…", October 30, pp. 23–25.

———. (2017c) "Is Trudeau Losing His Mojo?", November 27, p. 35.

———. (2017d) "Putin Has a Problem in His Own Backyard", December 4, pp. 46–47.

Booth, John A. (1998) *Costa Rica: The Quest for Democracy* (Boulder, CO: Westview Press).

Brumby, James and Richard Hemming (2013) "Medium-Term Expenditure Frameworks", in Richard Allen, Richard Hemming, and Barry H. Potter (eds), *The International Handbook of Public Financial Management* (New York: Palgrave Macmillan), pp. 219–236.

Bykov, Yury (2014) "Durak", (The Fool) (Locarno: 67th Festival del Film Locarno)

Caiden, Naomi and Aaron Wildavsky (1974) *Planning and Budgeting in Poor Countries* (New York: Wiley).

Campbell, Larry and George M. Guess (2012) "Jordan GFMIS Project: Post Implementation Review". (Bethesda, Maryland: Development Alternatives Incorporated DAI).

Campbell, Matthew (2018) "All the Zollars in the World", *Bloomberg Business Week*, January 8, pp. 48–51.

Carothers, Thomas (2014) "Shortchanging Democracy", *The Washington Post*, December 23, A20.

Cary, Joyce (1939) *Mr. Johnson* (London: Thistle Press).

Cercas, Javier (2017) "What's a Spaniard These Days?", *New York Times*, December 17, p. 9.

Champion, Marc (2017) "Erdogan Tries to Bully the Central bank", *Bloomberg Business Week*, December 25, p. 39.

Chang, David W. (1965) "U.S. Aid and Economic Progress in Taiwan", *Asian Survey*, Vol. 5, No. 3 (March), pp. 152–160.

Chua, Amy and Jed Rubenfeld (2014) "What Drives Success?", *New York Times*, pp. 1, 6, January 26.

City of Milwaukee, Office of Budget and Management (2005) *2005 Plan and Budget* (Milwaukee, WI: Milwaukee OBM). Available at www.city.milwaukee.gov/budget; www.city.milwaukee.gov/mayor/issues/fiscal-management.htm (accessed 2015).

———. (2003) "Plan and Budget Summary 2003"; "2003–2008 Capital Improvements Plan". (Milwaukee, WI: Milwaukee OBM).

Cohen, Richard (2017) "American Jews vs. the Israeli Government", *The Washington Post*, December 6, A23.

Collier, Paul (2007) *The Bottom Billion: Why the Poorest Countries are Failing and What Can be Done About It* (New York: Oxford University Press).

Constable, Pamela (2017) "After Protests, Pakistan Forces Out Law Minister", *The Washington Post*, November 28, A8.

Corning, Gregory P. (2011) "Managing the Asian Meltdown: The IMF and South Korea". (Washington, DC: Institute for the Study of Diplomacy, Pew Case Study Center), Case #235.

Crozier, Michel (1964) *The Bureaucratic Phenomenon* (Chicago, IL: University of Chicago Press).

Cust, James and David Mihalyi (2017) "The Presource Curse", *Finance and Development*, Vol. 54, No. 4 (December), pp. 37–40).

Da Cunha, Euclides (1944) *Rebellion in the Backlands* (Chicago, IL: University of Chicago Press).

Dener, Cem, Joanna Watkins, and William Dorotinsky (2011) *Financial Management Information Systems: 25 Years of World Bank Experience on What Works and What Doesn't* (Washington, DC: IBRD).

Development Alternatives, Incorporated (DAI) (2013) "Public Financial Management Fiduciary Risk Assessment Framework: Stage 2 Risk Assessment, Government of Kosovo, Technical Proposal". (Bethesda: DAI).

Diamond, Jared (1999) *Guns, Germs and Steel: The Fate of Human Societies* (New York: Norton).

Dickens, Charles (1967) *Little Dorrit* (New York: Penguin).

Downs, Charles (1988) "Negotiating Development Assistance: USAID and the Choice between Public and Private Implementation in Haiti", (#117) (Pew Case Study/Institute for Study of Diplomacy, Georgetown University, Case #117).

Ebel, Robert D. and Gabor Peteri (editors) (2007) *The Kosovo Decentralization Briefing Handbook* (Budapest: Local Government Initiative of the Open Society Institute; Pristina: Kosovo Foundation for Open Society).

Finkler, Steven A. (2010) *Financial Management for Public, Health and Not-for-Profit Organizations*, 3rd edition (Upper Saddle River, NJ: Pearson).

Fisher, Ronald C. (2007) *State and Local Public Finance*, 3rd edition (Thomson South-Western).

Foner, Eric (2015) "Why Reconstruction Matters", *The New York Times*, March 29, pp. B1–4.

Fukuyama, Francis (2017) "Why Populist Nationalism Now?", *The American Interest*, November 30.

———. (2014) *Political Order and Political Decay* (New York: Farrar, Straus and Giroux).

Gerson, Michael (2017) "Our Political Parties are in Crisis", *The Washington Post*, November 7, A19.

Gomez, James M. and Kateryna Choursina (2018) "Stalin's Legacy is Choking the Ukrainian Economy", *Bloomberg Business Week*, January 8, pp. 29–30.

Good, Kenneth (1994) "Corruption and Mismanagement in Botswana: A Best-Case Example?", *Journal of Modern African Studies*, Vol. 32, No. 3, pp. 499–521.

Goodhart, David (2017) *The Road to Somewhere: The Populist Revolt and the Future of Politics* (London: Hurst).

Gregory, Peter (1994) "Diagnosis with Limited Information: Government Pay and Employment Reform in Somalia", in David L. Lindauer and Barbara Nunberg (eds), *Rehabilitating Government: Pay and Employment Reform in Africa* (Washington, DC: IBRD), pp. 33–62.

Grupo Propuesta Ciudadana (2006) *Seminario Internacional: Democracia, Descentralizacion and Reforma Fiscal en America Latina y Europa del Este* (Lima: GPC).

Grygiel, Jakub J. (2018) *Return of the Barbarians: Confronting Non-State Actors from Ancient Rome to the Present* (New York: Cambridge University Press).

Guerrero, Christi Rangel (2007) "Decline of Federalism in Venezuela", *Federations* (October/November), pp. 24–27. Available at forumfed.org (accessed 2018).

Guess, George M. (2015) *Government Budgeting: A Practical Guidebook* (Albany, NY: State University of New York Press).

———. (2014) "How to Support Democracy", *The Washington Post*, December 25, letter to the editor, A18.

———. (2007) *Training of Trainers for Local Government Public Financial Management* (Budapest: Local Government Initiative of the Open Society Institute).

———. (2005) "Reducing Local Government Corruption by Improved Fiscal and Service Information", Brasilia: 4th Global Forum on Fighting Corruption, June 7–10.

———. (2005a) "Comparative Decentralization Lessons From Pakistan, Indonesia and the Philippines", *Public Administration Review*, Vol. 65, No. 2 (March/April), pp. 217–230.

———. (1992) "Centralization of Expenditure Controls in Latin America", *Public Administration Quarterly*, Vol. 16, No. 3, pp. 376–394.

———. (1991) "Poverty and Profit in Central American Forestry", *Public Administration and Development*, Vol. 11, No. 6, pp. 573–589.

———. (1987) *The Politics of United States Foreign Aid* (New York: St. Martin's) p. 1 (republished by Routledge Development Library edition, Vol. 7, 2011).

Guess, George M. and Paul G. Farnham (2011) *Cases in Public Policy Analysis*, 3rd edition. (Washington, DC: Georgetown University Press).

———. (2000) *Cases in Public Policy Analysis*, 2nd edition. (Washington, DC: Georgetown University Press).

Guess, George M. and Husted, Thomas (2017) *International Public Policy Analysis* (New York: Routledge).

———. (2011) "Fiscal Incentives for Aid Management", ASPA Conference Paper, Baltimore, MD.

Guess, George M. and Joel Jutkowitz (1999) *Evaluation of USAID Latin American Regional Financial Management Improvement Project II* (Bethesda, MD: DAI), February, 78 p. 49.

Guess, George M. and Jun Ma (2015) "The Risks of Chinese Subnational Debt for Public Financial Management", *Public Administration and Development*, Vol. 35, pp. 129–139.

Guess, George M. and Costel Todor (2005) "Capital Programming and Budgeting: Comparative Local Government Perspectives", in Jack Rabin (ed.),

Encyclopedia of Public Administration and Public Policy (New York: Marcel Dekker) (E-EPAP-120040385), 9 pp.

Hamilton, Alexander, James Madison, and John Jay (1961) *The Federalist Papers (1788)* (New York: New American Library), p. 322.

Harrison, Lawrence E. (1985) *Underdevelopment as a State of Mind: The Latin American Case* (Lanham, MD: Center for International Affairs).

Haussmann, Ricardo (2017) "Iconoclast with a Mission", *Finance and Development* (September), pp. 31–33.

Hemming, Richard (2013) "The Macroeconomic Framework for Managing Public Finances", in Richard Allen, Richard Hemming, and Barry H. Potter (eds), *The International Handbook of Public Financial Management* (New York: Palgrave Macmillan), pp. 17–37.

Herring, Hubert (1972) *A History of Latin America From the Beginnings to the Present*, 3rd edition (New York: Alfred Knopf).

Hirsch, Seev (2017) "Two-State Resolution", letter to *The Economist*, June 10, p. 20.

Hirschman, Albert O. and Richard Bird (1971) "Foreign Aid: A Critique and a Proposal", in Albert O. Hirschman (ed.), *A Bias for Hope: Essays on Development and Latin America* (New Haven, CT: Yale University Press).

Huntford, Roland (1999) *The Last Place on Earth: Scott and Amundsen's Race to the South Pole* (New York: Random House).

Huntington, Samuel P. (1965) "Political Development and Political Decay", *World Politics*, Vol. 17, No. 3.

Inglehart, Ronald (1997) *Modernization and Postmodernization: Cultural, Economic, and Politcal Change* (Princeton, NJ: Princeton University Press).

International Center for Human Development (ICHD) (2006) "Citizen's Participation in Local Government Budget Policy Development: A Case Study on Involving Citizen's Voice Into the Policymaking Process". (Yerevan: ICHD; Budapest: Local Government and Public Services Reform Initiative).

International Monetary Fund (2015) Government Financial Statistics Yearbook (Washington, DC: IMF).

———. (2012) "Liberia: Public Expenditure and Financial Accountability (PEFA) Assessment". (Washington, DC: IMF).

Jeffrey, James (2017) "The State of State", *The American Interest*, Vol. XII, No. 6, July/August).

Judt, Tony (2005) *Post War: A History of Europe Since 1945* (New York: Penguin).

Kaplan, Jacob J. (1967) *The Challenge of Foreign Aid: Policies, Problems and Possibilities* (New York: Praeger).

Kaplan, Robert (2016) *In Europe's Shadow: Two Cold Wars and a Thirty-Year Journey Through Romania and Beyond* (New York: Random House).

Kassabova, Kapka (2017) *Border: A Journey to the Edge of Europe* (Minneapolis, MN: Graywolf Press).

Key, V.O. (1940) "The Lack of a Budgetary Theory", *American Political Science Review*, (December), pp. 11–37.

Kifordu, Henry Ani (2011) "Ethnic Politics, Political Elite and Regime Change in Nigeria", *Studies in Ethnicity and Nationalism*, Vol. 11, No. 3, pp. 427–450.

King, John, John Noble, and Andrew Humphreys (1996) *Central Asia: A Lonely Planet Travel Kit* (Hawthorne, Australia: Lonely Planet Publications).

King, Matthew Taylor (2017) "All Africa Could Be", *The American Interest*, Vol. XIII, No. 2, November/December, pp. 67–78.

Krauthammer, Charles (2017) "Revolt of the Attorneys General", *The Washington Post*, March 3, A17.

Levy, Brian (2014) *Working With the Grain: Integrating Governance and Growth in Development Strategies* (New York: Oxford University Press).

———. (2008) *Public Sector Reform: What Works and Why?* (Washington, DC: World Bank).

Marx, Axel and Jadir Soares (2013) "South Korea's Transformation From Recipient to DAC Donor: Assessing Korea's Development Cooperation Policy". (Geneva: Institute for Development Policy, Graduate Institute), pp. 107–142.

Mead, Walter Russell (2015) "The Paradox of American Democracy Promotion", *The American Interest*, Vol. X, No. 5, (May/June), pp. 50–59.

Michel, R. Gregory (2001) *Decision Tools for Budgetary Analysis* (Chicago, IL: Government Finance Officers Association).

Mikesell, John L. (2014) *Fiscal Administration, Analysis and Applications for the Public Sector*, 9th edition and 2011, 8th edition. (Boston, MA: Wadsworth Cengage).

Milbank, Dana (2016) "The Flint Tragedy Is a Failure of Governing, Not Just Government", *The Washington Post*, January 26, A2.

Morison, Samuel Eliot (1994) *The Oxford History of the American People, Volume 1 (Prehistory to 1789)* (New York: Penguin).

Muller, Jerry Z. (2015) "The Costs of Accountability", *The American Interest*, Vol. 11, No. 1 (September/October), pp. 18–32.

Musgrave, Richard A. (1959) *The Theory of Public Finance* (New York: McGraw-Hill).

Musil, Robert (1995) *The Man Without Qualities (Volume 2)* (New York: Knopf).

Nelson, L.E. (1983) "Send Accountants to El Salvador", *The Miami Herald*, November 8, 19A.

North, Douglass C., John Wallis, and Barry R. Weingast (2009) *Violence and Social Orders: A Conceptual Framework for Interpreting Recorded Human History* (New York: Cambridge University Press).

Oates, Wallace E. (1972) *Fiscal Federalism* (New York: Harcourt Brace Jovanovich).

Organization for Economic Cooperation and Development (2016) "Indonesia: Asia Pacific Unitary Country". (Paris: OECD).

———. (2005) *Paris Declaration on Aid Effectiveness* (Paris: Development Cooperation Directorate DCD-DAC).

Overman, Sam E. and Donna T. Lorraine (1994) "Information for Control: Another Management Proverb?", *Public Administration Review*, Vol. 54, No. 2 (March/April), pp. 193–196.

Packenham, Robert A. (1973) *Liberal America and the Third World: Political Development Ideas in Foreign Aid and Social Science* (Princeton, NJ: Princeton University Press).

Paddock, William and Elizabeth Paddock (1973) *We Don't Know How, An Independent Audit of What They Call Success in Foreign Assistance* (Ames, IA: Iowa State University Press).

Pastor, Robert A. (2004) "Democracy and Elections in North America: What Can We Learn From Our Neighbors?", *Election Law Journal*, Vol. 3, No. 3.

Perrow, Charles (1974) *Complex Organizations: A Critical Essay*, 3rd edition. (New York: McGraw-Hill).

Peterson, Stephen B. (2015) *Public Finance and Economic Growth in Developing Countries: Lessons from Ethiopia's Reforms* (New York: Routledge).

Piketty, Thomas (2014) *Capital in the 21st Century* (New York: Belknap Press).

Pradhan, Bibhudatta (2018) "Can India Turn Garbage into Cash?", *Bloomberg Business Week*, January 15, pp. 33–34.

Pressman, Jeffrey and Aaron Wildavsky (1984) *Implementation*, 3rd edition revised and expanded (Berkeley, CA: University of California Press).

Radelet, Steve (2016) "Africa's Rise: Interrupted?", *Finance and Development*, Vol. 53, No. 2.

Ramirez-Djumena, Natalie (2014) "Moving on Up", *Finance and Development*, Vol. 51, No. 4 (December), pp. 42–43.

Reynolds, Justin R. (2017) "Training Wreck", *The American Interest*, Vol. 12, No. 4 (February).

Riggs, Fred A. (1964) *Administration in Developing Countries: The Theory of Prismatic Society.* (Boston, MA: Houghton Mifflin).

Rodden, Jonathan A. (2006) *Hamilton's Paradox: The Promise and Peril of Fiscal Federalism* (New York: Cambridge University Press).

Rosenthal, Brian M. (2017) "The Most Expensive Mile of Subway Track on Earth", *New York Times*, December 28, p. 1.

Rosenthal, Brian M., Emma G. Fitzsimmons, and Michael LaForgia (2017) "The Making of a Meltdown: How Politics and Bad Decisions Plunged New York's Subways into Misery", *New York Times*, November 19, p. 1.

Rozner, Steve (2018) Bureau of Economic Growth, Education and Environment, USAID E3, Email communication, January 16.

———. (2018a) "Domestic Resource Mobilization: Getting Back to Basics", presentation in International Management course at George Mason University, April 3.

Schiavo-Campo, Salvatore (2017) *Government Budgeting and Expenditure Management: Principles and International Practice* (New York: Routledge).

Schiavo-Campo, Salvatore and David Tommasi (1999) *Managing Government Expenditure* (Manila: Asian Development Bank).

Sewell, David and Christine I. Wallich (1995) "Fiscal Decentralization and Intergovernmental Relations in Albania", Richard M. Bird, Robert D. Ebel, and Christine Wallich (eds), *Decentralization of the Socialist State* (Washington, DC: World Bank), pp. 251–281.

Silber, Laura and Alan Little (1995) *The Death of Yugoslavia* (London: Penguin/ BBC).

Silverman, Craig (2017) "Trump has Released Unprecedented Levels of Polarization in How People View the Media, Says This New Survey", *BuzzFeed News*, December 4. Available at www.buzzfeed.com/craigsilverman/trump-has-unleashed-unprecedented-levels-of-polarization-in?utm_term=.ftNv6120X#.tm2jWJAMO (accessed 2017).

Skidmore, Thomas E. and Peter H. Smith (2004) *Modern Latin America*, 6th edition. (New York: Oxford University Press).

Staronova, Katarina (ed.) (2007) *Training in Difficult Choices: Five Public Policy Cases from Slovakia* (Bratislava: Institute of Public Policy).

Stevens, Mike (1994) "Public Expenditure and Civil Service Reform in Tanzania", in David L. Lindauer and Barbara Nunberg (eds), *Rehabilitating Government: Pay and Employment Reform in Africa* (Washington, DC: IBRD), pp. 62–82.

———. (1994a) "Preparing for Civil Service Pay and Employment Reform; A Primer", in David L. Lindauer and Barbara Nunberg (eds), *Rehabilitating Government: Pay and Employment Reform in Africa* (Washington, DC: IBRD), pp. 103–119.

Tarnoff, Curt (2015) "USAID Background, Operations and Issues". (Washington, DC: Congressional Research Service) July 21, #7-5700.

Tartar, Andre (2017) "Europe: March of the Radical Right", *Bloomberg Business Week*, December 18, pp. 40–41.

The Americas (2016) "Criminal Justice in Mexico: Trials and Errors". (New York: Cambridge University Press), June 18.

The Economist (2018) "Briefing: Education in Pakistan, Stepping Up", January 6, pp. 13–14.

———. (2018a) "Feudalism in Pakistan", January 6, pp. 24–25.

———. (2018b) "India's economy: The Missing Middle Class", January 13, p. 16.

———. (2018c) "Protests in Tunisia: Austerity Bites", January 13, p. 44.

———. (2018d) "Accountancy in Afghanistan: Cultivating Bean-Counters", January 13, p. 67.

———. (2018e) "Special Report: Universal Health Care: An Affordable Necessity", April 28, p.5.

———. (2017a) "Ethnic Tension in Ethiopia: Unity vs. Diversity", October 7, pp. 50–51.

———. (2017a1) "Border Blues: Brexit Explodes the Ambiguity that has Underpinned Stability in Northern Ireland", November 25, p. 49.

———. (2017b) "Liberia's Election: Into a Vague Future", October 7, p. 49.

———. (2017b1) "The Budget: Out of Ammo", November 25, pp. 51–52.

———. (2017c) "Special Report: India and Pakistan", July 22, p. 8.

———. (2017c1) "Capital in the 80th Century BC", November 25, p. 68.

———. (2017d) "Separatism in Catalonia: How to Save Spain", October 7, p. 18.

———. (2017d1) "Banking in Afghanistan: Building Credit", November 25, p. 71.

———. (2017e) "Balkan Autocrats: Wrong and Stable", July 1, p. 45.

———. (2017f) "Elections in Papua New Guinea: Wantok and No Action", July 1, pp. 34–35.

———. (2017f1) "Brazil's Development Banks: A New Year's Resolution", December 2, p. 64.

———. (2017g) "Political Fragmentation: Going to Bits", January 14, p. 48.

———. (2017g1) "Education in Myanmar: No Questions Asked", December 2, pp. 34–35.

———. (2017h) "Special Report on the Future of the EU", March 25, pp. 1–16.

———. (2017h1) "Who Supervises the Supervisors?", December 9, pp. 45–46.

———. (2017i) "Bagehot: Bagehot vs. Brexit-Walter Bagehot Would Have Loathed Government by Referendum", October 21, p. 58.

———. (2017i1) "Turmoil in Ukraine: Revolution Devolution", December 9, pp. 51–52.

———. (2017j) "Lord Make Me Free—But Not Yet", October 14, p. 49.

———. (2017j1) "Trade in Africa: Africa Unite!", December 9, pp. 70–71.

———. (2017k) "Briefing: Left-Behind Places", October 21, pp. 21–25.

———. (2017k1) "Sugar in the Caribbean: Nearly Sweet Nothing", December 16, p. 32.

———. (2017l) "Closing in on Cancer", p. 11.

———. (2017l1) "Electrification: Shock Therapy", December 16, pp. 41–42.

———. (2017m) "Hurricane Irma: Too Little but Not Too Late", September 16, pp. 30–31.

———. (2017m1) "Nationalism: Vladimir's Choice", December 23, pp. 53–58.

———. (2017n) "Licensing Laws: Locking Up Firefighters", October 28, p. 31.

———. (2017n1) "Venezuela: Maduro's Dance of Disaster", January 28, pp. 29–30.

———. (2017o) "Briefing: Enter Tsar Vladimir", October 28, pp. 23–25.

———. (2017p) "The National Health Service: Policy Transplant", November 4, pp. 56–57.

———. (2017q) "Household Debt in Asia: Mutable Values", November 4, p. 70.

———. (2017r) "Special Report: Technology in Africa, The Leapfrog Model", November 11, pp. 1–14.

———. (2017s) "Malaysian Politics: Eyes on the Prize", November 11, pp. 33–34.

———. (2017t) "China: Center-Local Relations, The Walking Debt", November 18, pp. 37–38.

———. (2017u) "Zimbabwe: The Man who Wrecked a Country", November 18, pp. 39–41.

———. (2017w) "Bagehot: Power to the People", November 18, p. 50.

———. (2017x) "South Africa's Coming Crisis", in "The World in 2018", December, pp. 77–78.

———. (2017y) "Why No Catalonia? Explaining the Absence of Separatism in Latin America", November 25, p. 32.

———. (2017z) "Justice in Egypt: Of Puppets and Parasites", November 25, p. 44.

———. (2016) "Iraq Unravels: The Ungovernable Country", May 7, pp. 41–42.

———. (2016a) "Fiscal Devolution in Scotland: A Taste for More", April 9, pp. 56–57.

———. (2016b) "Way Jose", May 28, p. 32.

———. (2016c) "African Cities: Left Behind", September 17.

———. (2016d) "The Breakdown of Arab States: The War Within", May 12, pp. 7–8.

———. (2016e) "Politics in the Middle East: The Arab Winter", January 9, pp. 37–40.

———. (2015) "Scottish Nationalism: How to Scotch It", May 23, p. 10.

———. (2015a) "England's Sensible Slumber", June 20, p. 57.

———. (2015b) "Arab Bureaucracies: Aiwa (Yes) Minister", November 14, p. 47.

———. (2015c) "Schumpeter: Digital Taylorism: A Modern Version of Scientific Management Threatens to Dehumanize the Workplace", September 10, p. 36.

———. (2014) "You Kant do That", September 13, pp. 60–61.

———. (2014a) "Exorcising the Deadly Fever", December 13, pp. 49–50.

———. (2013) "Stubborn Facts on the Ground", April 20, p. 46.

———. (2013a) "The Multiplexed Metropolis", September 7, p. 24.

———. (2005) "Economic and Financial Indicators: Aid", April 15, p. 90.

The Washington Post (2017) "Metro's Leashed Watchdog", December 4, A24.

————. (2014a) "Obama: Islamists' Rise Was Misjudged", September 29, A1.

————. (2014b) "Islamic State Seizes Another Airbase", October 14, A12.

Tommasi, Daniel (2013) "The Coverage and Classification of the Budget", in Richard Allen, Richard Hemming, and Barry H. Potter (eds), *The International Handbook of Public Financial Management* (New York: Palgrave Macmillan), pp. 164–192.

United Nations Development Program (UNDP) (2001) "Rebuilding State Structures: Methods and Approaches: The Trials and Tribulations of Post-Communist Countries". (New York: UNDP).

U.S. Agency for International Development (USAID) (2017) "Ethiopia: Country Development Cooperation Strategy: Accelerating the Transformation toward Prosperity", (CDCS). (Addis Ababa: USAID).

————. (2017a) "Domestic Resource Mobilization: Helping Countries Sustainably Finance Their Own Development". (Washington, DC: USAID).

————. (2014) "PFMRAF: A Mandatory Reference for ADS Chapter 220". (Washington, DC: M/CFO, USAID), July 28.

————. (2013) "Evaluation at USAID", Report #PD-ACX-099 (Washington, DC: USAID/Department of State).

USOMB (U.S. Office of Management and Budget) (2012) "Guidance on Collection of U.S. Foreign Assistance Data", #12-01 (Washington, DC: OMB), September 25.

Vaughan, Liam (2016) "Wanted Accountants with Hearts of Stone", *Bloomberg Business Week*, July 1.

Vazquez, Jorge Martinez and Jamie Boex (2001) "Russia's Transition to a New Federalism". (Washington, DC: IBRD).

Wade, Francis (2017) "Myanmar's Enemy Within: Buddhist Violence and the Making of a Muslim 'Other'", *The Economist*, October 14, p. 75.

Wang, Xiao and Richard Herd (2013) "The System of Revenue Sharing and Fiscal Transfers in China", Working Paper 1030 (Paris: OECD).

Weick, Karl E. (1979) *The Social Psychology of Organizing* (Reading, MA: Addison-Wesley).

West, Rebecca (1993) *Black Lamb and Grey Falcon* (London: Canongate).

White, Jenny B. (2015) "The Turkish Complex", *The American Interest*, 10: 4 (March/April), pp. 15–23.

Wood, R.E. (1980) "Foreign Aid and the Capitalist State in Underdeveloped Countries", *Politics and Society*, Vol. 10, No. 1, pp. 1–34.

World Bank (2016) Available at https://data.worldbank.org/indicator/ny.gdp.pcap.cd (accessed 2018) (Washington, DC: World Bank).

————. (2015) "Total Natural Resource Rents as % GDP". (Washington, DC: World Bank). Available at https://knoema.com (accessed 2018).

————. (2004) *World Development Report 2004: Making Services Work for Poor People* (Washington, DC: The World Bank).

————. (1997) *The Public Expenditure Management Handbook* (Washington, DC: IBRD).

Wright, Glen (2002) "Introduction to Public Management", in Glen Wright and Juraj Nemec (eds), *Public Management in the Central and Eastern Transition: Concepts and Cases* (Bratislava: NISPAcee).

Wright, Glen and Juraj Nemec (2002) (eds) *Public Management in the Central and Eastern Transition: Concepts and Cases* (Bratislava: NISPAcee).

Yilmaz, Serdar, Francois Vaillancourt, and Bernard Dafflon (2012) "State and Local Finance: Why it Matters", in Robert D. Ebel and John E. Petersen (eds), *The Oxford Handbook of State and Local Finance* (New York: Oxford University Press), pp. 105–136.

Zhang, Jian (1994) "U.S. Aid and Taiwan's Development", *American Studies*, Vol. 1.

Zimbardo, Philip and Ebbson B. Ebbe (1970) *Influencing Attitudes and Changing Behavior* (Reading, MA: Addison-Wesley).

Index